The Vivid Air

# The Vivid Air
## The Lafayette Escadrille

## Philip M. Flammer

**The University of Georgia Press**
*Athens*

Copyright © 1981 by the University of Georgia Press
Athens 30602

Set in 10 on 13 point Melior type
Designed by Gary Gore

Printed in the United States of America

Library of Congress Cataloging in Publication Data

Flammer, Philip M
  The vivid air, the Lafayette Escadrille.

  Bibliography: p.
  Includes index.
    1. European War, 1914–1918—Aerial operations,
French. 2. European War, 1914–1918—Regimental
histories—France—Escadrille Lafayette. 3. France.
Armée. Escadrille Lafayette—History. I. Title.
D603.F55 1981      940.54′4944      80-22059
ISBN 0-8203-0537-5

To

Colonel Paul Ayres Rockwell, who,
as much as any man, typifies all
that was good and grand in the
Lafayette Escadrille,
and to
Colonel Charles H. Dolan II,
one of the squadron's distinguished
fliers and its last survivor.

Born of the sun they travelled a short while towards the sun,
And left the vivid air signed with their honour.

—Stephen Spender

# Contents

# Preface

Few segments of military history have provided as much glamour, excitement, and financial profit as aviation during the Great War, 1914–18. Though ignored for a time as part of the antimilitary reaction following the war, the books and articles began piling up with remarkable rapidity; the old planes were resurrected, photographed, and sometimes flown; societies for the study of World War I aviation came into existence; and a goodly number of buffs regularly pursued various aspects of the story with dedicated zeal.

Not all of this activity has been beneficial. Glamour has often overwhelmed reality, and the resultant misconceptions and falsehoods have largely obscured the true value and drama of this important period. The Lafayette Escadrille, N-124, is a case in point. It numbered only thirty-eight Americans and four French officers among its flying personnel. Yet over the years, more than four thousand Americans have claimed membership in it. Most people still think that the squadron included all Americans who flew for France during the war, even though many American airmen flew for France in units other than the N-124.

Lafayette Escadrille pilots have been characterized as American privateers, vicious men who loved to kill, and again as steel-eyed adventurers who faced danger for the sheer excitement of it all. Such conclusions are based more on fantasy than fact. Actually, the pilots of the Lafayette Escadrille, with two or three exceptions, were perfectly normal human beings, frightened in combat, but willing to fight because they felt it was their duty to do so. If anything, they were by and large an elite group, not because of any superlative combat record— other squadrons did more and paid a greater price—but because, given the time and the place and the activity, they were elite men. Almost all of them were well educated, came from fine families, and could look forward to quiet futures of relative ease and influence. Love of adventure lured some of them on, but it was mostly idealism that drew them into the upheaval, and it was idealism that led so many to fight so well for so long. Adventure without the dangers of combat was open to any airman. The American pilots did well because, by and large, they viewed the conflict as a crusade, a contest, as it were, between good and evil. In a position to take part, they felt a compelling obligation to do so. Quite by accident they were fortunate enough to fight in a new medium, one so exciting and individualistic that it would have made heroes of them had they been merely mediocre men.

In this history of the Lafayette Escadrille, I have not attempted to seek out and destroy the many misconceptions about the squadron. These will fall by the wayside as the true story is told. Nor have I felt compelled to dwell upon the human frailties which appear almost automatically in men under combat, but which always seem scandalous to a public not acquainted with the realities of war. In this story, as in perhaps few others, the facts speak for themselves.

It remains to be noted that I have made no special attempt to weave into this narrative the closely parallel story of those Americans who flew for France in squadrons other than the Lafayette. No doubt this will be criticized by some, but the two stories are not the same. Men of the Lafayette Escadrille, with one or two exceptions, volunteered before America came into the war; the others, again with a few exceptions, volunteered after their country joined in the fight against Germany, or at least after it was apparent that it would do so. Suffice it to say here, the story of all the Americans who flew for France, grouped under the unofficial title of the Lafayette Flying Corps, is worthy of a book by itself. Someday their story too will be told.

Many people have given me valuable assistance in the preparation of this work, for which I am deeply grateful. Not all can be mentioned here, but I am particularly indebted to the late Dr. M. Hamlin Cannon, who suggested the subject and guided me through my early research, and to the former pilots of the Lafayette Escadrille—Edwin C. Parsons, Charles Dolan II, Henry S. Jones, Edward F. Hinkle, Harold B. Willis, Kenneth Marr, and Frederick H. Prince, Jr., who extended the hand of fellowship and willingly gave information of great value, often at considerable personal inconvenience. Others, too, graciously supplied me with information or assisted me in other ways from time to time. Among them: Mme Georges Thenault of Paris and Harwicksport, Massachusetts; the late William W. Hoffman of New York City; Mme Jean Dudeon, Paris; Mr. Oliver-Martin of Paris; the late Emil Marchal of Pegomas, France; Mme Marcelle Guerin of Monte Carlo; Capt. Louis Richard of the French Air Force; and Mrs. Robert Soubiran of Washington, D.C. deserve special mention.

I also have reason to be grateful for assistance rendered by the editors of the *Cross and Cockade Journal* (particularly H. Hugh

Wynne), and officials of the National Archives of the United States, the Office of the Air Attaché, U.S. Embassy in Paris, the Archives Historique de l'Armée de l'Air at Versailles, the Archives de Bureau Central d'Incorporation et d'Archives de l'Armée de l'Air at Compiègne, and the French Ministry of War, which greatly facilitated my research in many ways.

Others who contributed much to this work by helping to make it possible or lessening the burdens it entailed include Gen. Paul Stehlin of the French Air Force; Gen. Mark Bradley, Col. Wilbert Ruenheck, Col. Eldon Downs, Lt. Col. John R. Sala, and Col. Silas Molyneaux, all former U.S. Air Force officers.

To several people I owe a special debt of gratitude that defies adequate expression. My precious wife Mildred cheerfully assumed enormous burdens in order that I might have the proper surroundings and adequate time. She has been glorious. Col. Charles H. Dolan II and the late Adm. Edwin C. Parsons, both former pilots of the Lafayette Escadrille, went far beyond ordinary courtesy supplying much information and carefully reading the manuscripts. Col. Paul A. Rockwell, of Asheville, North Carolina, has done likewise. While not a member of the Lafayette Escadrille, this remarkable man has always been closely associated with it. He cheerfully and generously shared with me his time, efforts, knowledge, and collection of documents, asking only in return—and then only once—that I do as complete and as accurate a job as possible. His support has been a strong incentive, as has that of Dr. William R. Emerson, a truly profound scholar, magnificent lecturer, and able leader, who was generous with his time and wisdom and who guided me safely through heavy academic seas.

Finally, I owe much to Dr. William R. Leary of the University of Georgia. A scholar of unusual wisdom and courage, he provided some critical perception and incentive.

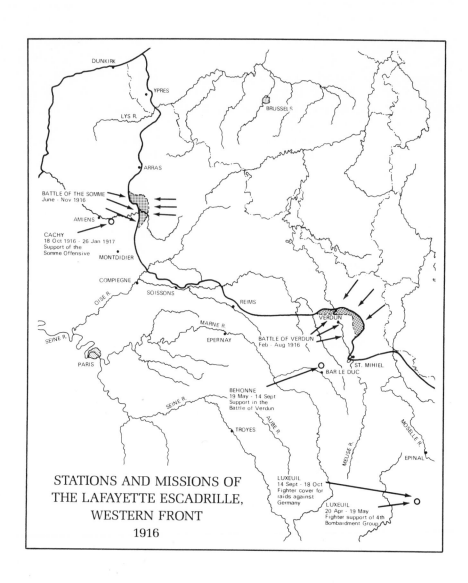

DUNKIRK

YPRES

LYS R.

BRUSSELS

ARRAS

BATTLE OF THE SOMME
June - Nov 1916

AMIENS

CACHY
18 Oct 1916 - 26 Jan 1917
Support of the
Somme Offensive

MONTDIDIER

COMPIEGNE

OISE R.

SOISSONS

REIMS

MARNE R.

SEINE R.

EPERNAY

PARIS

VERDUN

BATTLE OF VERDUN
Feb - Aug 1916

ST. MIHIEL

BAR LE DUC

BEHONNE
19 May - 14 Sept
Support in the
Battle of Verdun

SEINE R.

AUBE R.

MEUSE R.

MOSELLE R.

TROYES

EPINAL

STATIONS AND MISSIONS OF
THE LAFAYETTE ESCADRILLE,
WESTERN FRONT
1916

LUXEUIL
14 Sept - 18 Oct
Fighter cover for
raids against
Germany

LUXEUIL
20 Apr - 19 May
Fighter support of 4th
Bombardment Group

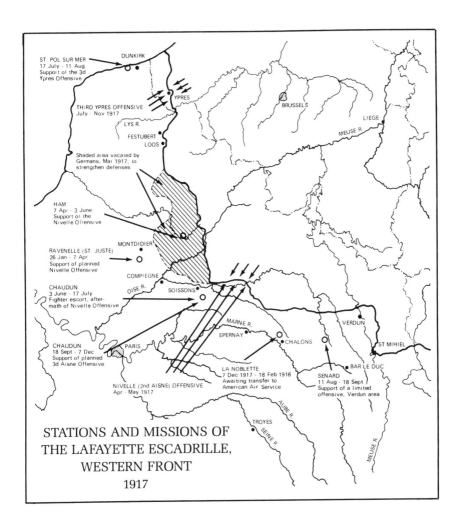

STATIONS AND MISSIONS OF
THE LAFAYETTE ESCADRILLE,
WESTERN FRONT
1917

# 1      The Genesis of the Lafayette Escadrille

*The First Volunteers*

When the crises that led to World War I erupted into that tragic upheaval, the United States, following a traditional policy, hastened to declare itself neutral. But in the Great War, a war unlike any previous war, a simple declaration of neutrality was not enough, as President Woodrow Wilson well knew. On 19 August 1914 he issued a "solemn word of warning" to the American people.

> We must guard against any breach of neutrality that may spring out of partisanship. . . . The United States must be neutral in fact as well as in name during these days that try men's souls. We must be impartial in our thought as well as in action, must put a curb on our sentiments as well as upon every transaction that might be construed as a preference of one part of the struggle before another.[1]

This presidential proclamation and others like it no doubt helped to pacify some people, but a great many Americans rejected neutrality, and, emotionally at least, allied themselves with one of the belligerents. Most of them preferred France and Britain, their allegiance favoring the country of their birth or ancestry; others, assuming Germany's role as the aggressor and the main cause of the war, associated the Allied cause with that of justice and humanity. Both groups favored assistance or intervention of some sort, but with varying degrees of enthusiasm. Still others adopted a softened attitude, insisting that something be done, but keeping their own activity humanitarian. This seems primarily true of those Americans associated with relief organizations such as the American Relief Clearing House, the American Relief Commission, and the American Hostels for Refugees. All were one-sided, however, and there is evidence that one acted as a recruiting station for French and British armies while another secretly offered to organize and equip a complete aero squadron for France.[2]

Partisan support, more direct and more active, came from field organizations such as the American Ambulance Corps, a medical unit organized in the fall of 1914 by the strongly pro-French American colony in Paris, with financial support from students at several American universities, including Yale, Princeton, and Harvard.[3] Ostensibly organized for strictly humanitarian purposes, these organizations performed valuable and consequential services by picking up wounded men at front-line first aid stations and transporting them to hospitals. Certainly the Germans were not inclined to applaud humanitarian activity which released able-bodied Frenchmen for military duty and increased the likelihood that some of the wounded would return to the lines.

Finally, there were a number of young men who for various reasons spurned neutrality and openly rejected what they liked to call the feeble policy of the United States.[4] Paul Ayres Rockwell and his brother Kiffin, two outstanding and dedicated young men from Asheville, North Carolina, were representative of this group.

In the summer of 1914, Paul, age twenty-five and a graduate of Washington and Lee University, was a promising reporter for the *Atlanta Constitution*. Kiffin, the younger by four years, had also studied at Washington and Lee and at the Virginia Military Institute. Both men could point to a proud family tradition that included military service from the French and Indian war through the American Civil War.[5]

On 3 August, the day before the German assault on Liège and the opening battle of the war, the two brothers, grieviously distressed at the world situation and believing that the cause of France was indeed "the cause of humanity, the most noble of all causes,"[6] wrote the French consul in New Orleans, offering their services to the French Foreign Legion. But the following day, learning that the war had begun, they elected not to wait for a reply. Two days later, they sailed for France aboard the S.S. *St. Paul*.[7]

In Europe, the Rockwell brothers found they were not alone in their desire to fight with the French. A regular movement of volunteers had begun, gathering in its ranks Italians, Turks, Russians, Greeks, Syrians, Americans, and a variety of others. Indeed, on 1 August, the day before general mobilization, the following appeal, drafted by a committee of volunteers appeared in the Paris newspapers.

The hour is grave.
Every man worthy of the name should act today, should forbid himself to remain inactive in the midst of the most formidable conflagration history has ever enregistered.
Any hesitation would be a crime.

A few days later, a group of Americans gathered in Paris and issued a similar appeal to their countrymen.[8]

Volunteers responded to the appeals with enthusiasm. More than forty Americans were among those who enlisted in the Foreign Legion in August 1914, moving the Count Albert de Mun, a leading member of the Chamber of Deputies, to exclaim, "La France a des volontaires étrangers, l'Allemagne, elle a des déserteurs."[9]

The motives that prompted these young men to enter a war under colors not their own are complex and often ill defined. Once, when a friend asked Eugene Bullard, a black and an ex-boxer who in 1914 was in Paris, hungry and broke, why he enlisted in the Legion, Bullard replied, "Well, I don't rightly know but it must have been more curiosity than intelligence."[10] Perhaps this answer could provide the central theme for a whole chorus of variations, since in August 1914 war propaganda had not yet taken hold and everyone expected the conflict to be over in a matter of weeks. Moreover, the love of adventure, as expressed in such pastimes as travel and flying, while not confined to the upper class was nonetheless an expensive taste that not every young American could satisfy. No doubt this love played a role for many of the volunteers; however it does not match the idealism many displayed when they willingly risked assured futures of profit and influence to undergo the dangers and hardships of combat. Nor does it explain why they fought so long and so well under the most trying combat conditions of modern times. Victor Chapman, for example, came from a very prominent New York family and was a promising student at the École des Beaux Arts in Paris when he enlisted. René Philizot had a reputation to match his many trophies as a big game hunter, Robert Soubiran was an expert mechanic and racing driver, Jules Bach a mechanical engineer, and Dennis Dowd a young lawyer.

Edward Stone, a Harvard graduate, had served with the American Diplomatic Service, John Casey and James Carstair were well-known artists in the Paris Latin Quarter, and Achilles Olinger had been instructor of languages at Columbia University. Many of the men, particularly those well traveled and well educated, enjoyed emotional ties with France, while others, such as the Rockwell brothers, regarded France as a symbol and their enlistment as an assist to justice and humanity.

Not all motives were as lofty as idealism, which remains, nonetheless, the most conspicuous among the Americans who enlisted in the legion. Bert Hall had a spotty past and was dissatisfied with his job as a Paris taxi driver. Paul Pavelka apparently wished to add another adventure to his already impressive list, as did Billy Thorin. Others no doubt came out of curiosity. Yet no one came except in response to his own desires and conscience, and whatever the mixture and blend of the various motives, it is safe to say that all but a few of the ninety Americans who fought in the famed Foreign Legion did so because they felt a moral obligation to fight for what they felt was right, even though it meant considerable personal sacrifice. One of the more idealistic of the Legionnaires, the tender poet Alan Seeger, who had his rendezvous with death at the Battle of the Somme in 1916, explained the motives of his fellow American Legionnaires in the following words:

Yet sought they neither recompense nor praise,
Nor to be mentioned in another breath
Than their blue-coated comrades whose great days
It was their pride to share, ay, share even to the death.
Nay, rather, France, to you they rendered thanks
(Seeing they came for honor, not for gain),
Who, opening to them your glorious ranks,
Gave them that grand occasion to excel,
That chance to live the life most free from stain
And that rare privilege of dying well.[11]

Although the Great War soon disintegrated into an ordeal that still defies imagination, the American Legionnaires overall gave a good account of themselves. As Paul Rockwell, one of the participants, put it,

Of the fourscore and ten American volunteers who served honorably at the

Front in France in the ranks of the Foreign Legion, thirty-eight were killed in action or died of wounds. Most of the survivors were wounded from one to four times. Eight were decorated with the Cross of the Legion of Honor, twenty-one with the *Médille Militaire,* and fifty-two with the *Croix de Guerre.* The little band of fighters won over one hundred citations in the Orders of the Day.[12]

At any rate, the initial enlistment of these Americans into the Foreign Legion had a side effect not reckoned at the time. When the all-American squadron of volunteers came into being in the spring of 1916, no less than four of the seven original members came out of the Legion.

## The Neutrality Issue

With the United States of America officially neutral, the entrance of American men into the ranks of the Foreign Legion as combatants brought into question the status of the volunteers. A law of 1907 stated that an American citizen "shall be deemed to have expatriated himself when he has been naturalized in any foreign state in conformity with its laws, or when he takes an oath of allegiance to any foreign state."[13] But like most laws, this one was subject to interpretation, particularly since it recognized the fact that mere enlistment did not of itself constitute a change of allegiance. The question, as yet unanswered, was whether the oath taken by men entering the Foreign Legion to "serve from this day with honor and fidelity for the duration of the war" made such a change.

It was a touchy issue, since theoretically the men would be bound to France if, for whatever reason, the United States found itself on the side of the Germans. President Wilson had made the official position clear on numerous occasions. However, by avoiding the mention of sanctions, he was obviously exhorting and not threatening. Thus the way was open to the would-be Legionnaires, but a possible stake in the gamble was their U.S. citizenship.

Fired with enthusiasm, the American enlistees chose to disregard President Wilson's pleas, but not before they had put the matter to Myron T. Herrick, the U.S. ambassador to France. As the ambassador recalled the story,

I got out the law on the duties of neutrals . . . read it to them and explained its passages. . . . It was no use. Those young eyes were searching mine, seeking, I am sure, the encouragement they had come in the hope of getting. It was more than flesh and blood could stand, and catching fire from their eagerness, I brought down my fist on the table saying, "That is the law, boys; but if I was young and stood in your shoes, by God I know mighty well what I would do."

This declaration was apparently what the young men had come to hear. They hastily shook the ambassador's hand and hurried off to the place of enlistment.[14]

Mr. Herrick, a temporary carryover from the Taft administration, was an avid Francophile who had assisted in the organization of several pro-French relief organizations.[15] The State Department never asked the ambassador to explain his actions or modify his views. Indeed, at this point, the State Department seemed to take a rather liberal view of the law of 1907. The absence of documentary material in the State Department section of the National Archives indicates that the authorities chose to ignore the problem except, as one document brings out, they were glad to learn that the French did not regard the oath taken by the Legionnaires as a permanent political allegiance.[16]

Ambassador Herrick was replaced in November 1914 by William G. Sharp, a successful Ohio businessman who shared his predecessor's enthusiasm for the French cause, but who, in the words of his son,

sought loyally to represent Wilson and our country's policies, and he did this throughout, . . . regardless of the fact that his private sympathies were with the Allies from the beginning. On the other hand he, I am sure, never gave the Lafayette Escadrille or any member of it, a basis to believe that our government or he, as representative of our government, supported the Squadron either overtly or covertly or encouraged anyone to join.[17]

Thus, under Ambassador Sharp, the strict neutrality which characterized the State Department home office now properly extended to the level of the American embassy in Paris. Men who sought encouragement or assistance in joining the French military no longer received it, a circumstance that they often interpreted as cold if not hostile indifference. From the viewpoint of the Legionnaires, certain officials, such as Major (later General) Frank Parker, the military attaché, were "unfailingly kind," but the overall treatment was "very unpleasant." When Alice Weeks, who was very active in relief work, went to the Embassy in the summer of 1915 to seek information about her son Kenneth, listed as missing in action, Robert Bliss, the first secretary, told her bluntly, "Mrs. Weeks, this embassy knows nothing about those Americans who have volunteered in the Foreign Legion . . . and makes it a point to know nothing about them."[18]

Under Ambassador Sharp, the issue of American volunteers and the duties of neutrals entered a sort of limbo. The creation of an all-American flying squadron in 1916, however, resurrected it for discussion at the ministerial level.

## The Idea of an All-American Squadron

In view of the widespread sympathy for France among the American people, the active participation in the war by some United States citizens, and particularly by the nature of the war itself, it was perhaps inevitable that some attempt would be made to form an American squadron of pilot volunteers. As the stalemate developed, aviation rose in glamour in direct proportion to the growing slaughter on the ground, on which few men, even early on, could look without a shudder. The trading of lives in trench warfare, where the losses as measured against the insignificant gains were stunning, the physical hardship of life in the trenches, and, above all, the loss of individuality among the millions of soldiers, proved a powerful repellent. Thus a soldier seeing his life wasting away to no apparent purpose in the trenches might well look to the sky, not merely as a release from his torment—attrition in the air soon proved even greater than on the ground—but as an opportunity to make an obvious and positive contribution. The individualistic Americans would hardly be immune to such feelings.

To most of the unnumbered souls on the ground who looked longingly to the sky, this dream was beyond realization. Forces greater than their personal desires determined their time and place of service. Besides, who could say how long the war would last? Early in the war, predictions that the end would come in the very near future kept life bearable for most. As a result, it largely fell to air-minded men, that is, to those men who had flown before or who recognized the flimsy flying machines as weapons of great potential, to channel their efforts toward the struggling concept of air power. The genesis of the Lafayette Escadrille is a case in point.

Credit for first mention of the idea of an all-American squadron of volunteers properly belongs to William Thaw II of Pittsburgh, although aviation writers have long credited Norman Prince of Prides Crossing, Massachusetts, with the honor.

Thaw, a great natural leader, came from a very wealthy family—his father was a director of the Pennsylvania Railroad and held executive positions in a number of other business concerns—and his background included education in private schools in New York and Pennsylvania, and two years at Yale University. While a student at Yale, he became interested in flying and left his studies in 1913 to learn to fly at the Curtiss school at Hammondsport, New York. Although he became proficient only in the Curtiss Model E hydroplane, he had found his calling, and henceforth listed his occupation as aviator.[19]

After gaining something of a reputation as a daredevil pilot in the United States, Thaw went to France in 1914 with his brother Alexander to market Alexander's invention of an automatic stabilizer. But while the Thaw brothers were following this business venture and William was doing some flying along the southern coast of France—his friends thereafter called him "the playboy of the Riviera"—the war broke out.[20]

William firmly believed that France was in the right and that he could not sit idly by. He forthwith offered his services as an aviator, only to be rejected on the grounds that France had more than enough volunteers to man the pitifully few airplanes then in service. Also, the French were truly fearful of the German spy network and were inclined not to take chances with foreigners wanting to fly. Naturally they did not mention this point to Thaw.[21]

Disappointed, Thaw nonetheless resolved to do his part. Along with forty-two other Americans, he marched to the Hôtel des Invalides on 21 August 1914, and enlisted in the Foreign Legion as a common *soldat*.[22]

To hurry his departure to the front, Thaw, like many of his fellow Americans, claimed to be a veteran. He avoided the outlandish, like Herman Chatkoff's claim of five years' sterling service with the Salvation Army, but he did claim prior service with the Mexican army. The French soon wondered about his obvious lack of proficiency in drill, but he countered with the observation that fighting in Mexico was always guerilla warfare.[23]

In late October the Second Regiment of the Foreign Legion, with Thaw as a member, was holding a section of the front line at Verzenay, in the Champagne sector. One afternoon, concealed under a tree with some comrades a short distance behind the lines, Thaw watched a German airplane move slowly overhead. "One day soon," he announced, "a squadron of American volunteers will be flying for France."[24]

It is not clear whether Thaw's first efforts to get such a squadron organized extended beyond this fateful announcement and subsequent mention of the idea to friends and minor French officials. His main effort at this time was directed toward getting into aviation himself, a goal that had been uppermost in his mind since the failure of his first attempt.[25]

Meanwhile, shortly after Thaw's brief mention of a volunteer squadron, another American came up with the same idea. Norman Prince of Prides Crossing, Massachusetts, was a Harvard graduate, lawyer, and like Thaw, a member of a prominent and wealthy family. He became interested in flying while a student at Harvard and experimented with it under the assumed name of George W. Manor so as to "escape an undesired notoriety."[26] He kept the interest alive even after the news broke, and soon qualified for the pilot's certificate of the Aero Club of America.

Prince's family maintained an estate near Pau in the Basses-Pyrenees, and Norman, having spent many delightful summers there, knew the French well and loved the country like his own. News of the war turned his thoughts to France, and as a result he left his law practice in the fall of 1914 and enrolled in the Burgess Flying School at Marblehead, Massachusetts, with the announced intention of perfecting his flying ability and offering his services to France.[27] He apparently had not heard of William Thaw's troubles, for he anticipated no difficulty.

It was while learning to fly at Marblehead that Prince conceived the idea of forming a squadron of American volunteers. As nearly as can be determined, he first mentioned the idea in late November or early December 1914 to Frazier Curtis, a friend from Boston, who had recently returned from England after an unsuccessful attempt to fly with the Royal Naval Air Service. Like Prince, Curtis hoped to perfect his flying at Marblehead. Then he would try again.[28]

Prince and Curtis apparently discussed the idea at some length, the latter approving it in principle but withholding his active support until he had again attempted to fly for England, where the language would not be a barrier. In mid-December 1914 Curtis suddenly terminated his schooling at Marblehead, and the day before Christmas sailed for England to have another go at it. Prince likewise left the Burgess Flying School in December, but spent the holidays with his family before sailing for France on 20 January 1915.[29]

Prince arrived in Paris the latter part of January, full of enthusiasm for his project. Uncertain about the reception he might receive from French authorities, however, he sought first to enlist the support of several influential Americans. Robert Chandler, a prominent member of the American colony in Paris and a man with connections at the U.S. Embassy, promised his full support, but others whom Prince hoped to win over did not find the idea feasible. Some flatly rejected the proposal as a violation of American neutrality. In the meantime, however, Prince had won the unqualified support of two Frenchmen, Jacques and Paul de Lesseps, both well-known aviators and members of the Paris Air Guard.[30]

Through the de Lesseps brothers and Chandler, Prince was able to meet and speak with some minor officials of the French War Department. He was full of enthusiasm and argued convincingly, but without success. The authorization of an all-American squadron of volunteers was inherently a matter of high policy and as a result the interviews were with the wrong people. The French were naturally noncommittal, and at the end of the first round the whole issue appeared depressingly uncertain.[31]

On 9 February Frazier Curtis suddenly appeared in Paris with the woeful announcement that he had been checkmated by the British, who would not allow him to fly with the Royal Naval Air Service unless he renounced his American citizenship, a step that he was unwilling to take.[32] He therefore joined forces with Prince in approaching the French authorities for a second time.

The new approach was decided upon at a dinner given by the de Lesseps brothers in early February. A letter offering the services of an entire squadron of American volunteers was drawn up and addressed to Étienne Millerand, the minister of war.[33]

Apparently the French felt no particular need to weigh the proposal carefully. A prompt reply to the Prince-Curtis letter politely but firmly informed the two Americans that no volunteers could be admitted into aviation because that particular service was popular with French servicemen and there were more applicants than aircraft and crew positions.[34] Thus for the time being at least the issue of an all-American squadron appeared dead, with little hope of resurrecting it.

It remains to be noted that, quite independent of Thaw and Prince, yet another American was thinking in terms of a volunteer squadron, a strong indication that the idea was a natural and not at all as revolutionary as many people believe. This man, a San Francisco–born physician named Edmund L. Gros, had spent many years in Paris and knew the French language and customs well. His occupation and double allegiance to France and America brought him prosperity in the American colony in Paris, and his close ties with the American Ambulance Corps gave him considerable standing with French authorities.[35]

It was while working with the American Ambulance Corps that Gros, early in 1915, first thought of organizing a squadron of American volunteers. According to his own testimony, the idea occurred to him when he noticed among the ambulance drivers some "splendid lads" who would be interested in expressing their sympathy for France "in material form."[36]

If Gros ever took his idea to the French in the form of a proposal, no record of it has been found. Since the doctor was not one to withhold credit for himself, it is likely that he, like Legionnaire Thaw, did not carry the idea beyond his immediate circle of friends—that is, not until Thaw, Prince, and Gros became acquainted with one another and consolidated their efforts.

## The Basis for French Reluctance

The French were perfectly sincere when they told Thaw and Prince that there were more French applicants for aviation duty than could be effectively utilized. As one American airman put it, "There was really no place or need for volunteer aviators. Hundreds of young Frenchmen were clamoring for admittance to this new and romantic branch of the service, which, above all, offered surcease from the horrors of the trenches, to say nothing of the chance to wear fantastic uniforms and impress the pretty girls almost to the point of tears."[37]

There was much more to the French rejection of potential American fliers than this basic argument. As mentioned earlier, the French feared the renowned German spy network. According to one French officer, "The French at that time fancied they saw spies everywhere. They were afraid even of their best friends." To make matters worse, there was some foundation to these fears. Early in the war one German airman had entered French aviation by means of a forged American passport and had caused "untold damage" before he was discovered and executed.[38]

Also, the French authorities were particularly suspicious of Americans, and again not without reason. Despite what they told Thaw about the surplus of volunteers for aviation and despite the law forbidding the entrance of foreigners into units other than the Foreign Legion, they had allowed a few foreigners into the Service Aéronautique during the early months of the war, apparently restricting it, however, to those who could provide their own airplanes.[39] Among this group was an American pilot by the name of Frederick C. Hild.

According to his own testimony, which must not be accepted without qualification, Hild came to France in September 1914, offering himself and his monoplane to the French. Not willing to stand on formality at a time when trained pilots, and particularly airplanes, were in great demand, the French accepted Hild, taking care, however, to first enter his name on the rolls of the Foreign Legion. Already licensed, Hild was given a short period of training and by the middle of October found himself flying a two place observation craft on the front.[40] The air war, however, which was just beginning, was something Hild apparently had not bargained for. After one or two trips over the lines, he asked for release from the Service Aéronautique, ostensibly for the purpose of flying with the British.[41] When this was denied him, he deserted, fleeing to Spain and thence to the United States where he compounded his error by giving out false and sensational information, including the announcement that after serving a "short time" with the French, he was "politely and kindly rejected because he was not a native of France."[42] Worse yet, he was seen talking with a German military attaché in Washington, and as a result was suspected of selling vital security information. This suspicion in turn was naturally carried over by the disappointed French to other Americans attempting to enter the French military service, leading one Legionnaire to later write of Hild, "His desertion did untold harm to the brave American boys who entered French Army aviation later on."[43]

Finally, the neutrality of the United States entered into the initial rejection of the proposed all-American squadron. While Article 6 (Chapter I, Convention V) of the 1907 Hague Convention expressly permitted "persons . . . to offer their services to one of the belligerents," the formation of a group such as an American squadron was a different matter. The Germans could argue quite convincingly that any official French show of enthusiasm or marked hints of encourage-ment—inherent in the authorization of an American unit—was a direct violation of Article 4 of the same chapter and convention in that the French were recruiting "corps of combatants" in a neutral country through the power of the press. They could also argue that the French already had a service unit designed for foreigners in the Foreign Legion, a unit where nationality traditionally meant very little. Aviators, on the other hand, and particularly a squadron of American volunteers, could hardly avoid having a "national character."

Then, too, as long as the United States government adopted a strict interpretation of neutrality, as evidenced by the legalistic attitude of Ambassador Sharp, there was a distinct danger that active encourage-ment of American volunteers by French officials might have an adverse effect on American public opinion. Citizen Genêt, they recalled, had pulled just such a diplomatic blunder in 1792, when the French had far greater reason than they had in 1914 to expect widespread American sympathy and support.

The French worried long and hard about this one. Not until mid 1915, when it was evident that the war might very well be a long one, did they conclude that authorization of an all-American squadron did not violate the Hague Convention.[44] Until that decision had been made, the French were naturally unwilling to approve a project that involved the neutrality of the United States. Little wonder, then, that French officialdom, with one or two exceptions, did not tumble to the idea at first.

## The Door Is Opened

Meanwhile, if the French were firm in their refusal to allow an all-American squadron, they seemed to have lost focus on Frederick Hild and were slowly modifying their position about Americans enter-ing military aviation on an individual basis.

In late October 1914, shortly after his fateful prediction of a squad-ron of volunteers, William Thaw launched his second attempt to enter French aviation. Somewhat secretly, it seems, he joined forces with Bert Hall and James Bach and successfully gained permission to visit the Escadrille D-6,[45] a French squadron stationed nearby. Apparently the three men intended to win support for their application and perhaps even to secure a "name request" to have them assigned to that particular squadron.

With his impressive background in aviation and sterling record in the Foreign Legion, Thaw could afford to be honest, feeling he had every reason to expect a sympathetic hearing. Hall and Bach, on the other hand, had no aviation background whatever. Undaunted, they fell back on a tried and proven procedure by inventing one.[46]

Among the personnel of the Escadrille D-6, the three men met Lt. Félix Brocard, the senior pilot of the squadron. Brocard, soon to be an important official in the Bureau du Sous-Secrétaire d'État de l'Aéronautique, liked their enthusiasm and promised his support.[47] Greatly heartened, the three Americans returned to the front anticipating an almost immediate transfer to aviation.

The visit proved rewarding, at least for James Bach, who learned of his pending transfer the following month. Hall waited yet another month, while Thaw sat fuming. The kind of person who could rejoice in another man's good fortune, Thaw nonetheless could not understand why he, easily the best qualified of the three, had been passed over. As soon as possible, he arranged another leave of absence, and, this time alone, walked the thirty-two kilometers to the D-6. The walk was a sign of grim determination, since Thaw detested the more exhausting modes of travel and ordinarily considered it a mild form of torture to walk further than across the street.[48]

On his second visit to the D-6, Thaw again spoke with Lieutenant Brocard, who assured him that he had not been forgotten and that orders for his transfer would soon be forthcoming.[49] With this bit of good news, Thaw returned rejoicing to the front lines.

The day before Christmas, Thaw finally received the glad tidings. Unlike Hall and Bach, who still had no word as to when they would begin training, he was to enter aviation immediately—in the Escadrille D-6, of all units. With some sadness, however, he noted that he was to serve not as a pilot, but as an observer and *soldat-mitrailleur*, or gunner.[50]

Thaw flew with the D-6 for only one month. He was a pilot and could not be satisfied with less. Thus, although he had flown only the Curtiss hydroplane, he borrowed a page from Hall and Bach and set about convincing the French authorities that he could fly just about anything. The French accepted him at his word and on 1 February he was sent to Saint-Cyr to learn to fly the Caudron, a two-place reconnaissance and bombardment craft. As his first efforts at deceit were a rousing success, Thaw decided to try again. "I told them that my name was W. Caudron Thaw," he reported in a letter home, "and finally persuaded them to give me a try." Naturally Thaw failed to mention that he had "never flown on land, never with a rotary motor, never with a propeller in front and never with that control."[51]

Thaw lived through this initial flight and through the others that followed. On 15 March he received the coveted military *brevet* (license), the first American other than Hild to be so honored.[52]

Meanwhile, Bert Hall received his orders and left the regiment on 28 December 1914 for pilot training. His claims to prior aviation experience had preceded him, and upon arrival at Pau he found himself faced with grim reality. He was told to climb into a waiting airplane and show what he could do.

At this point, Hall probably displayed as much raw courage as at any time in his life. While climbing into the cockpit, he is reported to have said, "I'll drive this thing like a baby carriage."[53]

Like many a fledgling pilot, Hall soon found that flying was not easy. The airplane "zig-zagged across the field like a drunken duck" and, completely out of control, dashed itself to pieces against a hangar wall. Hall was not injured, except for his dignity and a scratched knee, but he endured a period of intense embarrassment while a French officer poured out invectives upon his head, ending the scathing lecture with an invitation to stay in aviation. "You have never even been in an aeroplane," he shouted at Hall, "but you have guts, that much I will say for you."[54]

James Bach joined Hall at Pau in early March and the two men became partners in misfortune. Their claims to past flying experience were now known to be false. This, together with the fact that they wrecked a distressingly large number of training planes, brought them under the suspicious eyes of French authorities, who began to wonder if the two men were not really spies, sent to "sabotage our material and interfere with the training of pilots." As a counterplay, security agents posing as student pilots were brought into the camp and billeted next to the two Americans.[55]

Despite their initial troubles, both Bach and Hall received their military *brevets*. Bach, free of all suspicion, graduated from flying training on 4 July 1915. Hall, still under a cloud, finished his schooling on 19 August.[56]

The entrance of Thaw, Bach, and Hall into aviation actually brought to five the number of Americans in the Service Aéronautique. The other two were Gervais Raoul Lufbery of Wallingford, Connecticut, and Didier Masson of Los Angeles, both unusual men and both native French, which may in part account for their acceptance into aviation in preference to other Americans.

Lufbery, the third son of an American father and a French mother, was a most unusual person. Doomed by a series of misfortunes to a lonely life, he had been virtually on his own since childhood. At the age of fourteen he became a world wanderer. By the time he was twenty-seven, he had lived and worked in Africa, the Near East, the Balkans, continental Europe, the United States, and the Far East, and had served with the United States Army in the Philippines.

While in Saigon in 1912, Lufbery met Marc Pourpe, the famed French flier, and became his devoted friend and mechanic. As a team the two men gave exhibitions throughout the Near and Far East, but in August 1914 they were back in Paris to buy a new airplane before undertaking a new tour. The war interrupted their plans. Pourpe, a true-blue patriot, hastened to join up as a pilot. Lufbery attempted to follow his friend into the Service Aéronautique, only to be checked by the law precluding a foreigner from serving in other than the Foreign Legion. Lufbery marched to the Hôtel des Invalides with the forty-one other Americans on 21 August 1914 and enlisted in the Legion, but through Pourpe's influence he was assigned "detached" duty with the Service Aéronautique the following week. In a matter of days he was again serving as Pourpe's mechanic.[57]

The unusually strong friendship between Lufbery and Pourpe came to a tragic end on 2 December 1914, when Pourpe was killed while attempting a night landing in a fog. Lufbery was devastated. Somehow blaming the Germans for the accident, he swore eternal vengence. From that day forth, to quote one acquaintance, "Raoul Lufbery flew, fought and died for revenge."[58]

There was no revenge to be had as a mechanic, so Lufbery applied for pilot training. It was an auspicious time, for the mushrooming Service Aéronautique needed pilots. Perhaps to his surprise he was accepted, entering flying training the following May. Two months later he received his *brevet* in the Maurice Farman, a slow and clumsy bombardment machine.[59]

Like Lufbery, Didier Masson had a most unusual past. He was a young man when he immigrated to California in 1905. Four years later he took up flying. A true daredevil and exhibition pilot, he lived through so many crashes that he became known as "the Rubber Man."[60]

In 1913, Masson went to Mexico where he signed on with General Obregon in the campaign against General Huerta. As Obregon's entire air force, Masson flew an antique Curtiss, primarily scouting for the general, although on his own initiative he tried dropping a can of dynamite down the smokestack of Huerta's one-gunboat navy. This was surely one of the first attempts at serious aerial bombardment, but, not surprisingly, it was as ineffective as it was crude.[61]

At the outbreak of the war in August 1914 Masson, now an American citizen, hurried back to the land of his birth, where he successfully enlisted in the infantry of the regular army. He wanted to fly, however, and after several months fighting in the trenches he managed to get assigned to the Service Aéronautique. He took his military *brevet* on 10 May 1915 in the Caudron, the same lumbering machine Thaw was flying.[62]

The fact that Thaw, Bach, Hall, Lufbery, and Masson had found their way into French military aviation by the beginning of 1915 represents an important landmark in the formation of an all-American squadron of volunteers. Their overall performance, along with that of other Americans in the Foreign Legion, several of whom had already lost their lives, was more than enough to overcome the contagious distaste of Hild and to re-create confidence in the American volunteer per se. Moreover, by acting on their own initiative and gaining entrance into aviation, they had opened the door, as it were, thereby creating an invaluable precedent. Through their conspicuous devotion to duty they convinced the French that they could be very useful in the Service Aéronautique, so much so in fact that the French soon proved willing to circumvent the law forbidding foreigners to serve outside the Foreign Legion. With the same bit of bureaucratic maneuvering they used with Lufbery, they now accepted as a matter of policy that the Americans could enlist in the Legion with detached duty to the Service Aéronautique. Gone too was the standard argument that there was no place for the Americans in aviation because of the abundance of French volunteers. Indeed, a mushrooming air service, now suffering impressive combat losses, had such a pressing need for aviators that some squadrons were encouraged to train observers and even mechanics as pilots while at the front.[63]

In this regard, a second major step was taken in late February and early March 1915, when Frazier Curtis and Norman Prince enlisted in French aviation. The importance of this step lay not in any intrinsic value of the two men as qualified pilots, but in the manner in which they were allowed to enlist.

After the French War Department had officially rejected the proposed all-American squadron in mid-February 1915, Prince and Curtis, who now knew of Thaw and the other American student pilots, discussed the advisability of enlisting in the Service Aéronautique themselves and working on the project from within. The problem was that neither had any inclination to enlist in the Foreign Legion and serve in the trenches, even as a prelude to entering aviation.[64]

Sometime between the fifteenth and the twentieth of February 1915, Robert Bliss, the first secretary of the American Embassy in Paris, and a man not known for favoring the American Legionnaires, introduced Prince to Jarousse de Sillac, an undersecretary of the French Ministry of Foreign Affairs. De Sillac, a career diplomat, had considerable influence, along with an outstanding reputation for patriotism and prudence.[65] This introduction, as later events would have it, not only solved Prince's and Curtis's personal problem about getting into aviation, but a great many other problems associated with the founding of the proposed squadron as well.

De Sillac listened to Prince's proposal with more than ordinary interest. Recognizing in it a possible center of mutual pride and interest for both Americans and Frenchmen, he promised his complete support. Equally important, he was in a position to do something about it. A few days later, he wrote an important letter to his friend, Col. Paul Bouttieaux of the Ministry of War.

I beg to transmit to you herewith the names of six young men, citizens of the United States of America, who desire to enlist in the French Aviation—an offer which was not accepted by the Minister of War. Permit me to call your attention to this matter, insisting upon its great interest. It appears to me that there might be great advantages in the creation of an American Squadron. The United States would be proud of the fact that certain of her young men, acting as did Lafayette, had come to fight for France and civilization. The resulting sentiment of enthusiasm could have but one effect: to turn the Americans in the direction of the Allies. There is a precedent in the Legion of Garibaldi, which has had an undeniably good influence on Franco-Italian relations. If you approve these considerations, I am confident that it will be possible to accept these young men and to authorize their enlistment in such a manner that they may be grouped under the direction of a French chief. In doing this you will contribute to the happiness of these six Americans.[66]

De Sillac attached a memorandum to this letter, containing the names of the six Americans alluded to above. Besides William Thaw, Bert Hall, and James Bach, who were already in aviation but were included so that they might be "grouped under the direction of a French chief," the list included Norman Prince, Frazier Curtis, and Elliott C. Cowdin. Cowdin, the son of a bankrupt New York silk merchant and a close friend of Norman Prince, was then driving for the American Ambulance Corps.[67]

Colonel Bouttieaux's reply was dated 24 February. It proved encouraging, but considering its wording and the short time taken in answering de Sillac's letter, could hardly be taken as the official War Department view. "I think," the colonel wrote, "that your candidates will be welcomed. They should contract an engagement in the French Army for the duration of the war, and should fly only the aeroplanes customarily used in the French Aviation Service."[68]

The letter did not mention the possibility of authorizing an all-American squadron, nor did it discuss the ways and means of enlisting under the terms suggested by Colonel Bouttieaux. Nevertheless, the letter was significant, for it meant that an important ally had been gained in the War Department, which in turn bade fair for the future of the proposed squadron. Also, it was sufficient guarantee for both Curtis and Prince to enlist in the Service Aéronautique, the former on 2 March, the latter two days later. Cowdin followed on 5 March. All entered directly into aviation without the formality of first serving as infantrymen with the Foreign Legion.[69]

## The French Relent

In sponsoring the group of American aviators, de Sillac had assumed a personal responsibility for the integrity and good faith of the volunteers. So had others, among them Georges Leygues, a Deputy and president of the Foreign Affairs Committee, whose daughter had met and married Paul Ayres Rockwell.[70] No doubt this support marked a most important advance in the genesis of the Lafayette Escadrille. The

French obviously reversed their earlier stand against Americans entering directly into aviation, largely because of support by such men as de Sillac and Leygues. At the same time, it seems equally safe to say that such high-level sponsorship did much to insure the future integrity of the squadron once it was organized. Given its inception as an elite unit, there was every reason to keep it that way.

Meanwhile, the French were making some effort to keep the American trainees together—Hall and Bach were transferred to Pau, where Cowdin, Prince, and Curtis were located—although no authorization for an all-American squadron had, in fact, been promised or implied. The agitation for authorization continued, however, with the activity now taking two distinct avenues of approach. On the one hand, de Sillac and other French officials used their positions and influence in an *action systematique,* although initially at least they were more than offset by the Minister of War's basic rejection of the idea. He had already voiced his opinion, and later was joined in it by the Minister of Foreign Affairs.[71] Thaw, Prince, and Curtis, on the other hand, were agitating from their respective squadrons and training schools, attempting to personally present their case to some officials while writing letters to others. Among the airmen, however, there was little coordination and direction to their efforts, although Thaw early recognized this weakness and worked hard for the formation of a central committee to deal directly with the French.[72]

In the spring of 1915 Curtis was suddenly forced to change to the other camp. While training at Avord, he experienced an unfortunate series of accidents that undermined his health and forced his retirement from aviation. Sent to Paris to recuperate, he appointed himself a committee of one to visit young American men and urge their enlistment in aviation, apparently on the premise that the more Americans there were in aviation, the more likely it was that an all-American squadron would be authorized. On one such excursion to members of the American Ambulance Corps, he learned of Edmund Gros's aspirations for getting a big aviation corps of volunteers. He tried to speak with the doctor, but failing in the attempt, left a note indicating a desire to meet and discuss the matter of volunteers, suggesting that "we ought to be able to work together" and offering to "introduce you to one of my friends who is pretty much running this enlarged Corps."[73]

Dr. Gros lost no time in reaching Curtis, and a few days later was rewarded with an introduction to de Sillac. It proved a most fruitful and consequential meeting, for Gros and de Sillac, both admirably equipped to deal with French officialdom, agreed to unite their efforts. The happy result was the organization of the Franco-American Committee, with de Sillac as president, Gros as vice-president, and Frederick Allen, a prominent member of the American colony in Paris, the remaining member.[74]

The organization of the Franco-American Committee stands as another milestone along the pathway leading to the authorization and organization of an American squadron. It unified the efforts of those working to this end, and by combining in it persons of influence and understanding, gave overall direction and cohesion to the movement.

More than four months had now passed since Colonel Bouttieaux's encouraging letter, and yet no firm commitment on the authorization of the proposed squadron had been made, nor did there appear to be any prospect for it in the immediate future. The Franco-American Committee therefore sought to hurry things along. Their first step in this direction was a giant one.

On 8 July 1915 Gros and de Sillac sponsored a luncheon at the home of a friend, Senator Gaston Menier. Those present included Colonel Bouttieaux, Senator Menier, Dr. Gros, de Sillac, Leon Bourgeois, Robert Bacon, and Dr. William White, the latter a visiting physician from Philadelphia. The guest of honor, however, was Gen. Auguste Hirshauer, the chief of French military aeronautics. Before the evening was over, new hope had been injected into the plan for a squadron of American volunteers. The general, now persuaded of the plan's feasibility and benefits, agreed to give orders for the formation of just such a squadron, to be known as the Escadrille Américaine.[75]

The way seemed open at last. Although almost everyone, including the ministers of war and foreign affairs, soon approved the idea in principle,[76] much remained to be done. Problems concerning organization, command, equipment, and the like, would have to be resolved before it could become a reality. This took time, and to the Franco-American Committee and the American fliers in training and at the front, another oppressive period of delay set in.

In a way, this was an unusually tense period. Some important Frenchmen had yet to be persuaded, and a great deal hinged on the performance of the American airmen already at the front. If there were even one bad experience the project would almost certainly collapse.

Fortunately there were no such incidents. In fact, the American airmen soon ran up such an impressive record that in September 1915 the French Minister of Foreign Affairs referred to them in an important memo as an elite group. Elliot Cowdin, for example, flying with the Escadrille Voisin B-108, was cited in July 1915 as an "excellent pilot who often attacked enemy aeroplanes," an impressive accomplishment, since the VB-108 was a bombardment squadron. A month later, Norman Prince, flying in the same unit, was described in a citation as an "excellent military pilot who has consistently displayed great audacity and presence of mind."[77]

James Bach added some luster to himself by volunteering to land French spies behind German lines, one of the most dangerous missions available. He came to ruin on his first attempt, but still handled himself in such a way as to make the French proud. Bach and another pilot named Mangeot had successfully landed their aircraft in a field covered with bushes and small trees and discharged their dangerous cargoes. Bach got off the ground safely, but Mangeot's airplane flipped over. Bach returned and again landed safely. This time, however, his own wing struck a tree on takeoff and the hapless pilots found themselves stranded. Both were captured and twice tried as spies, but with the help of an able German lawyer they survived the ordeal and ended up legitimate prisoners of war.[79]

Meanwhile, William Thaw had set a standard for all. In one month—May 1915—he earned three citations and promotion to the rank of sergeant for "piloting his machine with remarkable mastery" and for his "outstanding qualities of *bravoure* and *sang-froid*." In one instance, Thaw and his officer observer regulated artillery fire for half an hour while under such intense fire that when they returned, the machine was found to be shot up beyond repair.[79]

In the aggregate, the record of the American airmen was as impressive as it was critical. The French Minister of Foreign Affairs, who had some serious reservations about the proposed squadron, nonetheless wrote the Premier that the American fliers then in combat "distinguished themselves as aviators of great merit."[80] Under the circumstances, it is difficult to avoid the conclusion that the combat record of this elite group further softened the French attitude and thus helped make the formation of the Escadrille Américaine a reality.

Meanwhile, the Franco-American Committee could also point to some progress. On 21 August it had reached an agreement with the Ministry of War and the Ministry of Foreign Affairs that henceforth the

Committee would represent the American interests touching upon the proposed squadron.[81] The consolidation of effort was now complete.

There was also some progress within the Ministry of War, although this was essentially unknown to the Americans. On 21 August 1915 General Hirshauer, writing to the Minister of Foreign Affairs "for and by order of the Minister of War," announced the decision to "group the American aviators presently serving in the army into a single squadron." The general further laid down some ground rules for establishing the squadron and accepting further volunteers.

Enlistments will be made on an individual basis. Authorization for same will be given by my office after examination of the references [a required item of all American volunteers] with particular emphasis on nationality and moral integrity. Enlistment . . . will be under the colors of the Foreign Legion with the provision, in all cases, for transfer to aviation. . . . The enlistees will be united in a single aviation group and will be placed under the same administrative and disciplinary regulations presently used by our army. Student pilots will go to the same schools as French pilots.[82]

When this news reached the Franco-American Committee, the sponsors of the proposed squadron took heart, but expressed some disappointment. The Committee, thinking big, had an aggressive recruitment program in mind, which entailed mailing brochures to prominent American sporting clubs, universities, and individuals, encouraging Americans to come to France to fly.[83] Before such a program could even hope for success, some guarantees regarding the treatment of the volunteers were essential.

The French War Department had already discussed this matter to some extent,[84] but now went so far as to ask the Franco-American Committee what it had in mind. The Committee requested in reply:

1. That every care be taken to settle at Paris their medical fitness for flying.
2. That if, once enlisted, they show ineptitude for flying, it be made possible to release them from further obligatory service.
3. That they be treated, insofar as possible, with courtesy inspired by their generosity in offering their lives in the service of France.[85]

By this time the French were generally aware of the value an all-American squadron would have towards the French war effort. High-level government documents now mentioned the "sympathy and favorable public opinion" that would be generated in America by the formation of the squadron, and the "fine results" produced by Americans flying at the front. Recognizing the "moral and military arguments which favored it," the French were showing a willingness not only to authorize an all-American squadron, but were actually looking to the possibility of allowing an increase in aviation volunteers.[86] Still, there can be no question but that the French remained concerned about the neutrality issue. Great care was taken to incorporate the Americans into the Foreign Legion before "detaching" them for duty with the Service Aéronautique.

For these and allied reasons, the Franco-American Committee did not have much trouble getting the French to grant special consideration to the volunteers. Whereas in August, General Hirshauer had declared himself unable to authorize individuals who proved inept in flying to return to civilian status because "present laws do not permit it," the following December an official wrote the Committee,

> It gives me pleasure to inform you . . . that the Direction of Infantry has admitted the possibility of releasing Americans serving in French Aviation . . . if they do not satisfy the conditions demanded of the flying personnel. . . . The following solution, which should be satisfactory to those interested, has been authorized: The letter sent to Americans, authorizing their engagement in the French Aviation will contain the following clause: "It is guaranteed to you that this act of engagement may be rescinded, either on your demand, or on demand of the military authorities, in case of proven inaptitude for service in the flying personnel of the Military Aviation."[87]

## The Christmas Leave Incident

With things going smoothly at last, Thaw, Prince, and Cowdin returned to the United States in December 1915 for a thirty-day leave. The visit did much to confirm the view that American public opinion was favorable to Americans flying for France. At the same time, it also temporarily resurrected the neutrality issue. Indeed, with a little misfortune thrown in, it could easily have brought the whole process to an abrupt halt.

To their surprise, the three airmen were given considerable publicity, much of it on the front pages and nearly all of it highly favorable. Thaw in particular received a great deal of attention, and with good reason. For one thing, the name was well known. Harry Thaw, a cousin to William, had been involved in one of the most celebrated murders of the century nine years before. Also, William had made a few headlines himself as a young man for flying under bridges. Now he returned as a hero from abroad, a combat airman and newly promoted *sous-lieu-tenant*, the only American so far to achieve officer rank with the French forces.[88]

Not everyone, of course, was happy to see the young Americans treated as heroes. Their presence and applause alarmed the strict neutralists and angered those advocating support of the Central Powers. Thaw himself had a brief, cold encounter in a New York barbershop with Count Johann von Bernstorff, the German ambassador to the United States, during which the count suggested that the American pilots voluntarily intern themselves in order to avoid an international incident. Thaw walked out on the ambassador, but Bernstorff, an able diplomat, dutifully brought the issue of the American volunteers before Robert Lansing, Secretary of State.[89] Concurrently, George Viereck, the editor of the strongly pro-German newspaper the *Fatherland*, sent an open telegram to the Secretary of State which aggravated as well as outlined the problem, since it was published in the leading New York newspapers.

These men, though of American birth, are officers in active service in the French army, and it would be a gross violation of American neutrality if they were not at once detained so as to prevent their return to the front. In view of the fact that the neutrality of the Administration has been seriously questioned, both here and abroad, I trust that you will take immediate action in the case and that you will hold these three officers in confinement unless they give their parole not to leave American territory without permission.

Inasmuch as you have so ardently championed the rights of neutrals as against the Central Powers, I feel sure that you will gladly avail yourself of the opportunity to demonstrate to the world that the United States Government is also alive to its neutral duties. In fact, I am advised that we have no other choice in the matter unless we regard international conventions as "scraps of paper."[90]

While Secretary of State Lansing was contemplating what action, if any, he should take, the three airmen, alarmed at the furor, secretly boarded ship in New York and sailed for Europe. In departing, they left behind a protest "in the name of American youth against the feeble policy of their country."[91]

From the standpoint of the Franco-American Committee, these events gave cause for some satisfaction and some concern. On the one hand, an aggressive move by the State Department could easily cancel the whole program. On the other, the idea of an all-American squadron had virtually received a public vote of confidence. That was enough to continue the movement for authorization and activation of the proposed squadron unabated.

## Success

The State Department chose not to press the issue and the movement picked up momentum throughout January and February 1916, until authorization seemed a certainty. As James R. McConnell, one of the airmen flying at the front, put it, "Every day somebody 'had it absolutely straight' that we were to become a unit at the front, and every other day, the report turned out to be untrue." Finally on 14 March 1916, Col. Henri Regnier, the new director of military aeronautics, gave the word everyone was waiting for. He wrote to the Committee:

> General Headquarters has just replied, informing me that an American squadron will be organized, with the pilots whose names follow: William Thaw, Elliot Cowdin, Kiffin Rockwell, Norman Prince, Charles C. Johnson, Clyde Balsley, Victor Chapman, Lawrence Rumsey, and James R. McConnell. . . . I have every reason to believe that the . . . squadron will be constituted rapidly . . . and I will keep you posted as to what is done in this matter.[92]

There was still a delay of more than a month, primarily because the great Battle of Verdun then in progress made the necessary accumulation of men and equipment extremely difficult.[93] These problems were eventually overcome, however, and the squadron became a reality on 16 April 1916. It received the official designation of Escadrille N-124, but virtually everyone called it the Escadrille Américaine.

While the military factor cannot be ignored, political motives were the primary factor behind French recognition of the new squadron. Top French officials clearly recognized that an elite squadron of American volunteers fighting at the front would almost automatically bring France and the United States closer together, although in retrospect it is certain that they seriously underestimated this effect and therefore failed to exploit the matter fully.[94] As a step in that direction, however, they activated the Escadrille Américaine not in reconnaissance, artillery ranging, or bombardment as one might expect—they customarily recruited fighter pilots from bombing and observation squadrons—but in *avion de chasse*, easily the most glamorous and publicized aspect of military aviation. Also, the squadron was given the Bébé Nieuport,

France's first real fighter plane. This aircraft, the French answer to the Fokker Eindecker with its synchronized machine gun, was in critical demand. Small (hence the name *Bébé*), with only 16 square yards of wing surface and an 80 (later a 110) hp Le Rhône rotary engine that gave it a top speed of around 100 miles per hour, it handled superbly. Though it could not match the Eindecker in firepower, it was clearly the superior airplane, and only four months after its appearance at the front, had won the nickname of "machine of aces and ace of machines."[95] Certainly the pilots of the Escadrille Américaine were both flattered and honored to receive it.

## The Originals

Colonel Regnier's letter of 14 March 1916 to the Franco-American committee had mentioned the names of nine American pilots who would constitute the original Escadrille Américaine. For reasons not yet clear, however, three of the men specified—Charles C. Johnson, Clyde Balsley, and Lawrence Rumsey—did not make the first roster. Bert Hall was added, together with the two French officers who would command the unit, again bringing the number of "originals" up to nine.[96] These men who launched the famed Lafayette Escadrille deserve special mention, for by any standards, they were an unusual group.

Capt. Georges Thenault, the squadron commander, came from the small village of Celles l'Evescault, in the Deux-Sèvres department. A graduate of St. Cyr and a career army officer, he had been associated with French aviation from the beginning of the war and was one of the first regular army officers to learn to fly.[97]

By nature a friendly man but always an officer, Thenault was a pilot of proven experience and ability when William Thaw knew him as commanding officer of the Escadrille Caudron 42 in 1915. Thenault had heard Thaw speak of his hope for an all-American squadron and, approving the idea, manifested some interest in becoming its commander. Thaw in turn liked and respected Thenault. He therefore passed the captain's name along when discussing the proposed squadron with French authorities.[98]

Thenault's chosen second-in-command was Lt. Alfred de Laage de Meux, a close friend. De Laage came from a Poitevine family of ancient military aristocracy and glorious traditions. He was born in the family chateau near Clesse, in the Deux-Sèvres department, and was a scientific farmer by occupation when the war broke out. Born to command and to lead, he entered combat as an officer with the 14th Dragoons, but a painful leg wound in August 1914, a long period of convalescence, and the inactivation of the Dragoons in early 1915 left him free to look for some other way to serve. In March 1915 he entered the Service Aéronautique as an observer and machine gunner. Still not satisfied, he set out to become a pilot and so perfected his flying skills while carrying on his other duties that he became one of the few to qualify as a combat pilot without a single day in the training schools.[99]

Already recognized for his flying ability during the first months of the Battle of Verdun, de Laage de Meux was a standout with the Lafayette Escadrille. One pilot who knew him well called him "the man in the French Army," and Hall and Nordhoff wrote that he "represented all that is best in French character and had a power of personal magnetism which made him a natural leader."[100]

William Thaw was another standout. His record before becoming part of the Escadrille Américaine has already been mentioned, but with the latter assignment came responsibility, something which brought him into full blossom. As the only American holding officer status, Thaw had the unusually difficult task of serving as mediator between the intensely patriotic and strict disciplinarians of the French army, and the individualistic, adventuresome, and fun-loving Americans. It was a delicate position to be in, one that kept him in "hot water most of the time."[101]

Yet Thaw was not only highly respected by the French. No other pilot in the Escadrille Américaine was so beloved by his comrades in arms.

> I can never speak or write about Bill [one acquaintance wrote] without a certain feeling of awe, amounting almost to reverence. . . . When the Gods that be finished making Bill, they broke the mold. . . .
> He never lost, except by death, a friend once made, man, woman or child. With a magnificent record, he emerged from that seething cauldron without a trace of swelled head, still just "plain ole Bill." It is hard to write about Bill Thaw without becoming maudlin.[102]

Kiffin Rockwell, also mentioned earlier, was another distinguished member of the Escadrille Américaine. After suffering a leg wound in the Artois Offensive of May 1915, Rockwell found himself unable to make the long marches and carry the sixty-pound pack demanded of members of the Foreign Legion. Thus, the following July, when Thaw suggested aviation to his fellow Legionnaire, Rockwell welcomed the idea.[103]

Rockwell was an excellent aviator, but it was his personality that added the most luster to the squadron. He was enthusiastic, seemingly fearless—his basic tactic was to hold his fire until he was extremely close to the enemy—and thoroughly idealistic. One individual insisted that he was the soul of the squadron and Captain Thenault, at Rockwell's funeral, referred to him as the "best and bravest of us all."[104]

Rockwell's enthusiasm and idealism were matched by Victor Chapman, another individual who would have stood out in any crowd. The son of John Jay Chapman, a prominent lawyer, poet, and essayist, Victor had been educated at St. Paul's and Harvard before going to Paris in 1913 to study architecture. With his father's permission, he enlisted in the Foreign Legion in September 1914, where he soon earned an enviable reputation for tenacity and devotion to duty.[105]

Chapman transferred to aviation in August 1915 because he felt his ten months in the trenches had "neither helped the French nor injured the Germans." He was marvelously sensitive to the sufferings of others, yet he seemed to love danger, traits that made it nearly certain that he would not survive the war.[106] Of him, one friend wrote, "The mantle of civilization was never stripped from him as from so many others. Despite the searing horrors of war, his artistic soul was able to see the beauty in anything; in shell-torn earth, in ruined villages, in a sea of clouds, in the stark skeletons of fire-blackened forests. Just as in humans, he saw only the best in nature and overlooked the unpleasant."[107]

This assessment, by a fellow pilot in the Lafayette Escadrille, is hardly an overstatement. His letters, preserved and later published by his father, are flush with a kind of rosy zest for life and include such things as some gruelling maneuvers being held in "a charming wood with the leaves just popping out, and the early blossoms and ground flowers out."[108]

James R. McConnell of Carthage, North Carolina, also fell into the category of the well-educated, idealistic, and devoted individuals who were so conspicuous among the early members of the Lafayette Escadrille. The son of a prominent judge and railway president, his education included study at preparatory schools in New York, and later study at the University of Virginia, where he became known for his brilliant mind, warm personality, and great sense of humor.[109]

McConnell's love for France and his belief in the Allied cause brought him to France in 1915 to drive ambulances, and his demeanor on the battlefield earned him an impressive citation. He enlisted in aviation in October 1915 because, as he put it, "All along I had been convinced that the United States ought to aid in the struggle against Germany. With that conviction, it was plainly up to me to do more than drive an ambulance. The more I saw of the splendour of the fight the French were fighting, the more I felt like an *embusque*—what the British call a 'shirker.' So I made up my mind to go into aviation."[110] McConnell also excelled in aviation. A citation called him a "pilot as modest as he is courageous," and one comrade stated flatly that he was a "man of infinite courage and devotion."[111]

Like so many of the early members of the Escadrille Américaine, Norman Prince entered the squadron having already demonstrated his love for France, his personal bravery, and sense of responsibility. Citations dating from his early days in aviation, of which there were several, mentioned his bravery, audacity, impatience to get into the air, and fondness for danger. Friends described him as a "brilliant pilot," adding that "he was sparing of speech but practically oozed personality and his energy and enthusiasm were unbounded."[112]

Prince also had an intense desire to excel and gain preeminence, a trait that served him well in battle, but which hinted of arrogance and jealousy to his comrades in the Escadrille Américaine. Thus were sown some of the seeds of dissension that somehow seem unavoidable in a unit under the tensions of war.[113]

Weston Bert Hall and Elliot Cowdin, the two remaining members of the original Lafayette Escadrille soon proved to be a notch below the others. Hall in particular had his ups and downs. At low ebb as a taxi driver in Paris, he served honorably but without distinction in the Foreign Legion. As mentioned earlier, he did poorly in flying training, but he served with some distinction during his first flying days at the front. His basic problem was an abrasive, almost repulsive personality that made him something of a misfit among his more cultured colleagues. Eventually his fellow Americans forced him out of the squadron.[114]

Elliot Cowdin, it will be recalled, came directly into aviation from civilian life. Like Hall, he had a good record in combat, at least in the beginning, earning three impressive citations which mentioned such things as energy and bravery. He liked to have things his own way, however, and was something of a troublemaker when he didn't get it. He had been in four different squadrons before coming to the Escadrille Américaine, nor did he remain long with that one.[115]

In an elite squadron like the Escadrille Américaine personality was important, and both Hall and Cowdin helped to initiate a change in the selection process. Henceforth, when a replacement was needed or the number of pilots were to be increased, Captain Thenault personally visited the flying schools and interviewed the more likely prospects. These in turn were largely determined by the original members of the squadron or the more reliable members who took their places.[116] Thus in a very real way the squadron helped determine its own composition. The process was not infallible, of course, and two or three mistakes were made, but in these cases the flaws appeared only after the men were in the squadron.

Looking back, it is safe to say that any defects of personality among the originals, however irritating, were more than offset by the unusually high caliber of the first men to make up the Escadrille Américaine. With the exception of Bert Hall, all were well educated, with good family backgrounds. And, with some allowance for lack of consistency on the part of Hall and Cowdin, all were devoted soldiers, perfectly willing to die, if need be, for what they felt was a worthy cause. Little wonder that the French were much impressed that such men would volunteer their services. Little wonder too that the Escadrille Américaine was considered an elite group from the beginning.

# 2      The Air War

On the evening of 17 April 1917, a group of young Americans gathered in a Paris restaurant to celebrate the activation of the N-124 and to bid farewell to William Thaw, Norman Prince, James McConnell, and Kiffin Rockwell, who would be departing for the front the next morning. Besides the four guests of honor, the group included Paul Rockwell, Kiffin's brother; Clyde Balsley, who was then at the Reserve Générale Aéronautique (RGA) awaiting assignment; Charles C. Johnson, on his way to the RGA; Lawrence Rumsey, in a reserve unit awaiting transfer to the front; and a young Frenchman named Michel who was to be Prince's mechanic.[1] All save Paul Rockwell and Michel were pilots who were or soon would be members of the N-124, but the two, like the others, had a prime interest in the unit that would be so much a part of their future.

The gathering was a joyful one. All were lighthearted with the realization that something remarkable and unique, their "fondest ambition" as one of them termed it, was now a reality. Soon the airmen would be flying for France against Germany, the great "enemy of mankind." Moreover, they would be fighting in a new medium, one so inherently individualistic and exhilarating that they could look forward to an exciting, heroic future.

It is doubtful that, in their enthusiasm, they paused to give consideration to the other side of the story, namely, that in 1916 combat flying was no longer a sport. In a logical but unexpected way, it had grown to be a grim and bloody business, although it somehow never lost its intense aura of glamour. Indeed, so rapidly had military aviation come of age and so emeshed were the agony and ecstasy of it all, it is necessary to briefly review the background of the so-called air war if one is to understand the future role of the Escadrille Américaine.

## The Beginnings: 1914

On the eve of the Great War, it hardly seemed possible that military aviation would play other than a minor role in the coming conflict. All major belligerents had aircraft assigned to their military organizations, and the potential of the airplane had been discussed by military theorists and demonstrated in maneuvers. But in the quick war of movement anticipated by the belligerents, with its prime emphasis on the headlong offensive culminating in one great, decisive battle, aviation had little to offer. As a result, when the war began, no nation had aircraft specifically designed and constructed with military purposes in mind. Moreover, the airplanes then available for duty in the field were comparatively few in number. The 7 German armies concentrated in the west had 30 field aviation sections with a total of 180 machines; the British had 4 squadrons with a nominal strength of 12 planes each; and the French had 136 machines divided up into 21 army *escadrilles* and 2 cavalry *escadrilles*.[2]

In the war plans of 1914, airplanes could best be used to gather reconnaissance information, to assist in dispelling what military people aptly called the "fog of war." Naturally this fact did not escape those nations priding themselves on up-to-date armies. To all major belligerents of 1914, the first and primary duty of their respective air services was, as the British put it, "observation from the air." Thus the Germans initially limited the maximum cruising altitude of their airplanes to 2400 feet, high enough to gain some immunity from ground fire, yet not so high as to preclude good aerial observations.[3] The same logic, at least in the beginning, left both sides well satisfied with the slow, lumbering aircraft then in use. Indeed, at this point the authorities could hardly see any reason for wanting other than what they had. In their view, the airplane would have to fit the brief, vicious ground war they had in mind.

It is not surprising that the "experts" failed to foresee the lengthy and bitter struggle of trench warfare, from which airpower received most of its emphasis. Few individuals, civil or military, even imagined such a thing. Even so, it is safe to say that they were quite correct in their emphasis on aerial reconnaissance as the primary function of the airplane. Aerial reconnaissance remained the prime function throughout the war, in some ways gaining in importance as the war dragged on. And it was this importance, in turn, that triggered the air war.

In theory aerial reconnaissance promised to be an easy yet invaluable tool to lift the "fog of war." It certainly seemed inherently better than the cavalry, the traditional mode of reconnaissance. Whereas the cavalry not only had limited perspective, usually took considerable time to get where they were going, and now had to face fearsome automatic weapons fire as well, the airmen supposedly enjoyed easy access to enemy positions and a wide, panoramic view when they got there. In practice, however, aerial reconnaissance did not live up to expectations, particularly in the early months of the war. The limitations were many, the failures legion and, in some instances, nearly disastrous. The French, for example, had a detailed plan for "strategic reconnaissance" which would, in theory at least, pinpoint the place and strength of German concentrations in the west before actual combat began. This plan, if successful, might very well have detected the nature and scope of the famed Schlieffen Plan, thereby alerting the French to the danger on the left flank. The plan failed, not from willful negligence, but from several limitations which, largely representative of all belligerents, were as logical for the time and circumstances as they were regrettable later on.

In the first place, because of insufficient aircraft and fear of violating Belgian neutrality, the French aviation forces were so deployed as to be unable to detect the important buildup on their left. Also, at this early date the airmen themselves were simply not properly equipped or trained to recognize with certainty what they saw. As a result, they made some spectacular mistakes, errors that the army leaders could not fail to notice. Moreover, the airmen themselves often gave conflicting reports. Indeed, the overall performance was such that neither side felt they could use aerial observations as prima facie evidence of enemy dispositions and intentions.

Secondly, the French—like the British and particularly the Germans—lacked the proper coordination between the air units and various echelons of the army. Good information as well as bad was often mislaid, and information of particular value to one army might be buried in the files of a neighboring one. (The German official history, for example, estimates that fully 50 percent of the air reports available during the critical Battle of the Marne never reached the headquarters of the German First Army.)[4] Moreover, there were a dozen places between the operational air units and supreme headquarters where an officer, largely on his own initiative and with his own limited experience as a guide, could stop the flow of information which he considered valueless. One need hardly add that a good aerial observation had no value whatever unless authorities on the ground put it to use.

Finally, and most important, the overwhelming emphasis on the offensive, both in the German Schlieffen Plan and in the French Plan XVII, automatically relegated initial enemy troop concentrations to minor importance. Since the initiative lay with the attacker, it was argued, the enemy would be forced to conform the the threat, hence what the troop concentrations would be in the near future could be predicted with considerable certainty. Thus, until the great offensive plans had proven bankrupt, aerial reconnaissance was simply not important enough to get officially excited about.

In the great, chaotic clashes of August and September 1914, aerial reconnaissance clearly revealed both its initial limitations and its critical potential. Both sides became extremely active, of course, with the French (who can be taken as representative of the others) flying nearly 10,000 reconnaissance missions in the first six months of the war. There were failures on both sides, such as the time some British fliers of the 6th Squadron mistook gravestones for tents and spots of tar on the roadways for marching soldiers. And there was an instance when airmen reported "large hostile forces" north of Château Thierry during the German retreat to the Marne, a report that led the British commander of the 1st Corps to proceed with great caution when in reality the enemy troops numbered only two brigades and were in a very vulnerable position.[5]

On the other hand, the successes clearly outweighed the failures during the critical months of 1914. It was air sighting of an advance German column between Brussels and Ninove, for example, which gave warning of an ambitious German turning movement. Aerial reconnaissance helped to indicate and then confirm the fact that the German forces would swing east of Paris, a critical event that helped doom the Schlieffen Plan. Also, allied airmen revealed, in part at least, the terribly important gap that developed between the German First and Second Armies during the Marne campaign, a gap that played a vital role in bringing the German offensive to a halt.

On the other hand, if the British and French missed some opportunities to exploit this gap, it was partly because German airmen were able to pinpoint the threat, thereby giving the Seventh Army time to close it. And finally, although there is still some debate about the details, a particular aerial report by one Lieutenant Berthold of Field Aviation Section 23 helped convince General von Bülow, commander of the Second Army, that the time had come to implement a conditional agreement with a representative of the General Staff and withdraw from a threatened position. So critical was this report that Lieutenant Berthold, having reported his findings to General von Bülow personally, noted in his diary, "I have never seen a man in such agony as His Excellency v. Bülow."[6]

It was in this critical period that airpower in the form of reconnaissance came of age in war. Walter Raleigh, one of the official historians of the Royal Flying Corps, was not being overly generous to the "air arm" when he wrote, "The value of reconnaissance to the army was so great and our military airplanes so few that it was impossible to spare any of them for less essential work."[7] And John R. Cuneo, one of the few military historians to look at airpower in relation to the war as a whole, summed it up as follows:

> From a supplementary means of information relied upon principally for confirmation, the air weapon had begun to become the principal means of operational reconnaissance—an important factor in forming army commanders' decisions. Despite its inexperience and inconsiderable forces, the fallacy of the headlong offensive and the futility of cavalry reconnaissance had assured the air weapon of a permanent place with field armies, and to a lesser extent with corps.[8]

Moreover, both the Entente and Central Powers, when put to the test, proved willing to fight each other in the air in order to maintain air reconnaissance capability. And the impetus for this significant escalation came primarily from the ground forces.

## The Impact of Trench Warfare

In the first weeks of the war, pilots and observers were essentially noncombatants. Aviation writers have tended to overemphasize this remarkable though brief period wherein opposing airmen ignored each other, saluted, or perhaps waved a friendly greeting. It has even been suggested that the airmen were inherently part of an international

though unofficial brotherhood that transcended international bound-
aries, and that combat, when it did come, was largely accidental.
According to one apocryphal story current during the war—in this
instance, picked up by James Norman Hall, who got it from another
bed-ridden aviator who naturally had it first hand—it all began this
way:

A friend of his [the French pilot said] . . . attached to a certain army group
during August and September, 1914, often met a German aviator during his
reconnaissance patrols. In those Arcadian days, fighting in the air was a
development for the future, and these two pilots exchanged greetings, not
cordially, perhaps, but courteously: a wave of the hand, as much as to say, "We
are enemies, but we need not forget the civilities." Then they both went about
their work of spotting batteries, watching for movements of troops, etc. One
morning the German failed to return the salute. The Frenchman thought little
of this, and greeted him in the customary manner at their next meeting. To his
surprise, the Boche shook his fist at him in the most blustering and caddish
way. There was no mistaking the insult. They had passed not fifty metres from
each other, and the Frenchman distinctly saw the closed fist. He was saddened
by the incident, for he hoped that some of the ancient courtesies of war would
survive in the aerial branch of the service, at least. It angered him too; therefore, on his next reconnaissance, he ignored the German. Evidently the Boche
air-squadrons were being Prussianized. The enemy pilot approached very
closely and threw a missile at him. He could not be sure what it was, as the
object went wide of the mark; but he was so incensed that he made a *virage*
[quick turn], and drawing a small flask from his pocket, hurled it at his boorish
antagonist. The flask contained some excellent port, he said, but he was repaid
for the loss in seeing it crash on the exhaust-pipe of the enemy machine.
     This marked the end of courtesy and the beginning of active hostilities in
the air. They were soon shooting at each other with rifles, automatic pistols,
and at last with machine guns.[9]

Actually, aerial combat was inevitable, and the airmen themselves
were partly to blame. From the beginning, they tended to carry
weapons aloft to defend themselves, should they go down behind
enemy lines, and this, together with the seemingly omnipresent temptation to drop something from a plane or shoot at a moving target, were
enough to trigger a spiral of challenge and response. Thus, the initial
weapons included not only pistols, muskets, and rifles, but also bricks,
grenades, and other assorted missiles. The French authorities approved, ordering their airmen to carry objects to drop on the enemy and
providing them with grenades and steel darts called *flechettes*, which
were supposed to rain down on the enemy like hailstones.

No one can state with certainty what the air war would have become had the airmen been left to themselves, primarily because the main impetus towards true combat in the air came not from the airmen, but from the growing importance of airpower, particularly in reconnaissance and artillery ranging. This importance, in turn, grew largely from the advent and distresses of trench warfare.

The advent of trench warfare caught civil and military leaders on both sides completely by surprise. So certain had they been of their plans for quick and decisive victories, they had no alternative plans, and hence, after the "race to the sea" had stretched the lines from the Swiss border to the channel coast, literally millions of men, to quote the eloquent Winston Churchill, "sat facing one another at close quarters without any true idea of what to do next."[10] It was, in fact, a new kind of war, one which immediately displayed an incredible ability to absorb undreamed of quantities of men and materiel while yielding little or no gains in return.

This catastrophic situation, carrying with it consequences that have not yet run their full course, naturally had a great impact upon airpower. The failure of the headlong offensive to channel enemy troops and resources made reconnaissance more important than ever. Yet with no flanks to turn, and facing a solid cordon line of defense, the use of cavalry to scout the enemy positions was out of the question. However much certain army commanders may have questioned the efficaciousness of airpower, they now had no choice but to rely heavily on it.

This increase in importance naturally carried an increase in responsibility. Heretofore almost all aerial reconnaissance had been collected for consumption at the army level. Now, for the purpose of sound defense and the necessary probing offensives up and down the line, the need was also felt at the corps level.[11] At the same time, the various commanders began demanding more exact and detailed information than aerial observers customarily brought back. No longer was it as simple as locating large bodies of troops and determining their direction of march, if any. With the soldiers burrowing into the earth and the increasing use of camouflage, a new trench, a change in gun positions and numbers, a pattern of vehicle tracks entering a forested area could all be important clues. The airmen could not be expected to notice all these details, let alone remember what the terrain looked like the day or the week before. Thus, aerial photography came to be an integral part of the reconnaissance mission.[12]

Actually, aerial cameras had been used, though sparingly, since the war began. But in the first few months of the conflict, when important things such as troop movements could be seen with the naked eye, when aerial photographers were largely unskilled, and when the developing of the film and the distribution of the prints were time-consuming, the camera played little part. With improved training and techniques, however, and in the face of necessity, aerial photography came to be of primary importance. Trench warfare soon taught the various army commanders and intelligence specialists to appreciate recurring photographs of enemy lines and emplacements. On the lower level, soldiers on both sides took little comfort in the knowledge that their positions were now inked in on the enemy's artillery maps.

Aerial ranging of artillery was another potential function of airpower given great emphasis by the advent of trench warfare. This art, for such it was, was designed to furnish long-range artillery batteries with a well-placed observer near the impact area. Like aerial photography, it had been demonstrated before the war, but had received only minor emphasis during the months of maneuver. The stalemate in the trenches made its need a compelling one, particularly since the early years of the war were characterized by a chronic shortage of artillery ammunition.

Artillery ranging from the air might well have become the primary function of airpower in World War I, for artillery, matching range with firepower, was easily the most formidable weapon of the war. The basic problem was one of accuracy. The range of the guns required an observer in or near the impact area to "regulate the fire," that is, to send information back to the gun crews on how to correct their aim. In World War I, this meant regulation by air, for there was no other way. But even in the air there was a serious technological limitation, i.e., the lack of suitable air-to-ground communications. Wireless sets, the obvious answer, were not unknown in the early days of the war, but they had not been refined to the point where they could be regularly carried aloft except by dirigibles.

Until better sets and more powerful airplanes were available, airmen used a variety of methods to signal the batteries, including acrobatic maneuvers, flares, signal lights, and the time-consuming method of simply flying back to the guns and dropping a note. Since none of these proved anywhere near satisfactory, continuing emphasis had to be placed on the wireless sets.

By December 1914, some French and German aircraft were equipped with wireless sets, although it is said that the airmen didn't much like them at first. Rumor had it that they attracted lightning.[13] Nevertheless, they used them as required, and in time, artillery ranging came to be a recognized and important function of airpower, even though the problem of unreliability with the sets themselves plagued the belligerents throughout the war.

The advent of trench warfare had yet another influence on airpower, not as direct, perhaps, as fostering aerial photography and artillery ranging, but important nonetheless. This was its effect on the development of a functional concept in aviation itself.

Considering the variety of airplanes in use by the belligerents in 1914, some of them obviously better suited to certain purposes than others, it is likely that some sort of functional concept and organization would have developed without the additional impetus created by trench warfare. At least there was a trend in that direction even before trench warfare set in, particularly in the bombing and scouting units. Nevertheless, by forcing a clearer definition of the various functions of airpower, increasing their importance and demanding specialized equipment in the form of camera mounts and wireless sets, the process was accelerated. Thus, by early 1915 the French had gone over to a rather hazy functional organization, grouping their airplanes into bombing, reconnaissance, combat (protection), and artillery ranging squadrons; however, all were charged, if need be, with the gathering of reconnaissance information. In time, the British and Germans also followed suit.

## The Air Weapon in the 1915 Offensives

Since the air weapon had grown to recognized importance by the end of 1914, it would seem that the time had also come to fight, if need be, to use it and to deny it to the enemy. But, as two eminent French air historians summed it up, "Throughout 1915, pursuit aviation was indisputably neglected, both from the standpoint of technique and industry. If there was progress during this period, it was due to the efforts of individuals such as Rose, Garros and Morane."[14]

The trouble lay not in the lack of appreciation for what fighter aircraft could do if given the chance, but in certain technological limitations which largely restricted their development and use despite a crying need throughout the 1915 offensives. Airpower, in short, like the later ICBMs, initially developed a conspicuous offensive capability but lacked a comparable defense capability. Without that, there could be no real air war.

The 1915 Allied offensives on the western front—the Germans held to the defensive in the west while conducting offensive operations against the Russians—were largely variations of a single theme. Failing to recognize the existence, let alone the nature, of a deadlock, they launched several major assaults against the German lines. Basically, these were attempts to use the infantry to exploit breeches made by artillery bombardment. They naturally expected a breakthrough with each assault and were naturally disappointed when the offensives produced abundant casualties but meager gains. In February and March 1915 the French conducted an offensive in the Champagne sector, while in March the British struck the German lines near Neuve Chapelle. In April the French suffered a costly failure at St. Mihiel, and the following month, both the French and British shared an offensive—and failure—at Souchez and Festubert. Finally, in September, the French struck a major blow against the Germans in the Champagne sector, while the British joined in with secondary attacks at Vimy Ridge and Loos. All failed. The deadlock remained firm.

In this series of assaults, airpower played a role of increasing importance, although it would be too much to say that its capabilities were everywhere recognized and its potential appreciated. Nevertheless, more and more commanders came to depend on it. In January 1915, for example, Hugh Trenchard, the officer who would soon command the entire Royal Flying Corps at the front, was called in by Sir Douglas Haig, the cavalry-oriented commander of the newly designated First Army. Trenchard was asked to explain "the use of aircraft in battle."

> I tried to explain what I thought they would do in future besides reconnaissance work, how our machines would have to fight in the air against German machines and how we should have to develop machine-guns and bombs. He was interested.
>
> Then he said he was going to tell me something that only three or four people in the world yet knew; in March, somewhere in the neighbourhood of Merville and Neuve Chapelle, we were going to launch an attack on the

Germans. I was not to tell anybody. He asked, "What will you be able to do?" I explained rather badly about artillery observation (then in its infancy), reporting to gun batteries by morse and signal lamps, and of our early efforts to get wireless going. On the map I showed him the position of my squadrons and what their several tasks could be.

I remember very well his Chief Staff Officer, General Sir John Gough, coming into the room and Haig's saying to him, "Don't interrupt me now. I'm finding out what can be done in the air." When I'd finished he said: "Well, Trenchard, I shall expect you to tell me before the attack whether you can fly, because on your being able to observe for artillery, and carry on reconnaissance, the battle will partly depend. If you can't fly because of the weather, I shall probably call off the attack."[15]

Even as reconnaissance and artillery ranging came into wide acceptance, other functional breakdowns were beginning to appear. Bombing on something of an organized scale came into being, and there were some attempts to use it in a role of interdiction to isolate the battlefield and prevent replacements and supplies from coming in.[16] By comparison with later developments the machines were crude, and the weather, the great nemesis of combat striking power, proved a critical restriction from time to time. Nevertheless, this was a significant step, for it heralded the extensive use of airpower, not strictly as a support weapons system, but as one with striking capability of its own.

## The Airmen Learn to Fight

Looking back on the history of military aviation in World War I, it is obvious that it followed the traditional development of the cavalry. First came the attempt to make use of the new weapon in its simplest and most obvious function, that of reconnaissance. Some success and much imagination combined to expand the weapon, to exploit it for other purposes as well—in this case, artillery ranging and aerial bombing. Finally, the growing success and hence importance of these efforts almost automatically brought countermeasures. Soon men were forced to fight for the privilege of using the weapon and to deny the same right to the enemy. In time this fight came to dominate the original purpose, since the effectiveness of the latter depended in large part on the outcome of the former.

As pointed out earlier, much of the impetus towards aerial combat came from the airmen themselves. The greater impetus came from the ground, however, and particularly from the soldiers on the receiving end of the bombs and aerial-directed artillery shells. Even those ground commanders who had so often downgraded aviation in the past added to the impetus by demanding more reconnaissance and artillery ranging, things which the enemy now was most anxious to prevent. At the same time, they demanded protection for their own supporting aircraft.

To this must be added the incessant demands of the soldiers in the trenches to have the skies cleared of enemy aircraft. This demand stemmed not from the aerial bombs or the steel darts once used, but from the reconnaissance missions, which returned with photos marking their positions, and the even more ominous artillery ranging machines, which invariably heralded the onset of the nightmarish artillery. According to John Cuneo, one of the foremost students of World War I aviation, the presence of any airplane "made the troops feel exposed to spying eyes from the air and any gunfire that came relatively soon after the aerial visitor had passed overhead was unhesitatingly attributed to air direction of the artillery."[17] Indeed, the demands for protective "air umbrellas" were sufficient to force both the French and German air forces to provide them from time to time, when the airmen themselves wanted to follow the more rewarding pursuit of pushing the offensive into enemy territory.

Thus, aerial combat was inevitable as soon as airpower became important enough to fight for; however, since the pressures that led to it were gradual, relatively few people realized what was taking place. That is why enterprising airmen, with considerable justification, have been given so much credit for their ofttimes crude improvisations. They, as much or more than anyone else, wanted air superiority over the enemy.

Technically speaking, the pistols, rifles, and other weapons carried aloft by the airmen early in the war qualified as armament of sorts, but the chances of success with these weapons were remote, to say the least. A delightful story from the German side of the lines illustrates the point.

Another time . . . [a certain German aviator] had to fight a protracted duel with a British machine. . . . When the combatants had exhausted all their rifle and revolver ammunition, they blazed away with their Very [flare] pistols, with which they made very poor showing. After a while, both pilots realized that the only chance of scoring a hit was to get close up, but when they laid their machines alongside, the humour of the situation struck von Leutzer forcibly, so that he roared with laughter at the sight of the two observers solemnly loading up and taking deliberate aim, a green light answering a red one. Evidently the observers were also too tickled to shoot straight, for neither got anywhere near his mark.[18]

The machine gun was the obvious answer to the problem of armament, but this weapon, in turn, posed several problems of its own. In the first place, they were heavy; one needed an airplane capable of carrying the gun aloft with ease, otherwise no advantage had been gained. For example, when Lt. L. A. Strange mounted a Lewis gun on his Maurice Farman in August 1914, it took him forty-five minutes to struggle up to 3,500 feet altitude and he could go no higher, even though the Aviatik he wished to intercept was cruising easily at 5,000 feet. In other words, Lieutenant Strange had made his machine ineffective as an interceptor by weighting it down with the one weapon that, under other circumstances, might have made it effective. His superiors properly ordered him to remove the machine gun and go back to the rifle.[19]

Bigger and more powerful airplanes, fully capable of carrying heavy machine guns soon made their appearance along the western front, but this in itself did not solve the enigma of armament. The problem was much more basic. In the case of the tractor type of airplane, which had the engine in front of the pilot, the whirling propeller completely blocked the forward field of fire, a major obstacle in that aerial combat inherently tended to end up in a nose-to-tail affair anyway. In the case of the "pusher," which had the engine behind the pilot, the ability to fire forward was more than offset by some serious considerations. Extra structural drag made the pusher relatively slow, and the engine, next to the pilot the most vulnerable part of the man/machine combination, sat completely unprotected from a rear attack. Moreover, the crew had to live with the disturbing fact that in case of accident, which was much too common to be ignored, they would be between the lethal engine and the equally lethal ground.[20] The heavier, two-seater, tractor type aircraft often carried an observer/machine gunner in the rear cockpit, but when it came to air-to-air combat, these machines were inherently defensive rather than offensive. The rear gunner might be quite effective in fending off an attack, but he rarely had the opportunity to take the initiative in making one, since it was virtually impossible for one such machine to overtake or maneuver around a similar one, unless both aviators, like von Leutzer and his opponent, accepted combat and pulled up alongside. And since air combat was not the primary mission of such machines, air crews rarely offered or accepted such challenges.

Thus, while fighting in the air began very early in the war, an "air war" was simply not possible until a fighter, designed specifically to be a destroyer of other aircraft, made its proper debut.

## The Advent of the Fighter

The willingness, even eagerness, to fight if need be to stop enemy airpower and protect one's own aerial forces wrought a remarkable change in the history of military aviation. It led directly to the advent of the fighter, the small, relatively fast, highly maneuverable ship especially designed to attack and overcome other aircraft. In this way, a new phase of military aviation came into being, which soon transcended all previous functions of airpower in interest, intensity, and, at times, importance as well. Indeed, the fighter pilot by and by became a breed apart, partly because of his glamorous assignment and partly because his activity, unlike reconnaissance, artillery ranging, bombing, and so on, was only indirectly tied to the war on the ground. The advent of the fighters signalled the beginning of the air war.

Despite the compelling need that finally produced the pursuit or fighter plane, such aircraft developed slowly, primarily because, of all problems facing military aviation during the war, arming the fighter proved one of the most difficult. Since speed, maneuverability, and rate of climb were directly related to the size of the airplane and particularly to the weight/horsepower ratio, the theoretical answer always pointed to the single-seater. After all, such airplanes had displayed remarkable performance even before the war. The British, for example, had one in 1914 which flew 130 mph and could climb at the astonishing rate of 1,600 feet per minute.[21] But this particular machine, like all other single-seaters, had been neglected during those first critical months of the conflict. They were simply not as good as the two-seaters for reconnaissance and artillery ranging, and except for those functions there was little for them to do. Now there was an urgent requirement for the fighter, but only if it could be properly armed.

In a two-seater, one man could fly the airplane while his partner did the shooting; in the single-seater, the same man necessarily did both. Each in its own right was a full-time job, particularly in combat. Indeed, it is safe to say that regardless of the performance of his machine, the single-seater pilot was at a disadvantage against a two-seater unless he could at least meet the machine guns of his opponent with a comparable weapon, comparably accurate in his hand. This meant that the gun would have to be fixed, that is, attached to the airplane in such a way that the pilot could fire it remotely and aim it by aiming the airplane. This by itself was not a formidable problem except for the fact, mentioned earlier, that the best airplane was the tractor type and the only favorable field of fire for the fighter pilot lay directly ahead, a field blocked by the whirling propeller.

One answer, though inherently an unsatisfactory one because of the reduced drag and the accident problem, was the single-seater pusher. Such a ship was put into production by the British, but it was February 1916 before its presence was felt on the front. In the meantime, the compelling need could not wait for such an answer. Airmen flying single-seater tractor types began taking to the air armed with fixed rifles, bolted to the side of the cockpit and angled to fire over or outside the propeller arc.[22] Then, in February 1915, the first airplane created specifically to destroy other airplanes made its appearance. Considering the technological limitations of the time, it is not surprising that this machine, the Vickers FB-5, was a two-seater pusher, with the gunner in the front cockpit. Nor was it surprising that the Gun Bus, as it was called, could not equal in performance certain German machines such as the Aviatik—a tractor type with a more powerful engine—which it was supposed to intercept and destroy.[23]

The solution to the single-seater problem obviously centered on some system for directing fire *through* the propeller arc. This in turn called for plenty of imagination, which is perhaps why an airman provided the first key. This airman was Roland Garros, one of France's most famous prewar aviators.

In early 1915 Garros was a member of the Escadrille MS-23, a squadron flying the Morane Saulnier monoplane. Garros, like other single-seater pilots, had experimented with fixed rifles, angled to fire over the propeller, but he recognized their limitations and continued his search for something better. Then, in February 1915, he hit upon a novel, albeit dangerous solution. He mounted a machine gun on the cowling of his Morane Saulnier so that he could aim the gun simply by maneuvering the airplane. Then, based on his calculation that only about 7 percent of the bullets would hit the propeller, he fastened steel deflector plates on each blade. These plates, cut in the form of a triangular wedge, were attached in such a way that they sat directly opposite the gun muzzle with the apex pointed towards the pilot.

In ground trials and later in the air, Garros proved that he could get a goodly number of machine gun bullets past the propeller without destroying it. On the other hand, it was clear that the device had certain disadvantages. By reducing the efficiency of the propeller, the deflector plates slowed the airplane and the ricocheting bullets were a hazard to both propeller and pilot.

In February and March 1915, Garros several times carried his device into the air without appreciable result. Then, on 1 April, he caught an unsuspecting German who felt he had no reason to fear an enemy aircraft approaching him head on, and shot him down. He shot down another German on 15 April and another two days later.[24] Garros was thus well on his way to becoming the most fearsome pilot on the western front when, on 18 April 1915, his propeller and engine, having taken more than the usual amount of punishment, failed behind enemy lines. Garros, his Morane Saulnier, and his wedge deflector system fell into German hands.

The Germans were more than a little interested in Garros's invention. They had long believed, though erroneously of course, that all French airplanes carried machine guns, but they had never understood how the weapon was made effective on a single-seater.[25] Now the secret seemed to be out.

The Germans hurriedly shipped the device off to Berlin, where the authorities passed the problem on to Anthony Fokker, a young Dutch aerial designer who had produced several airplanes of merit for his hosts. The Germans apparently expected Fokker to produce a similar though improved system of some sort, but Fokker saw the problem quite differently. He reasoned that the objective could be attained without the disadvantages of the deflector system if one momentarily interrupted the flow of machine-gun bullets when the propeller blade passed in front of the weapon. Careful computations convinced him that this could be accomplished simply and effectively by setting cams on the propeller shaft, with a mechanical linkage to the gun. The bump or cam on the shaft would set the linkage in motion in such a way as to momentarily interrupt the gun at the instant each blade passed in front of the muzzle.[26]

To an engineer like Fokker, the rest came easy. Two days after getting the assignment, he had burst the technological barrier that had kept the single-seater from becoming a true fighter. Indeed, it had gone so smoothly and so quickly that German authorities could scarcely believe it. They forced Fokker, who had mounted a Parabellum machine gun on one of his own Eindeckers (E-1), to demonstrate his device again and again, finally insisting that he prove it in combat by shooting down an enemy airplane. Fokker backed out at the last minute, leaving both the modified Eindecker and the honor of being the first to shoot down an enemy with a syncronized machine gun to Lt. Oswald Boelke. At any rate, it was a grand success. By the time Fokker arrived back in Berlin with his clear conscience, Boelke and the Eindecker had already sent a startled British air crew to their deaths.[27]

With the marriage of the single-seater and the synchronized machine gun, the stage for air war was properly set. Nevertheless, the Germans were not anxious to disclose their new weapons system. Fearing that the device might fall into enemy hands, they scattered the first Eindeckers with synchronized guns throughout various squadrons and forbade the pilots to cross the lines. At the same time, a series of fatal accidents in the E-1s led them to temporarily withdraw the machines from service. Before this had been straightened out in October, much precious time had been lost.[28]

By the end of 1915, however, the Fokker Eindecker and its synchronized machine gun had made a fearsome reputation for itself on both sides of the lines. French and British pilots began speaking of themselves as potential "Fokker fodder" and of a short life expectancy, while certain politicians at home vented their dismay by shouting that the airmen were being "murdered" by official negligence. Actually, the "deadly Fokker era" was largely a myth, even then. The Fokker never came close to wreaking havoc among the French and British air services, although many pilots and politicians thought it did, and hence allowed their morale to suffer accordingly.[29] The Germans had indeed won a limited "mastery" or "control of the air" over the western front, but this factor, later the grand objective of all fighter operations, was only partly understood and appreciated at the time.

To partially offset the advantage of the Fokkers, the British countered with improved pushers, while the French mounted a Lewis machine gun on a rack atop the upper wing of their new fighter, the Nieuport 11, so as to fire directly over the propeller. Both systems left much to be desired, however, and well into 1916, the Germans enjoyed an advantage in firepower that the French and British could not match. Not all odds were in favor of the Germans, however. The Nieuport, particularly the one with 110 hp Le Rhône rotary engine, proved far superior to the E-1, as did the Dehavilland D-2, a one place pusher brought into action by the British in February 1916.[30] At any rate, it was now clear that both sides were willing to fight, if need be, with what they had. Thus in late 1915 and early 1916 the air war began in earnest.

## The Ecstasy . . .

The appearance of the true fighter airplane carried in its wake one of the most fascinating phenomena of the entire war—the glamour of the *avion de chasse,* as the French called it, with emphasis on the so-called aces. As mentioned earlier, this was a tonic the people needed, a logical consequence, as it were, of the stalemate on the ground. Attritional warfare allowed almost no mark of individuality in its mass armies and great casualty lists. As a result, people automatically turned to the sky for their all-essential war heroes.

The sky had much to offer in this line. The very idea of two men locked in a savage and spectacular duel to the death high above the earth was enough to trigger even the tamest imaginations. Moreover, aerial warfare, having no precedent, and, initially at least, no firm tactics or doctrine to guide it, left the airmen largely on their own. To those who accepted the challenge, and particularly those with courage to the point of recklessness, renown was almost unavoidable. Unlike the masses on the ground, engaged in battles so huge and bloody that individuality was lost in large round numbers, the fighter pilots were as distinctive and individualistic as the medieval knight, and hence a ready source for the heroes important in any war but critically essential in this one. This need, even craving, for heroes whose courage was conspicuous is evident in the admiration and respect given an impetuous novice to air combat for "bounding" a dozen German fighters, even though in so doing he disobeyed orders and placed himself and his comrades in considerable danger. It is evident in the endless admiration given Charles Nungesser, a French ace who fearlessly went at the

Germans again and again even though his personal list of serious wounds and injuries would have done credit to a medical dictionary.[31] And it is inscribed dramatically and conclusively in the controversy that centered on René Fonck, France's greatest airman, and George Guynemer, easily France's most famous ace.

Fonck, who insisted on choosing the time and place for combat, considered bullet holes in his airplane a disgrace. "My airplane has never . . . been hit," he liked to say. "Not one single bullet." Through incredible airmanship, rigid training (he abstained from all alchohol, even wine) and marvelous marksmanship, he lived out the war with fifty-eight confirmed victories to his credit, including six in a single afternoon. Indeed, in view of his superlative record, one must agree with Kenneth Driggs that "no other man, dead or living, has equalled this marvelous pilot in air dueling."[32]

But as every French schoolboy knows, the greatest name in French aviation is not René Fonck, the "Master Airman," but Georges Guynemer, the "Miraculous," a man who, in many ways, was just the opposite of Fonck. Frail and sickly, he was a legend long before he vanished under mysterious circumstances in September 1917. He ran up an impressive list of fifty-three victories in a remarkably short time, but it was not his victories as much as his manner of fighting that triggered the imagination of his many admirers. Literally blind to danger, he would hurl himself without caution into enemy fire in order to get away a few shots at point blank range. Eight times he was shot down, more than any other ace. Fonck said of him: "I cannot count the number of shattered struts, the control wires cut by bullets, the fuselage holes, the rudder bar in sections, the holes in his windshield, in his motor and even through his flying clothes. His method was intrepid, superb—but how foolish."[33]

In a popularity contest, however, either during the war or after, Guynemer would win hands down over Fonck. In subsequent wars, when team effort became the standard, airmen would agree almost to a man that Fonck was right all along, that the mission comes before personal glory. But in the Great War most airmen, and particularly the aces, had an individualism that even military discipline could not curb, and the people were more than happy to accept them on that basis.[34] Few men have ever been lionized as they were, all of which is to say that the fighter pilots of 1915–18, and to a degree the other airmen as well, lived and were judged by standards that later generations would think foolhardly and almost incomprehensibly reckless.

## . . . and the Agony

In the glare and glamour of World War I aviation, it is all too easy to lose sight of the fact that flying also had its grim and dismal side. Indeed, the aircraft of the time were so uncomfortable and unreliable that it required considerable courage to fly them, let alone take them into combat. Meager instrumentation had to be supplemented by guesswork and the now forgotten art of "flying by the seat of the pants." If the open cockpit let the white scarf flutter in the slip stream, it also left the pilots exposed to the bitter cold of the winter, which according to one airman got so bad that "I often wished a German would come along and shoot me but when one did, I soon warmed up and got the hell out of there."[35]

The airplanes themselves, and particularly the engines, were terribly unreliable by modern standards. Motor failures, with the inevitable *panne de moteur,* or dead stick landing, were so common that they could be a matter of constant jest,[36] and even the worst airmen were forced to master this art. On the other hand, it could also be a deadly affair. Not all tales of terror that began in the air ended with a "happy landing." One airman, writing from his hospital bed, where he had lain for months with a badly wrenched back, put it this way:

> I know of no sound more horrible than that made by an airplane crashing to earth. Breathless one has watched the uncontrolled apparatus tumble through the air. The agony felt by the pilot and passenger seems to transmit itself to you. You are helpless to avert the certain death. You cannot even turn your eyes away at the moment of impact. In the dull grinding crash, there is the sound of breaking bones.[37]

For reasons that will become painfully apparent later on, the hazards of flying increased many fold under combat conditions. It was almost axiomatic that a pilot, anxious for a kill or to avoid being killed, could easily strain his machine beyond endurance. Also in being forced to fly without parachutes, many airmen were assured a particularly violent and tragic death, while all airmen had to face that possibility. It was not that parachutes were unknown. Balloonists used them on a regular basis. But there was a deployment problem for aircraft, a problem that could have been resolved in short order with proper encouragement from leaders up the chain of command. This encouragement was not forthcoming, however, primarily because the authorities, unwilling or unable to see what it was like for themselves, jumped to the conclusion that pilots would bail out rather than fight when the going got tough. This was an unfortunate assumption, one easily proven false by a few hours in the air, but it prevailed during the war except for the Germans toward the end. As it was, many an airman lost his life because his airplane came apart in the air, or worse yet, caught fire, in which case his choices were to ride the flaming craft to the ground, or, like the great Lufbery, take the quick way out and jump anyway. So real was this danger and so terrifying its prospects that it is said opposing airmen sometimes mercifully continued the attack and deliberately killed the pilot to spare him the long ride down.[38]

The combat pilots of this period were naturally not unmindful of the dangers they faced, dangers which were demonstrated time and again in the most awesome manner. Indeed, combat fatigue, though not recognized as such at the time, was often as evident in the airmen as it was in the forlorn and forsaken soldiers on the ground. The airmen, however, found it much easier than their counterparts in the trenches not to dwell on this dark and dismal side of life. They managed to adopt that stoic outlook which, devoid of virtually all sentimentalism, has become traditional for all combat airmen. They made elaborate arrangements to divide the property of one who might fall, and when one did, sometimes showed uncommon haste in spreading the spoils.[39] They toasted death in the barroom, giving bravos to "the dead already" and hurrahs for the "next man who dies." They also discussed with vigor what they would do if caught in a burning airplane, and they sang with gusto such songs as "The Dying Aviator."

The young aviator lay dying
And as 'neath the wreckage he lay,
To the mechanics assembled around him,
These last parting words he did say:

"Two valve springs you'll find in my stomach,
Three spark plugs are safe in my lung,
The prop is in splinters inside me,
To my fingers the joy stick has clung.

"Take the cylinders out of my kidneys,
The connecting rods out of my brain;
From the small of my back get the crankshaft,
And assemble the engine again."[40]

It was not possible for those young American pilots without combat experience to understand what they were getting into when they became part of the newly formed N-124 in April 1916. Their thoughts seem to have centered on the glamour of it all, on the fact that they would be heart and soul in the air war, which, for the moment at least, seemed "fighting at its best." And, in a way, that is precisely what it was, mixing the fighting with a blend of individualism and initiative in an environment unique in modern military history. A particularly unique squadron like the Escadrille Américaine, preparing to fight in a medium that had already captured the public fancy, was thus well on its way to world renown before it had flown a single mission or fired a single shot in anger.

# 3 Off to the Front: In the Vosges and Verdun Sectors

## April – September 1916

The Escadrille Américaine was ordered to assemble at Luxeuil-les-Baines, an ancient watering place and resort area nestled in the Vosges Mountains. The Luxeuil airfield, from which the squadron would be operating, was located in the comparatively quiet Vosges sector, a comfortable thirty-five miles behind stabilized lines. It was used principally as a staging area for French Farman and Breguet bombers.

The new squadron was badly needed at Verdun, where one of the greatest land battles of history was in progress. But with German pilots using the synchronized machine gun to keep the life expectancy of enemy airmen at a pathetically low figure, French authorities wisely selected a quiet sector for the N-124 to receive its baptism by fire. The squadron needed some time to develop the teamwork essential to all fighter units.[1] A cautious introduction to aerial combat was wise if the squadron was to survive its probation period and grow to maximum effectiveness.

Since several of the N-124 pilots were already seasoned veterans, the French did not consider the period at Luxeuil as strictly a training exercise. The squadron received the exacting and honorable responsibility of flying protective cover for one of the most famous bomb groups in French aviation history, the Groupe de Bombardement no. 4.[2]

The bomb group was already a legend in French aviation when the Escadrille Américaine came into being, with most of the fame centered around its commander, a red bearded Frenchman named Captain Happe. Happe was known on both sides of the front for his "mad recklessness"; the French called him "Le Corsaire Rouge," and the

Germans, recognizing him as more than a minor nuisance, placed a price of 25,000 marks on his head. It seems the Captain and his faithful mechanic Leleu had several times bombed the German cities of Frederickshafen, Rottweil, Colmar, and Freibourg. These cities were some distance behind the lines, yet the two men flew an old 80 hp Maurice Farman, nicknamed the "chicken coop" because of its many wires and braces. Its top speed was in the neighborhood of forty-five mph, but it had a high wing loading that permitted it to carry a four-hour supply of fuel and about a hundred pounds of bombs. As gunner, Leleu went aloft with a Winchester carbine or a cavalry musket, to be fired from the shoulder. And, reckless enough to go along on such missions in the first place, he was not averse to firing through the propeller arc, either.[3]

Captain Happe enjoyed an incredible amount of luck. German aircraft attacked the "chicken coop" almost at will, and antiaircraft batteries took their turns at it. Happe and Leleu were never harmed, however, and the French, unable to account for this miracle, somehow concluded that Happe's charmed life would extend to a bomb group built around him, making all his pilots equally immune to misfortune and death. They therefore created Bomb Group no. 4 with Happe as commander, taking special care to equip it with the same antique Maurice Farmans that Happe liked so well.[4]

Unfortunately, fate proved unkind, and Happe, still personally immune, began losing pilots so fast that the French sought emergency means to cut down the losses. New Farmans and Breugets were brought in, and when this proved inadequate, Happe and his men were forbidden to cross the lines except at night. In a final effort, the French decided on fighter protection and selected the newly formed Escadrille Américaine to do the job.[5]

Meanwhile, Captain Thenault had received his orders, and on 9 April 1916, began gathering the ten tractors, four trucks, two automobiles, and eighty-odd ground personnel that would support the ten to fifteen pilots he would be receiving. The equipment, except for the airplanes, which were to be delivered later, were shipped to Luxeuil by special train. By 19 April, when Rockwell, McConnell, Prince, and Chapman arrived, after a day wandering around in the Aisne Sector, all was in readiness.[6] Effective 20 April 1916, the N-124, better known as the Escadrille Américaine, took its place on the official rosters.

Life was pleasant at Luxeuil. Thenault had arranged quarters for the Americans in either a villa bordering the famous hot baths or the Hôtel Pomme d'Or, the "best hotel in town" according to James McConnell, where room and board could be had for four francs a day. Since the airplanes had not yet arrived (the Battle of Verdun was drawing most of the war materiel to the north), there was little for the pilots to do at first, and so Thenault took the men on motor tours up and down the countryside. These were not pleasure cruises, however. The men were scouting the best fields for the *pannes de moteurs* (forced landings, usually because of engine trouble) which were certain to come. The war itself seemed far away, however, and one eager airman wrote of this period, "I began to wonder whether I was a summer resorter instead of a soldier."[7]

Captain Thenault introduced one grim note of reality into this otherwise peaceful scene when he introduced the men to Captain Happe. Happe was in his office at the flying field when Thenault brought in the Americans, all full of anticipation, for, as Victor Chapman phrased it in one of his letters home, "[Happe] is a by-word in aviation and incredible are the stories told about him and his *bombardement escadrilles.*"[8]

Happe greeted the new pilots with an impromptu lecture on the advantages of accompanying the bombardment machines. "I know *escadrilles de chasse* do not like to accompany us," he said, "but it is my belief that they would find more game if they did. Now if you had been with us on my last trip, I should not have this sorry task." The captain pointed to a pile of yellow envelopes. "*Croix de guerre* and letters to the relatives of the eight fellows killed on my last raid," he said.[9]

Le Corsaire Rouge made a profound impression on his American visitors. "I thought his eye glittered as he related the satisfaction of his last victim," the tender Chapman wrote to a friend. "I believe he prides himself on having lost as many *pilotes* as any other two Captains in France." To James McConnell, with his more humorous approach to life, the incident "recalled the ancient custom of giving a man selected for the sacrifice a royal time of it before the appointed day."[10]

The Nieuport 11s assigned to the squadron did not arrive until the first week in May, although there was some flying before that. The Americans borrowed a "well-used" Nieuport from the Escadrille N-49, but that benefit ended when Norman Prince ran the airplane into a hangar wall. Six machines made up the initial shipment, three of them with the 80 hp Le Rhône engine and three with the 110 hp model. Thenault, de Laage, and Thaw, all officers, took the 110 hp machines; Rockwell, Chapman, and McConnell got the others, while Prince, Cowdin, and Hall waited.[11]

## The First Sortie

The arrival of the machines was followed by yet another period of impatience while factory representatives assembled the airplanes and instructed the mechanics in their care. Even after the machines were ready, there was armament to install, with the airmen more impatient than ever, for several German reconnaissance machines had lately flown over the field.[12] Finally, on 12 May, everything was ready. The squadron's first sortie was scheduled for early the next morning.

The formation, in the form of a huge V, left on schedule at sunrise. Rockwell led the group, with Chapman and McConnell on either side. Thaw and Thenault, the only members of the team with real combat experience, wisely brought up the flanks. Flying at 10,000 feet, the group flew to a checkpoint near the Swiss border, then north to Belfort and Roppe, where the presence of German and French "sausages" (balloons) marked the lines separating the two forces. About this time, McConnell lost contact with the others and wandered off towards the Swiss border and a breach of neutrality, but Thenault successfully herded him back. A short time later, the reassembled unit was over German territory.

To the airmen, the trenches below were "woodworm-like tracings on the ground" and careful observation revealed sporadic shell bursts. It all seemed remote and far away except for the antiaircraft bursts that suddenly began appearing on all sides. Thaw and Thenault, having learned to live with that sort of thing, regarded them with "impersonal" feelings, but to the three novices they were sources of amusement. With a dismay that must have approached despair, Thenault watched the three airmen "diving at the little smoke clouds."[13]

Enemy aircraft were nowhere to be seen. Rockwell dived down over the Habsheim aerodrome, daring the Germans to rise to the challenge. None rose to the bait, however, and finally, to the dismay of some

of the pilots and the relief of others, the patrol returned to Luxeuil.[14]
All in all, it was a very inauspicious beginning for a squadron that
would soon be world famous.

## First Blood

Only five days after the first sortie, Rockwell drew first blood in an
aerial combat that reportedly "caused a tremendous wave of excitement in Paris."[15] Alone over Thann on the morning of 18 May, he spied
a two-place LVG several hundred meters below and a short distance
inside the French lines. Since the German pilot and observer had
apparently not noticed the Nieuport, a more cautious pilot might have
attempted to work his way underneath and behind the adversary where
he would be relatively safe from the forward-firing synchronized gun
and the pivot-mounted machine gun in the rear cockpit. In this way,
the top-mounted Lewis could be used to best advantage. Rockwell,
however, was not a cautious pilot, and he knew that such an approach
required immense skill to escape detection, with the added risk of
losing the advantage and seeing his quarry race for his lines. Fearless
by nature and eager to get a kill, he took the approach that characterized him throughout his brief career. He plunged to the attack, intent
only on his objective. In a letter to his brother, written that same day, he
told what happened.

> [The German] saw me and began to dive towards his lines. . . . [The gunner]
> immediately opened fire on me and my machine was hit, but I didn't pay any
> attention to that and kept going straight for him, until I got within twenty five
> or thirty meters of him. Then, just when I was afraid of running into him, I fired
> four or five shots, then swerved my machine to keep from running into him. As
> I did that, I saw the *mitrailleur* fall back dead on the pilot, the *mitrailleuse* fall
> from its position and point straight up in the air, the pilot fall to one side as if he
> was done for also. The machine itself fell first to one side, then dived vertically
> toward the ground, and three or four minutes later saw a lot of smoke coming
> up from the ground just beyond the German trenches. I had hoped that it would
> fall in our lines for it is hard to prove when they fall in German lines.[16]

Although the LVG had fallen behind German lines, its fall had been
observed by the French, and by the time Rockwell returned to Luxeuil
to report the kill, the three or more ground witnesses necessary to get
the victory confirmed had already made their report.[17] Rockwell's
cheering comrades lifted him from his plane while his mechanic made

a routine check of the machine gun and then interrupted the rejoicing with a startling announcement; only four bullets were missing from the ammunition drum.[18]

To the men of the Escadrille Américaine and to a great many pilots up and down the line, it seemed an incredible story. A novice pilot, in his initial combat, had practically flown down the barrel of a German machine gun. With his main wing spar seriously damaged by gun fire, he had closed to within thirty meters and killed both pilot and gunner with four bullets. It was as if the daring of the great Guynemer had been coupled with the spectacular marksmanship of René Fonck.

No American rejoiced more in this impressive victory than did Paul Rockwell, Kiffin's older brother, who, having been forced from the trenches by wounds and illness, was now working with the French Ministry of Public Information. Tied to the squadron by strong bonds of blood and friendship, he expressed his profound pleasure in an unusual gift to his brother—a rare and precious bottle of eighty-year-old Bourbon.[19]

The whiskey received a proper welcome at Luxeuil, particularly since Rockwell was willing to share it. Someone proposed a round of toasts, but Chapman, who had little taste for alcohol, countered with a suggestion. "Lets save it for rare occasions," he said. "Naturally Kiffin gets the first drink, but from now on every man to bring down a German is entitled to one slug. It'll be something worth working for."[20] Thus, watered down with champagne, a ceremony was inaugurated that was oft repeated until the Bourbon was gone. In the meantime, many of those who helped drink it were gone, too. The "Bottle of Death," as it was called, was never replaced.

## The "Furnace of Verdun"

On 19 May 1916, the day following Rockwell's sensational victory, the N-124 suddenly received orders to move to Behomme, a field near Bar-le-Duc in the Verdun sector. The squadron had been in action less than a week and had not yet flown cover for Captain Happe's celebrated bombardment group, but that no longer mattered. The great Battle of Verdun, now three months old and growing in intensity, had priority call.

The Battle of Verdun was the brain child of General von Falkenhayn, Chief of the German General Staff. In presenting his plan to the

Kaiser, Falkenhayn argued that "France has almost reached the end of her military effort" and hence, "if her people can be made to realize that in a military sense they have nothing more to hope for, breaking point will be reached."[21] Falkenhayn therefore proposed a massive assault aimed at the ancient city of Verdun on the grounds that this symbol of national strength was a bastion "for the retention of which the French General Staff would be compelled to throw in every man they have." In Falkenhayn's eyes, the city itself was relatively unimportant as a strategic objective, but in luring the French into defending it, "the Forces of France will bleed to death—as there can be no question of withdrawal—whether we reach our [geographical] objective or not. . . . For an operation limited to a narrow front, Germany will not be compelled to spend herself so completely, for all other fronts are practically drained."[22]

On this foundation of logic, Falkenhayn launched his great attack on the morning of 21 February 1916. Woefully unprepared at first, the French fought back with everything available to them, just as Falkenhayn knew they would. Yet this impressive general, who showed uncommon wisdom about the war as a whole, made several serious miscalculations. Blood, he found, flowed heavily in both directions; the French were far from their breaking point; and Verdun, like so many attritional battles of the past, quickly absorbed so many lives that neither side could call it off without conceding a defeat of the first magnitude. Thus the possibility of withdrawal by either side decreased as more and more blood was invested. And since both nations felt compelled to redeem the blood lost by investing more of it, the Battle of Verdun came to be a colossal battle of attrition, earning for itself two of the grimmest nicknames ever given in war, "The Furnace" and "The Sausage Grinder."

In such a great struggle at that time and place, airpower naturally found extensive use. Even before the battle, German reconnaissance craft, enjoying their rather vague air superiority, photographed in fine detail the French lines, supply routes, and depots as far back as Bar-le-Duc. At the same time, the Germans sought to screen their own preparations for the offensive by establishing an "aerial blockade" to keep enemy reconnaissance out of friendly skies.

The German attack on 21 February achieved both strategic and tactical surprise, no mean accomplishment in itself. This was partly due to the aerial blockade which made French reconnaissance more difficult than usual. But this factor was less important than the faulty interpretation of intelligence information by the French, and particularly General Joseph Joffre's complacency, which seriously restricted proper recognition of the danger signals.[23] But once the battle was joined and all French efforts were turned towards stopping the German drive, aerial reconnaissance and artillery on both sides leaped to critical importance, along with a serious effort for air supremacy as well.

Since the Germans had the synchronized machine gun, the odds would seem to favor them in the struggle for air supremacy, but fortunately the French had a viable plan. Conversations between General Trenchard of the Royal Flying Corps and Commandant du Peuty of the Service Aéronautique in August 1915 had convinced the commandant that optimum use of airpower lay in the "strategic offensive," that is, carrying the fight to the enemy, destroying him wherever he might be found. This, the two officers concluded, made more sense than diverting a major portion of one's effort to safeguarding home territory. Unlike Trenchard, however, du Peuty felt that a defensive posture was not inherently unsatisfactory and in uncertain circumstances could be the optimum doctrine.[24]

The "strategic offensive" was a bold idea, for it meant that the fighters and bombers would operate offensively even though their comrades on the ground might be on the defensive. The idea worked, partly because Trenchard was right in believing that the airplane was inherently an offensive weapon, and partly because the Germans had made some erroneous conclusions of their own. An "aerial blockade," for example, was something of an absurdity unless hundreds of fighters were available. Thus, when French airplanes penetrated an in-flight blockading force of some thirty or so planes, the Germans initially blamed the failure on the fact that their fighters were not grouped together at select airfields and were positioned too far behind the lines to give them adequate time in the blockade zone. The Germans therefore regrouped their fighters into two commands and moved them closer to the lines.[25]

The French aerial offensive faded for a time, but came back strongly as they responded to the German move by sending their airplanes out in groups, the fighters to take on fighters while the reconnaissance and artillery ranging machines went about their business. Under the circumstances, the Fokker pilots, flying singly or in pairs to provide maximum coverage, simply could not cope with the situation, and

German ground forces began to complain bitterly about lack of protection. The German authorities responded, not by initiating a "strategic offensive" of their own, but by declaring that "barrage flying has precedence over all other work" and by taking many bombing and reconnaissance craft off their ordinary activities and making them part of what the Germans called an "aerial umbrella." "Enemy airpower," the future commander of the German Army Air Forces later wrote, "was not stopped by this."[26]

French doctrine had paid off. By May 1916, the French rather than the Germans had the brighter future in the air over Verdun. And, while the doctrine of the "strategic offensive" would undergo some variations during the remainder of the war, overall it had enormous implications for the French air service in general and the Escadrille Américaine in particular. Among other things, it meant that much of the flying by the *avions de chasse* would be behind German lines, where, if something went wrong, the pilot was either buried in enemy soil or became a prisoner of war. It also meant that many of the legitimate victories by French fighter pilots would never be confirmed.

It was at this point, with the air war full blown, that the Escadrille Américaine went into action over Verdun, after only a token baptism of fire in the Vosges sector. Actually, however, it was not as bad as it might seem. Of the nine pilots assigned to the N-124, only Rockwell, Chapman, and McConnell were without any real combat experience, and Rockwell had already given promise of a brilliant future. Moreover, since the N-124 was flying the Nieuport 11, at the time the best answer to the Fokker, the French had every reason to believe that the N-124 would make a solid contribution at Verdun despite the fact that the bitter contest in the air kept life expectancy of incoming pilots at a dismally low figure.

The squadron left Luxeuil on 20 May, in such a hurry that not even a German bombing raid on the field the night before slowed their departure. By noon the pilots were dining with men of the N-48 at Luneville, where they made a refueling stop, and where Chapman and Thaw interrupted the meal by dashing from the dinnertable in a futile attempt to intercept a German reconnaissance craft reported to be in the neighborhood. The unit was in place at Behomme by the evening of the 20th, but spent one day setting up the equipment that arrived during the night and in getting established in a comfortable villa on the outskirts of Bar-le-Duc. This villa, between the town and the airfield, was a convenient stopping-off place, and as a result, the squadron's reputation for hospitality, centering on its impressive mess, grew by leaps and bounds. "Comforts were plentiful as at Luxeuil," McConnell later wrote, but added, "The endless convoys of motor trucks, the fast-flowing stream of troops, and the distressing number of ambulances brought realization of the near presence of a gigantic battle."[27]

There were other reminders as well. The famous Cigognes (Storks) N-3, now commanded by Captain Brocard and containing such famous names as Guynemer, Dorme, Huerteux, Auger, Doullin, and de la Tour, was located on the field. The indestructible Nungesser and his N-65 were also there.[28] The French were obviously using the very best they had in the Battle of Verdun, but then, so were the Germans.

Ironically, the N-124 began combat operations in the Verdun sector on 22 May, by which time the French authorities, under pressure from ground troops and from bombardment and reconnaissance crews who wanted direct protection, temporarily adopted the practice of maintaining "offensive" patrols along the lines during the daylight hours. Each fighter squadron—and there were many in the Verdun area—was assigned a particular time and portion of the sector to patrol, a system which tended to duplicate the German system, but which the French hoped would work well, since all squadron headquarters were now equipped with wireless sets.[29] Nevertheless, it proved a great step backwards. Despite their offensive label, patrols of this type were inherently defensive, and the French paid a heavy price before du Peuty turned them again to the offensive.[30]

On 22 May the French launched a counteroffensive and the N-124 was assigned a morning patrol well inside the German lines and an afternoon patrol in the vicinity of Fort Douaumont, where the artillery duel was chiefly concentrated. The latter was an exciting and dangerous assignment. The airmen, charged with flying cover for reconnaissance and artillery ranging machines, flew at 1,000 feet, low enough to see the very heavy fighting going on below but also low enough to have the air "nervous and troubly" and to hear artillery shells passing them by on all sides.[31]

The panoramic view of the battle made a profound impression on the men of the Escadrille Américaine. "I am not even going to try to express my impressions," Kiffin Rockwell wrote to his brother. The sensitive Chapman, who had spent more than a year in the trenches, wrote a cousin that the landscape was "one wasted surface of brown powdered earth, where hills, valleys, forest and villages all merged into phantoms." It was "boiling with puffs of dark smoke," while "tiny sparks like flashes of a mirror, hither and yon, in the woods and dales, denoted the heavy guns which were raising such dust.[32]

The high point of the day, however, was a death struggle between Bert Hall and a German pilot over the Mort Homme. Both were amateurs at this sort of game, but Hall shot down his opponent and was credited with a victory. Other than a strained ceremony while Hall drained his authorized portion of the "Bottle of Death," however, there was little rejoicing over the event. By this time Hall was so unpopular with his comrades that almost to a man they ignored or downplayed the event.[33]

After this engagement, routine patrols, breath-taking aerial duels and escapes followed one after another in rapid succession. For the first time, the pilots of the N-124 began to experience the creeping mental and physical fatigue of intensive combat flying. No longer a sport, it had become a deadly game in which the object was to kill and avoid being killed, again and again and again.

This was made dramatically evident as early as 24 May, when Thenault took the entire squadron on a "grand scouting expedition" covering the entire length of the Verdun sector. Rockwell and Thaw had been out earlier in the day and Thaw had actually brought down a German Fokker, a signal feat, but one in which all gamesmanship was gone, and with it Thaw's sense of real accomplishment. "No credit to me," he told his comrades later. "I just murdered him. He never saw me." For a sortie that same afternoon, Thenault counseled caution. Aware that the great German ace Oswald Boelke might be out, and worried about the fledglings of the squadron, he made it clear that displays of individualism would not be appreciated. No one should attack unless given the order to do so.[34]

Near Etien, the formation spotted a dozen German two-seaters "flying low over their own lines." Thenault had decided not to attack, since they were "too low, too numerous and too far behind their own lines," but someone—Thenault always insisted he didn't know who it was—suddenly broke formation and dived down on the airplanes below. The others, not willing to sacrifice their rash comrade, had no choice but to follow and in a few moments, a wild melee was underway. It was every man for himself, with individual engagements ranging from 4,000 meters down to altitudes so low that German rifleman on the streets of Etien joined in.[35]

If the initial plunge by the anonymous airman appears rash and foolhardy in the extreme, the battle that followed was a model of bravery that won citations for Rockwell, Chapman, and Thaw. Rockwell had already fought seven individual engagements and was near the end of his fuel supply when he joined with Victor Chapman in attacking a group of several German airplanes. Rockwell followed his usual tactic of withholding fire until the last possible moment, but as he approached his target, an explosive bullet smashed into his windshield, spraying his face with fragments of glass and lead. Struggling to keep his vision clear, he continued his attack and shot down his adversary, although the victory was not confirmed.[36]

Still dripping blood, Rockwell nursed himself and his airplane back to Behomme, where he violently denounced the Germans for using the illegal explosive bullet. At the same time, however, he was more than a little relieved to learn that the face wounds were not serious and would not interfere with his flying.[37]

Meanwhile, Victor Chapman had attacked three German airplanes simultaneously. Unable to shoot one down, he continued the fight until his own machine was well shot up. He had a minor wound in the arm, and several bullets had passed through his clothing. It was a marvelous display of courage by the idealist whom Jim McConnell once called "the most conscientious [soldier] I have ever known." Like Rockwell, Chapman refused hospitalization, preferring to remain at the front.[38]

For his part. Thaw found three Fokkers at 4,000 meters and chased them down to a much lower level before discovering the attacking armada consisted of a single Nieuport. The German pilots then turned on him. He succeeded in breaking away by pressing the attack against the one nearest the French lines, but not before his airplane had been heavily damaged and a bullet had crashed through his left elbow. Weak from loss of blood and suffering from shock, he barely managed to crash land in the French lines near Fort Travennes.[39]

Thaw's failure to return to Behomme left the remaining members of the squadron fearful that they had lost their first man. The fears turned to rejoicing, however, when the news reached them that Thaw, lifted from his plane by French infantrymen, was safe in a field hospital. A short stay at the American Hospital in Paris and Thaw was again with the squadron, nursing an arm that never straightened out properly.[40]

## Buildup of the N-124

Even as the N-124 was beginning to make its presence felt in the Battle of Verdun, new men were coming into the squadron, which was still understrength by six pilots. Raoul Lufbery was the first of the new arrivals. He had flown Voisins with the Escadrille VB-106 before training in Nieuports for future assignment to the Escadrille Américaine. Surprisingly, this "master pilot" of the future had trouble with the fragile Nieuport and his instructors at first wanted to send him back to the Voisins.[41] Thus, when "Luf," as his friends called him, joined the N-124 on May 24 there was no hint of his eventual fame.

Among his generally affluent and cultured comrades in the Escadrille Américaine Lufbery was unique, if not odd. A squat figure with "muscles of steel," he rarely spoke, and when he did his accent betrayed contact with numerous nationalities. He was a mysterious sort of man who liked to take long solitary walks, collect mushrooms, and be alone, even in the air. One fellow pilot said of him, "In contrast to him the Sphinx was a child's primer. He kept his real self shut up like a clam in a shell. He was a man seemingly devoid of fear or, in fact, emotion of any kind. . . . I only know one certain thing about him. Raoul Lufbery flew, fought and died for revenge."[42]

H. Clyde Balsley, a gentle, almost fragile fellow from San Antonio, Texas, and Charles Chouteau Johnson, who came from the upper strata of St. Louis society, followed Lufbery into the squadron by a matter of days. Both were fine, courageous men who left comfortable homes to drive ambulances in France. They enlisted together in the Foreign Legion for immediate transfer to aviation in September 1915, and graduated with the coveted *brevet* in the Bleriot the following January. They then spent six weeks in the Paris Air Guard before reporting to Behomme and the N-124 the latter part of May 1916.[43]

Both proved welcome additions to the squadron, although their parallel careers soon separated. Balsley, whom Thenault said had all the shyness and gentleness of a girl, would be an early victim of misfortune, forced to display his great courage in a hospital bed. Chouteau Johnson, on the other hand, had long and faithful service with the N-124, although he too had his share of troubles. As Hall and Nordhoff put it: "Chouteau could probably make from memory a relief map of the Western Front, marking in all the aerodromes and the best landing-sites, in case of a *panne de moteur*. Some of these possible landing-fields he chose by experimenting with impossible ones, and others he had the luck to find at the first try; for he had more than his share of motor trouble during his seventeen months at the Front."[44]

Lawrence Rumsey, who joined the Escadrille Américaine in early June, came from a prominent Buffalo, New York, family. Like Balsley and Johnson, he served first the American Ambulance Corps, but desired a more active part in the war. He was breveted in the Caudron but was given later training in the Nieuport, and according to Colonel Regnier's letter announcing the formation of the N-124, was to have been one of the squadron's original members.[45]

By comparison with the others, Rumsey added little to the luster of the Escadrille Américaine. He was a capable man and his intentions were good, but he came into the squadron with an overgrown fondness for hard liquor. Able to hide the malady in the training schools, it rose to dominate him at the front. Often unwilling or unable to fly because of his condition, he was sincere in his oft repeated promises to do better. But in more than four months with the N-124, he flew less than half a dozen missions.[46]

Dudley Laurence Hill joined the squadron on 9 June. The son of a prosperous Peekskill, New York, stove manufacturer, Hill came to France in 1915 to drive ambulances. He stayed with the corps only a short time, however, before enlisting in the Foreign Legion for transfer to aviation. He had been breveted in the Caudron but was an unusually proficient pilot and required little training in the Nieuport before being sent to the front. Hill came to the Escadrille Américaine with an established reputation for tenacity and endurance. He had enlisted in aviation with defective vision in one eye and had passed the eye examinations only by cheating. The French discovered the defect some time later but not before Hill had proven himself worthy of further trust. He was therefore granted his military *brevet* and shipped off to the front.[47] Hill may have been something of an adventurer, and some of his comrades-in-arms came to believe that his family, disappointed that he did not enter the family business, preferred not to have him around.[48] With the N-124, however, he was a much better person and pilot than his monosyllabic nickname of "Dud" implies. He made a fine record with both the French and American flying forces.

Didier Masson, mentioned earlier, also joined the squadron in early June 1916. The first American after Thaw to receive the military *brevet*, he had already seen front-line duty with the Escadrille Caudron C-18 and later with the N-68, the first unit to receive the famous Bébé Nieuport. In some respects, Masson was an immediate sensation with the N-124. His comrades enjoyed his "unfailing good humor" and liked to hear about his "hectic exploits" with the Obregon forces in Mexico. Most important, however, he was already a reliable, highly skilled pilot, just the sort of person to have around during the Battle of Verdun.[49]

## The Battle Continues

N-124 pilots flew numerous missions between 24 May, when Rockwell, Chapman, and Thaw were wounded during a wild melee, and the middle of June, but without recording significant damage to themselves or the enemy. On 17 June, however, an event occurred which in some ways was a replay of the 24 May incident. Several pilots of the Escadrille Américaine were patrolling the left bank of the Meuse River with express orders not to cross over. The sight of a formation of several German aircraft in the forbidden area, however, was too much for Chapman. In a maneuver that strongly suggests that he was the unnamed airman who triggered the combat three weeks earlier, Chapman broke off the patrol and plunged to the attack. Again his fellow pilots were forced to follow, and all were soon in one of these mixed-up aerial duels in which teamwork counted for very little. Without loss or gain, the Americans finally made their way back to Behomme—all that is, except Chapman. Refueling at Vadelaincourt, he returned to the lines, and quite alone attacked a group of two Aviatiks protected by three Fokkers. It was a monumental if somewhat irrational display of courage, even for one who thrived on danger. Under the circumstances it was, in the words of one World War I ace, "almost certain suicide."[50]

Chapman enjoyed the element of surprise and actually sent one Aviatik down in flames before the others realized that a lone Nieuport was making the attack and acted accordingly. They hemmed him in and proceeded to work him over.

Chapman had exhausted one drum of ammunition and was in the process of fitting a new one—a necessary but extremely hazardous operation which allowed him to maintain only marginal control of the airplane—when a German bullet severed the right aileron control, ricocheted, and cut through his helmet, inflicting a deep scalp wound.

Dazed, with very little lateral control on the right side of his airplane, Chapman let the Nieuport fall away. As it spun down, the German pilots apparently concluded that the pilot was dead and that it would be both useless and unwise to sacrifice altitude by following him down. This no doubt saved Chapman's life. Although dazed, bleeding, and unable to fight back, he managed to gather the severed ends of the control rod, and holding them together, regained control of the airplane. He made it back to the French lines and landed his damaged machine at a small field near Froids. Undaunted, he ate lunch, had both his head and airplane repaired, and continued back to Behomme. Thenault strongly urged Chapman to take a rest in the hospital but Chapman would not hear of it. His will prevailed and he was soon in the air again, wearing a dazzling headdress of gauze bandages.[51]

The following day, the N-124 suffered its first serious casualty. The victim was H. Clyde Balsley, who had been with the squadron for more than two weeks. This was his first real excursion into German airspace. The patrol, made up of Balsley, Prince, Rockwell and Thenault, began normally enough and an ensuing air battle east of Verdun was not out of the ordinary. But in the melee, Balsley attacked a two-place machine. In his own words, "I fired once—twice. These were my first and last shots. My machine gun had jammed. Not a shot from the observer. Probably got him. I pulled away, caught my stick in my knees to reach for the collapsable mount to drop the gun and fix the jam, but a machine gun opened up on my left, another on my right."[52]

Balsley knew that the best thing would be to attack the German nearest the French lines and perhaps fight his way into the open. His gun was not yet rearmed, however, and he was hemmed in by at least four enemy airplanes. He put on a dazzling display of acrobatics, but

while I was standing on my head, the belly of my machine skyward, . . . something struck me. It felt like the kick of a mule. With the sensation of losing a leg, I put my hand down to learn if it was still there. I had the presence of mind to cut the motor. But as my right foot went back with the shock of the bullet, my left sprang forward. So, with my commands reversed, my leg knocked out, still standing on my head, I went into a spinning nose dive.[53]

His legs paralyzed, "bleeding like a pig," Balsley made a "supreme effort" and got the airplane on an even keel, only to see the enemy again take up the attack. This time he pushed the machine into a controlled dive that at times reached the vertical. A drum of cartridges tore from the cockpit and struck him in the arm but this misfortune was more than offset by the fact that he had left his pursuers far behind. The danger was not over, however.

I was bleeding badly and faint. Field of green—could I swing for it? Stick in one hand, right hand on the knee, I worked my rudder, turned and slid in for the field. Too late I saw that it was filled with barbed wire. I was landing between the front lines and the reserve. I pancaked it in.

Wheels in the wire, the Nieuport turned over and crashed. Gasoline was soaking me. I broke my belt and dropped out. Legs still paralyzed, afraid of fire, I tried to get to my knees. No hope. Caught onto the weeds, dragging myself along the ground like a dog with a broken back. Ten yards, no further. A burst of dust in the field, no sound. My ears were gone from that terrific dive. . . . The 77's dropped around me. A direct hit on the ship, the shelling stopped. Four French soldiers crawled out of their trench. They too had been waiting for the shelling to stop. Under the wire they came, caught hold of me and dragged me down. I had made my last flight for France.[54]

Balsley was taken to the big evacuation hospital at Vadelaincourt some ten miles behind the lines, where he saw his wound for the first time and learned that an explosive bullet had smashed against his pelvic bone. The sciatic nerve was partially severed and numerous shell fragments were scattered throughout the lower part of his body. The doctors did not expect him to live, and the day following his wound, a colonel hurriedly presented him with the Médaille Militaire and croix de guerre. "Now I knew what it all meant," Balsley later wrote, "those people grouped about me like the picture of some famous death-bed. Yesterday I had seen two men decorated. They died within an hour. So my time had come."[55]

Refusing to give up hope, Balsley responded to the medals by saying "Merci, but I am not going to die." He then clung to life through ten days of almost primitive conditions in the forward evacuation hospital at Vadelaincourt. He underwent several operations to remove fragments of metal from his body and endured long hours of high fever, intense cramps, and agonizing thirst. With the orderlies able to provide only minimum care, he lay for days at a time in his own sweat and blood, unable to move his body and too weak to brush the flies from his face. And all the while, day and night, there was the audible agony of dying men.[56]

Balsley's remarkable endurance, which was aided considerably by the special attention of an American nurse, won the admiration and respect of all who knew him at Vadelaincourt. When the other pilots of the Escadrille Américaine came to visit him, as they often did, the French would point to him and say, "Il est un brave petit gars, l'aviateur américain."[57] And the American pilots would return to Behomme, heartened by their comrade's courage and considerably sobered by the vision of what could easily befall any one of them.

Balsley never returned to the N-124, except for a brief visit. He spent many months and lived through several more operations in the American Hospital at Paris. Finally, his invalid state forced him out of the French military service. His two-shot assault on the German air forces had been costly, but in the aggregate, his real reward was the gratitude of the nation he had come to serve and the admiration of his comrades in arms.

## The First to Fall

During Balsley's stay at Vadelaincourt and partly as a consequence of it, tragedy in its final form struck the Escadrille Américaine. On 23 June 1916 Victor Chapman fell near Verdun in an air battle that was characteristic of this dedicated and reckless airman, one who displayed so well the virtues and defects of many World War I fighter pilots.

On one of his regular visits to the hospitalized Balsley, Chapman's capacity for compassion was aroused by his comrade's thirst, a consequence of the abdominal wound, for the doctors would not allow Balsley to take ordinary fluids. Chapman suggested sucking oranges and bullied the doctors into approving the proposal. Oranges, however, were hard to find at the front, and it was 23 June before Chapman had secured a few and was prepared to fly them to Vadelaincourt. Just as he was preparing to leave for the hospital, Chapman witnessed the departure of Thenault, Lufbery, and Prince on a regular patrol. Anticipating the possibility of an engagement with the Germans, he decided to tag along. He could always drop the oranges off on his way back. Thenault, Lufbery, and Prince ran into a group of two LVG's protected by three Fokkers, and after a brief engagement, retreated back to the French lines. Even as they withdrew, Chapman joined the fight, perhaps to aid his seemingly hard-pressed comrades, perhaps to carry on the fight alone. At any rate, it was five against one, or as Chapman may have phrased it, one against five. Either way, only immense skill and even greater luck could save him, for he was not one to retreat.[58]

The men of the patrol apparently did not know that Chapman had joined in, for there was little concern when he did not return to the field. Perhaps he had gone to drop off the oranges, and even if he had followed the patrol, he was always the last in, anyway. As time passed, the squadron grew more and more anxious. Finally their worst fears were realized. Late in the afternoon the crew of a Maurice Farman, which had been regulating artillery fire, telephoned to say that they had seen the air battle from a distance. A lone Nieuport, they said, suddenly appeared and dived down on a German fighter just as three other Nieuports were breaking away. But he, in turn, was bounced by three German fighters who came down on him from above. A big fight ensued with everyone mixing it up until the Nieuport abruptly fell away, obviously stricken. As it lurched past the Farman, the crew could see the pilot pitched forward in the seat with his head hanging over the side. The Nieuport then began coming apart in the air, continuing its fall until it crashed to earth some six kilometers behind the German lines.[59]

Chapman's death, which may have been at the hands of the great German ace, Oswald Boelke,[60] had a tremendous impact on the N-124. It was hard to get Cowdin into the air after that, and Bert Hall apparently realized for the first time that one could easily get killed doing this sort of thing.[61] All were naturally saddened, but with one or two exceptions they continued to fight as before, while paying extraordinary tribute to their fallen comrade. "Poor Victor was a prince of a fellow and as fine a pilot as there was in the Army," Chouteau Johnson wrote a friend, while Kiffin Rockwell, who knew well the meaning of valor, modestly wrote his brother, "There is no question that Victor had more courage than all the rest of us put together." "We talked in lowered voices after [Chapman's death]," is the way a subdued McConnell summed it up.

We could read the pain in one another's eyes. If only it could have been someone else, was what we all thought, I suppose. To lose Victor was not an irreparable loss to us merely but to France, and to the world as well. I kept thinking of him lying over there and of the oranges he was taking to Balsley. As

I left the field, I caught sight of Victor's *mechanicien* leaning against the end of our hangar. He was looking northward into the sky where his *patron* had vanished, and his face was very sad.[62]

Chapman's fellow pilots could be expected to grieve since, as Edwin C. Parsons later reflected, "The most beloved of all was the first to fall."[63] But there was also a surprisingly wide expression of grief and sympathy among Americans in Paris and among Frenchmen too, a solid indication of the impression then being made by the men of the Escadrille Américaine. The American Independence Day services, held at the American Church in Paris on 4 July 1916, was largely a tribute to Chapman, prompting a French woman to write a touching letter to Chapman's parents.

On all sides people speak with admiration and gratitude of the details, tragic and touching as they are, of his trip to his friend, of the little basket of oranges, of his headlong plunge to save his comrades. America has sent us this sublime youth and our gratitude for him is such that it flows back upon his country. Wherever I go, I am asked about him. Never since the outbreak of the war has public sentiment been more deeply aroused.[64]

Among French officials, Aristides Briand, the Prime Minister of France, mentioned Chapman when speaking to the American Chamber of Commerce on 4 July 1916, referring to him as "the living symbol of American idealism." "France will never forget this new comradeship, this evidence of a devotion to a common ideal," he said. While there may have been some Fourth of July rhetoric in the prime minister's statement, there was no such sentiment evident in the simple and heartfelt telegram the Chapman family received from the President of the French Republic. "I beg to offer to you my perfect sympathy. In your son who has died in the most just of all causes I hail a worthy rival of the brothers in arms of Lafayette."[65]

## Recognition

Meanwhile, the activity of the N-124 during its first weeks at Verdun had won official recognition in military circles, and on 28 June an appropriate ceremony was held at Bar-le-Duc. As a reward for shooting down the German two-seater on 23 May, Bert Hall was promoted and given the Médaille Militaire and the croix de guerre along with suitable plaudits. Rockwell, who had been at the front for less than two months, was promoted to sergeant and awarded the Médaille Militaire and the croix de guerre avec palme in recognition of his victory on 18 May. His citation described him as a "courageous and skillful pilot."[66] William Thaw was also decorated, but, as an officer, he was ineligible for the Médaille Militaire. He received the croix de guerre avec palme for his 24 May victory, along with a citation praising him for his "skill, his spirit and contempt of danger." Most important, however, he was named a Chevalier of the Legion of Honor, a special recognition indeed, for Thaw was the first American to receive it in the Great War.[67]

The only sad note of the ceremony was the posthumous awarding of sergeant's rank and the croix de guerre to Victor Chapman in recognition of his remarkable exploits on 24 May and 19 June. Praising him as a "model of audacity, energy and spirit," the citation did not fail to mention that he had found a "glorious death in the course of aerial combat."[68]

The intense fighting at Verdun that had cost Chapman's life and crippled Balsley declined with the opening of the Somme offensive on 1 July. The major emphasis on air fighting soon passed to the northwest, but there was still plenty of activity at Verdun. For many months to come, one could still kill or be killed anywhere in the sector.

It was in mid-July 1916 that sous-lieutenant Charles Nungesser, an ace whose name is forever associated with the famous N-65, joined the N-124 for a brief period. Flamboyant, so proud of his nine victories that he openly bragged about them and wore his medals on his flying suit,[69] he was already one of France's most famous airmen. The Americans were glad to have him around, particularly since he downed his tenth victim while with the N-124. Had it not been that Guynemer got number eleven the same day, the Escadrille Américaine would have had France's top airman on its roster.[70]

Two days after Nungesser's victory (which was never added to the squadron total) Bert Hall was credited with bringing down an enemy near the Fort de Vaux, and just four days later de Laage, one of the squadron's best and most determined pilots, brought down his first victim between Ornes and Bezonvaux.[71]

Two victories in five days; counting Nungesser's, three in seven days. It was a duplication of the flurry of activity in May when Rockwell, Thaw, and Hall each won a victory within a week's time. Thus the squadron was already falling in with a strange and unexplained phenomena of air fighting, i.e., that kills and deaths come in bunches. But even so, there was more to come.

On 31 July, as the squadron was enjoying lunch, a telephone message informed the unit that Raoul Lufbery, who had not yet returned from a patrol, had just brought down a Fokker, his first confirmed victim, near the Mace Forest.[72] There was naturally a period of rejoicing, for Lufbery was well liked. But for the happy pilot it was a monumental occasion. Living and fighting for the day when he could avenge the death of his friend Marc Pourpe, he had not found full satisfaction in his unconfirmed victory of 17 June. Indeed, on 30 July, after experiencing his fourteenth and fifteenth combats, he had written a friend as follows:

> At the moment, I am in a period of bad luck. I hope something happens to change it. Three days ago I had a bad accident and my aeroplane was smashed into bits of wood, iron and cloth. I wasn't scratched but it was a miracle since I was traveling at 160 kilometers per hour. I was attempting to evade a Farman, which was landing from the wrong direction. I attempted to make a steep climbing turn but I was so low that my wing hit the ground.
>
> I have had several unfortunate combats these last few days but no success. I attacked one machine from close in and fired 47 bullets into him but he wouldn't go down.[73]

Now the winds of fortune changed. Lufbery glowingly described his latest combat as follows: "I moved in rapidly, not giving him time to collect his wits. He didn't last long. He fell into a spin at the first burst of my machine gun and crashed to earth . . . just inside his lines. . . . The victory confirmed the same day . . . Imagine my joy. It took me two months and 16 combats to achieve this result."[74] It was the beginning of a brilliant career; Lufbery had apparently discovered that rare combination of skill and luck, which McConnell called a "secret formula." But evidently Lufbery was not the grim, remorseless avenger he imagined himself to be. Later, at the dinner table, McConnell heard him muttering to himself. "Those poor fellows."[75]

On 4 August, Lufbery got his second kill when he shot down an Aviatik east of Vaux. Within the hour, he sent another spinning to earth in the same vicinity.[76] It might have been beginner's luck, except that Lufbery had another victory on 8 August. Moreover, his account of that action points to skill rather than luck as the basic ingredient of his success. Having found a two-place Aviatik between Douaumont and Verdun he patiently waited to press the attack. He first scouted the area, aware of the possibility that the machine might be a tempting decoy. Then, convinced that it was not, he skillfully maneuvered his airplane in such a way that he passed unseen through the enemy gunner's field of fire. He was in excellent position, just below and behind the Aviatik's tail, when,

at this moment, [the pilot]saw me but it was too late. In vain he tried to bank the machine to permit his gunner to fire. . . . I fired 47 bullets into him.

I was now so close that I had to make a quick left turn to avoid a collision. I then leveled the machine and searched for my victim. He was there alright, under me. . . . His machine was coming apart and he was falling in large spirals. Black smoke and then flames came from the machine. . . .

He crashed in the Ravine of the Viper, a few meters inside the German lines.[77]

The student had at last become a master. The clumsiness that had marked him in his Nieuport training and threatened to send him back to the bombers was gone. In the words of two of his comrades, he now "flew as a bird flies, without any thought of how it was done."[78]

Lufbery's brilliant performance during the period between 31 July and 8 August naturally brought him considerable recognition, as well as reflecting great credit on the squadron he represented. Of the ten confirmed victories credited to the unit, the last four were his. As a consequence, on 16 August he was awarded the Médaille Militaire and the croix de guerre avec palme, but the citation mentioned only the victories up through 4 August. As his commanding officer put it, "He was scoring successes faster than they could recompense him."[79]

Meanwhile, as the German efforts to stop the Somme offensive were slowly siphoning both planes and pilots from the Verdun sector, the Germans took measures that hinted of desperation. In July and August they suddenly began sending bombers in groups of twenty and thirty to bomb French towns and airfields. Since the French no longer maintained the continuous patrols up and down the line, the bombers often got through. Bar-le-Duc and the Behomme airfield were bombed several times, each time suffering "serious damage." Neither the French nor the Americans were used to this sort of thing, and it was highly frustrating to endure the raids. Among other things, the lack of an adequate warning system and the proximity of Behomme to the front almost automatically insured that the whole business was over and done with before the Americans could rise to fight the invaders.[80]

## The Temporary Loss of McConnell

In mid-August, the N-124 temporarily lost the services of James R. McConnell, a "delightful" and courageous pilot, who was often in the fight, but somehow never tasted the fruits of victory. Returning from a patrol with Rockwell and Prince, a mission that carried them into the first hours of darkness, McConnell had the misfortune of a *panne de moteur.*

I made for a field [he later wrote]. In the darkness I couldn't judge my distance well, and went too far. At the edge of the field there were trees and beyond, a deep cut where a road ran. I was skimming ground at a hundred miles an hour and heading for the trees. I saw soldiers running to be in at the finish and I thought to myself that James's hash was cooked, but I went between two trees and ended up head-on against the opposite bank of the road. My motor took the shock and my belt held me. As my tail went up it was cut in two by some very low 'phone wires.[81]

It was characteristic of McConnell that he later wrote—from his hospital bed—"I wasn't even bruised."[82] Actually, he had a badly wrenched back, and although he continued to fly for several days, there came a time when he could no longer dress himself and had to walk with a cane. The malady worsened during a leave in Paris, and by the time he returned to the front, he could no longer walk. Thenault forthwith sent him to the hospital, where he lay for months, suffering from his wrenched back and rheumatism, and writing his delightful little book, *Flying for France.* Except for a brief period in November he remained bedridden until the following March, when he left the hospital without permission to return to his squadron and an untimely death.[83]

Elliot C. Cowdin also left the squadron about this time. Unable to get along with his fellow pilots, but willing to take advantage of French leniency toward the volunteers, he had overstayed his leave once too often and was brought back to Thenault under the technical charge of desertion. To avoid trouble, however, the charge was not pressed and Cowdin was allowed to resign.[84]

The gap created by the departure of Cowdin and the temporary absence of James McConnell was partially filled by the arrival of Paul Pavelka, a "real adventurer who laughed at danger," on 11 August. Raised on a small farm near Madison, Connecticut, Pavelka left home at the age of fourteen because of differences with his stepmother. During the ensuing years, he worked in the West as a cowboy, cook for a sheepcamp, and nurse. He then turned to the sea, living through a hundred adventures, including a walk clear across South America after a shipwreck, earning thereby the nickname that followed him to this death in Salonika—"Skipper."[85]

Pavelka was in a home for seamen in New York when the war broke out. He worked his way to England on a boat carrying cattle or horses, and in London encountered the Counani army, one of the most incredible units in military history.[86] Pavelka, who seemingly had a taste for the unusual, joined the small, undisciplined group led by Adolph Beaufort, the self-styled "president" of the Counani Republic, a Lilliputian territory between Brazil and French Guiana and claimed by both countries.

Along with the entire Counani army, Pavelka was absorbed into the French Foreign Legion when the unit was disbanded in late 1914. As a Legionnaire, he fought well in the trenches and was side by side with Kiffin Rockwell when the latter was wounded near Artois in May 1915. He was himself wounded by a bayonet in hand-to-hand combat the following month, but this did not prevent him from taking part in the Champagne offensives in September and October 1915. Encouraged by the Rockwell brothers, he transferred to aviation in December 1915, and eight months later was attached to the Escadrille Américaine.[87]

Pavelka's initiation into the brotherhood of combat pilots was not a pleasant experience. On 13 August, on his initial flight over German lines, his Gnôme Rotary engine "swallowed" one of its combination intake-exhaust valves, allowing raw fuel to spill over the hot cylinder casings. The engine caught fire almost immediately and Pavelka was faced with the most terrifying experience a World War I airman could imagine.[88]

Hurriedly shutting down his engine, Pavelka attempted to "slip" the airplane and by this means keep the windstream from blowing the flames directly back to the cockpit. Pushing the nose of the airplane down, he began a desperate race to get to the ground before he was fatally burned or the Nieuport quit flying on its own accord. It was almost a tie. With the hair singed from his face and hands, he maneuvered the fast disappearing machine into a "controlled crash" in a swamp, just within the French lines. Unbuckling his safety belt, he hurried to safety a few moments before the plane exploded and the German artillery began their customary practice of shelling the downed airplane.[89]

It was without question a combination of skillful flying and good fortune that saved him, but he was not overly disturbed. Back in the air the next day, he had some interesting things to say about the comparative safety of the trenches.[90]

## Last Days at Verdun

According to Captain Thenault, the Germans during the latter part of August and the first part of September were "much less numerous and above all showed much less dash" than heretofore. Even so, the squadron diary indicates almost daily contact with the enemy over Verdun. On 24 August, Chouteau Johnson fought an aerial duel, but left hurriedly when his machine gun jammed; Hall fought two combats, as did Lufbery, one of which was well behind the German lines. Prince also challenged a German airplane, returning home with several marks of battle. The following day there were more combats, with Prince forcing a "seriously damaged" enemy airplane to land behind the French lines. Then, after two days of inactivity due to rain, Hall brought down his third confirmed victory northeast of Douaumont.[91]

On 9 September Prince located an enemy machine near Fort Roether, and in a short engagement, sent it "turning and falling to earth, trailing grey smoke." He then found and attacked three enemy airplanes, but was forced to flee when one of them put a bullet through one of his cylinders.[92]

Meanwhile, Rockwell, out on a second patrol with Thaw and Lufbery, found an unsuspecting enemy, and "approaching very close to the aeroplane," killed the observer/gunner with the first shot. A wild plunge downward followed, with the German pilot desperately trying to evade his pursuer and Rockwell firing, swearing, and clearing his thrice-jammed machine gun.

At last, "riddled with bullets," the German machine fell off into a fatal spin, while Rockwell, faced with a faltering gun and two approaching German fighters, raced for the lines. His victim fell within the German lines, but not so far that French ground observers could not mark its fall.[93] Rockwell, who had won the squadron's first confirmed victory, also had won the last for the squadron during the great Battle of Verdun.

Three days later, the N-124 suddenly received orders to return to

Luxeuil, leaving their well-worn Nieuports at Behomme. [94] What did it mean? There was still plenty of activity around Verdun, and a transfer, if there be one, should obviously be to the Somme, where another gigantic battle was underway. The Escadrille Américaine had certainly given a good account of itself at Verdun, logging nearly 1,000 sorties, 146 combats and 13 official victories, all at the loss of one dead and three wounded. [95] Since the French had not spared the squadron in the past, there was little reason to believe that they would do so now. The pilots correctly guessed that something big was being planned for the Vosges sector, since there was news of a buildup at Luxeuil. Also, there was unquestionably some significance to the announcement that the squadron would soon be equipped with the Nieuport 17, France's newest and best fighter plane. [96]

With mixed emotions, the N-124 left Behomme by train at high noon on 14 September. The period just concluded had been a difficult one, a period in which the pilots hardly had time to eat, when they often slept "fully dressed in their flying suits beneath their planes so as to be ready to start at the first glimpse of dawn." [97] Nevertheless, they were true fighter pilots now. The campaigns of late 1915 had given comparatively few men experience with aerial combat, whereas Verdun was a veritable school for fighter pilots. Indeed, Verdun had witnessed the working-out of those basic principles which would build future fighters in the air for years to come. These principles, really a matching of logic and experience, were soon common to both sides of the lines. Oswald Boelke, one of the German masters of the art, summed them up as follows:

Try to secure advantage before attacking. If possible keep the sun behind you.

Always carry through an attack when you have started it.

Fire only at close range and only when your opponent is properly in your sights.

Always keep your eyes on your opponent, and never let yourself be deceived by ruses.

In any form of attack it is essential to assail your opponent from behind.

If your opponent dives on you, do not try to evade his onslaught but fly to meet it.

When over the enemies' lines never forget your own line of retreat. [98]

# 4

# Vosges and Somme Sectors

## September 1916 – January 1917

Since the Nieuport 17s assigned to the N-124 had not yet been delivered to Luxeuil, another period of waiting was inevitable. Several members of the squadron reasoned that part of this waiting period at least should be spent in Paris. They said as much to Captain Thenault, who approved both their logic and their request. "I was glad to give my pilots the pleasure of a visit to the capitol," the captain later wrote. "What an attraction Paris has exercised over all the fighting men during this war."[1]

All members of the Escadrille Américaine had taken leave in Paris at one time or another, but this was a special occasion. Heretofore they had been alone or in twos, virtual nonentities in the great city. Now they were going as a group, and, having covered themselves with glory, could expect a heroes' welcome, particularly from friends and relatives. In the latter category, Kiffin Rockwell's brother Paul was in Paris, as was Mrs. Laurence Slade, Thaw's sister. Prince had relatives there, and everyone had a friend and godmother in Mrs. Alice Weeks, an American who had lost her only son in the Foreign Legion.[2] Also, there was the indefatigable Dr. Gros, whose preference for men who had served in the Ambulance Corps did not sit well with those who had served with the Foreign Legion, but who never turned away an airman in need.[3]

Besides visiting friends, relatives, various bars, and the Nieuport factory, the men of the Escadrille Américaine acquired a pet. As distinctive as the squadron itself, this pet quickly became a legendary part of an already legendary group.

## Whiskey

Pets were common among World War I combat fliers. Virtually every French squadron had from one to a dozen, and the Escadrille Américaine was no exception. Thenault had a large pedigreed German police dog named Fram, a faithful friend who could endure everything except the captain's piano playing. Masson owned a red fox for a period, but the pet was a "general nuisance" until Fram killed it. And Thaw was once part owner of a "doctored" skunk that turned out not to be "doctored" after all.[4] But the squadron as such had no pet in which all could take pride.

During the leave in Paris, Thaw noticed an ad in the European edition of the New York *Herald* in which a Brazilian dentist was offering a four-month-old lion cub for sale. It seems that the cub, which the dentist kept in his office to amuse the patients, liked to roar and show his claws, feeble efforts to be sure, but enough to frighten his clientele.[5]

Joining with Rockwell, Prince, Johnson, and Hall, Thaw formed a syndicate to raise the necessary 500 francs. By nightfall, the N-124 owned a pet that in due time added a great deal of fun and fame to the life of the squadron.[6]

The cub was taken to Luxeuil in a cage, for although Thaw had put it on a leash and gotten it aboard the train by insisting that it was an "African dog," the lion gave one of its periodic roars, frightening the passengers and causing the conductor to change his mind. It was one of the few times the cub was ever in a cage, for the pilots liked the reasoning of James McConnell: "Why put him behind bars? He'll see all the bars he needs traveling with this mob."[7]

The cub acquired his unusual name shortly after the unit arrived at Luxeuil. One evening a pilot playfully placed a saucer of whiskey on the floor, and the cub, at first wary, began to lap it up. In a little while, "he roared like a lion should,"[8] and the name sort of fell into place. Henceforth he was everywhere known as "Whiskey."

Whiskey proved an unusually welcome addition to the squadron, for he provided considerable amusement, something that was sorely needed at the front. His first playmates were dogs, and in due time he became so gentle that Lufbery insisted that he didn't know he was a lion at all, but thought he was just another dog. He never bit or scratched and loved to be petted. He was also a good bed companion on

Bert Hall. *Courtesy of the Smithsonian Institution.*

Didier Masson. *Courtesy of the United States Air Force.*

Raoul Lufbery. *Courtesy of the United States Air Force.*

Raoul Lufbery.

James R. McConnell and Paul A. Rockwell. *Courtesy of Paul A. Rockwell.*

Kiffin Rockwell. *Courtesy of the United States Air Force.*

James R. McConnell. *Courtesy of the United States Air Force.*

Kiffin Rockwell, departing on a mission over German lines. *Courtesy of the United States Air Force.*

The original Lafayette Escadrille with pilots of the 4th Bombardment Group.

Chouteau Johnson in his Nieuport 11, with its top-mounted Lewis machine gun and Le Prieur rockets. *Courtesy of the United States Air Force.*

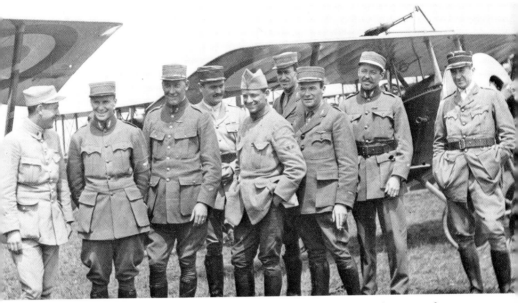

The Lafayette Escadrille at Bar-Le-Duc, July 1916. *Left to right*: de Laage de Meux, Chouteau Johnson, Lawrence Rumsey, James McConnell, William Thaw, Raoul Lufbery, Kiffin Rockwell, Didier Masson, Norman Prince, Bert Hall. *Courtesy of the United States Air Force.*

Poison gas attack on the western front. *Courtesy of the United States Air Force.*

William Thaw and Whiskey, with Paul Pavelka looking on.

Whiskey and Soda.

Victor Chapman, wounded 17 June
1916 and shot down six days later.
*Courtesy of the United States Air
Force.*

Paul Pavelka. *Courtesy of the United
States Air Force.*

The "tragic photograph"—within a few months after it was taken, the four
Americans were dead. *Left to right:* James McConnell, Kiffin Rockwell,
Georges Thenault, Norman Prince, and Victor Chapman.

The airfield at Chaudun. *Courtesy of the United States Air Force.*

A SPAD VII flown by Masson, Marr, and Lufbery. *Courtesy of the United States Air Force.*

cold winter nights, and was much in demand for this service despite the fact that he didn't keep himself very clean and had chronic halitosis. In fact, he smelled so bad that on state visits to other squadrons, in which the lion was invariably a guest of honor, he usually had to be rubbed down with eau de cologne.[9]

Although Whiskey was so gentle that the pilots played with him as if he were a baby kitten, he was enough of a lion to revert periodically to his natural instinct. He would chew on just about anything. Indeed, so incurable was this pernicious habit that the pilots had to attach pulleys to the ceiling of the barracks so that they might draw up their personal belongings when they were not around to protect them.[10] He once chewed a *kepi* (the French army cap) belonging to Lawrence Rumsey. Rumsey, angered and drunk, held the cub's head with one hand while striking him across the face with a heavy walking stick. Whiskey took the beating without attempting to retaliate, but the damage had been done. With an optic nerve damaged, the right eye began to cloud over and the best efforts of a veterinarian—when one was finally found who would do the job—failed to preserve the fading vision. Henceforth, Whiskey held his head cocked to one side like a listening parrot.[11]

In time Whiskey became so famous that many people visited the squadron just to see him. The fun-loving Americans soon discovered that this could be turned into considerable amusement. As Parsons tells the story,

> Hardly a day passed that we didn't have from twenty-five to fifty visitors, mostly poilus in rest camps and the like, curious to inspect the planes and attracted by stories of the Americans and their lion, stories which, before their arrival, few of them credited.
>
> Luf would wait for a good opportunity, then send Whiskey around the corner of the barracks out of sight, while we lined up to see the fun.
>
> His thoughts far away on other and perhaps more amorous matters, an unsuspecting poilu would stroll by the corner where Whiskey lay in hiding. Luf would give the signal. Whiskey, with a ferocious roar, would leap out, throw his huge paws over the shoulders of the victim and drag him to the ground by sheer weight.
>
> In most cases the unfortunate soldier would be so petrified with fear at the apparition of this savage beast springing out on him so unexpectedly, that his knees would simply collapse under him. He'd go down and lie like a log, stark fear in his eyes, as Whiskey poised over him, apparently ready to tear him to bits.
>
> Then Whiskey would put his head back and open his mouth wide, showing

all his yellowed fangs in a silent laugh. At least, Luf always said it was a laugh, although privately I though that Whiskey was just airing out his mouth after having gotten a taste of unwashed poilu.

Luf would quickly call Whiskey, and he'd come trotting over, purring over his achievement, begging for another victim. Sheepishly, the rescued victim would get up, come over and be urged to pet the savage-appearing but docile animal; which, if he did at all, would be done most gingerly and suspiciously. A tame lion was beyond the poilus' power of comprehension, but they were much too grateful to have escaped sudden death to be really angry at the trick. It was an unfailing source of amusement.[12]

The American pilots, anticipating how the lion must feel, concluded that he was lonely. After some searching, a female companion was found and purchased. Naturally she was christened "Soda." Soda, however, proved to be a cantankerous female. She refused to fit into the squadron routine and although Whiskey was reportedly "tickled pink" when they first met, she never returned the compliment. She had a mean disposition and barely tolerated the Americans.[13] Nevertheless, Soda and her mate became integral parts of the Escadrille Américaine, rivaling in popularity even the most famous members of the unit.

Meanwhile, just before leaving Paris, the N-124 acquired another pilot, a replacement for the gallant Chapman. This man was Robert Lockerbie Rockwell of Cincinnati, a distant cousin of the Rockwell brothers. A medical student before the war, he had terminated his studies in early 1915 and came to France to offer his services as an intern with the American Hospital. But "Doc" Rockwell, as he was called, was not satisfied as a medic. Desiring a closer and more personal contact with the war, he enlisted in aviation in February 1916 and was breveted in the Bleriot the following May. He then trained in the Nieuports for a period and was assigned to the N-124 in mid-September 1916.[14]

### Life at Luxeuil

The pilots of the Escadrille Américaine returned to their old and luxurious quarters at Luxeuil and again took up their numerous friendships with the townspeople. A new and very welcome addition to the surroundings, however, was the presence of about fifty British aviators along with more than a thousand ground personnel. The British pilots, flying the famous Scpwith, two-place, one-and-a-half strutters, were temporarily attached to the French and were obviously waiting for something big.[15]

At first the British and American fliers didn't know what to make of each other and there was what McConnell called a "feeling of reserve on both sides." But in a few days the ice had been broken and the bonds of friendship securely tied. "We didn't know what you Yanks would be like," one Englishman remarked one day. "Thought you might be snobby on account of being volunteers, but I swear you are a bloody human lot."[16]

While waiting for the Nieuport 17s to arrive, the American pilots lived a life of ease and luxury. "It was about as much like a war as a Bryan lecture [McConnell wrote from his hospital bed]. . . . I received a letter written at this time from one of the boys. I opened it expecting to read of an air combat. It informed me that Thaw had caught a trout three feet long, and that Lufbery had picked two baskets of mushrooms."[17]

The British pilots spent most of the daylight hours practicing formation flying, a pioneering effort in 1916, but in the evening they partied with their American friends and joined in organized dancing at one of the local hotels. As might be expected, some of the parties got a little out of hand, and on one occasion there was a "Homeric football match" played in an unlighted barracks at midnight. "The walls yielded to our shoulders and the players went head over heels outside," the dignified Thenault later wrote. "Personally, I was glad that the game had not been played in our own shed."[18]

The first of the new Nieuports arrived on 19 September. The airmen were naturally delighted, for the Nieuport 17s were larger and more durable than the earlier Bébés. The wings were flatter, allowing greater speeds while an additional 20 square feet of wing surface made up for the resulting loss in lift. The 110 hp Le Rhône rotary gave it an air speed ten to fifteen miles per hour faster than the Nieuport 11, yet it retained the maneuverability for which the Nieuports were famous. Its maximum altitude was in the neighborhood of 18,000 feet—not as high as some German airplanes—but it could climb to 7,000 feet in less than six minutes, a very important factor for a combat pilot whose life may depend on the ability to outclimb his opponent.[19]

Perhaps most important, the Nieuport 17 carried a Vickers machine gun, mounted directly in front of the pilot and synchronized to fire through the propeller arc. This gun, like the Lewis, was prone to jamming, and the engine needed to be partly dismantled to clear the breech. It was nonetheless a notable step forward and came close to neutralizing the technical advantage heretofore enjoyed by the Germans. The Americans appreciated this advancement, but like many of their French comrades, kept a Lewis machine gun mounted on the top wing just in case.[20]

It was 22 September before the machines were ready. Captain Happe, still in command of Groupe de Bombardement no. 4, expressed the wish that the Americans avoid contact with the enemy before the big event, which was still a closely guarded secret, but the squadron *Journal de Marche* indicates that Rockwell and Lufbery each flew twice that first day. As Thenault explained it, "Think of restraining fanatics like Lufbery or Rockwell when they had at their disposal superb new machines, fitted with the latest devices."[21]

## The Death of Kiffin Rockwell

Captain Happe knew what he was doing when he requested that the Americans not seek combat before the appointed time. He realized that despite the lack of fighting on the ground in the Vosges sector, one could still get killed in the air with remarkable ease. The massing of French and British bombers at Luxeuil had naturally been noted by the Germans, who felt obliged to concentrate fighters in the area. Best estimates were that more than forty Fokkers were located on the fields at Colmar and Habsheim alone. Moreover, the Germans in the Vosges sector had recently developed a highly effective decoy system in which a slow and highly vulnerable observation craft, obviously alone, was sent across the lines. The unsuspecting airman who took the bait soon regretted his failure to notice two or more Fokkers flying top cover.[22] It worked well, for a while anyway.

On 23 September, Lufbery and Kiffin Rockwell again took to the air, this time fully intending to challenge the Germans. They found several Fokkers over Hartmansweilerkopf, but Lufbery's Vickers jammed and he did not like the odds without it. He abandoned the contest and elected to fly to a nearby field at Fontaine, home of the Escadrille N-49, for quick repairs. Rockwell accompanied him to safety but declined to land, preferring to return to the lines. The Fokkers were nowhere to be seen, but near Rodern, Rockwell saw a swift, two-place Albatros, well situated below him.[23] Prudence would have counseled an attack from behind and below, for the Albatros carried a swivel-mounted machine gun in the rear cockpit, but Rockwell remained true to the tactic that matched his fearless nature. He simply reduced power and plunged to the attack.

The ensuing battle was witnessed by a French infantry captain using field glasses. He saw the German gunner begin firing as soon as Rockwell began his dive, but the Nieuport continued its approach until a collision appeared imminent. Only then did its pilot open fire. The German airplane appeared to be hit and started to fall, but the real victim was the Nieuport. It suddenly turned nose down and plummeted to earth. As it fell, one wing tore away from the fuselage and fluttered slowly to the ground.[24]

Rockwell fell in a field of flowers, a few hundred yards within the French lines and less than two and one-half miles from where he had killed his first German pilot four months before. German artillery immediately opened fire on the smashed airplane but some French soldiers braved the fire to recover Rockwell's body. There was no question as to how he had died. An explosive bullet had left a gaping hole at the base of his throat.[25]

The news of Kiffin's death, telephoned back to the squadron by an army doctor, was a staggering jolt for the American pilots. Captain Thenault was weeping quietly when he told the others that "the best and bravest of us all is no more,"[26] and James McConnell echoed the feeling of many when he wrote:

No greater blow could have befallen the escadrille. Kiffin was its soul. He was loved and looked up to not only by every man in our flying corps but by everyone who knew him. Kiffin was imbued with the spirit of the cause for which he fought and gave his heart and soul to the performance of his duty. He said: "I pay my part for Lafayette and Rochambeau," and he gave the fullest measure. The old flame of chivalry burned brightly in this boy's fine and sensitive being. With his death France lost one of her most valuable pilots.[27]

It was Rockwell's wish, expressed only the night before he died, that in case of misfortune, he be buried where he fell. But his was impossible, for the field was much too near the lines. Instead, his body, draped in a French flag, was brought back to Luxeuil for burial.[28]

The funeral, held two days later, was "worthy of a general." In it, Rockwell was named a *sous-lieutenant*, a rank he was to have received in the near future. There was also a citation, signed by General Joffre, praising him as "an American pilot who ceaselessly won the admiration of his chiefs and his comrades by his *sang-froid*, his courage and his daring."[29] The coffin was literally hidden by flags and flowers, while on the line stood fifty English pilots, eight hundred Royal Flying Corps mechanics, a regiment of French Territorials, a batallion of Colonials and hundreds of French officers and men. And as the slow-moving funeral procession passed from the village church to the cemetery, "airplanes circled at a feeble height above and showered down myriads of flowers."[30]

## Waiting for the Event

After Rockwell's death, it would have been most difficult for Thenault to keep the American airmen from flying. "There isn't space enough to tell you what kind of a man he was," Chouteau Johnson wrote his mother, adding, "You can rest assured the Huns have an account to pay and I think they will realize the Escadrille is seeing red and some of them are going to catch hell." Lufbery, who thrived on vengeance anyway, was so angered by the death of his friend and the role played by the illegal explosive bullet that only hours after Rockwell's death he flew alone to the German aerodrome at Habsheim and dared the Germans to come and get him. None took the challenge, nor was there any contact on the day following, when Lufbery, Thaw, Prince, and de Laage took to the air. Then the weather intervened. From the day after Rockwell's internment through the third of October constant rain made flying impossible, turning the period into one of frustrated boredom. There was one bright spot, however. On 26 September Prince received the Médaille Militaire and a citation praising him as "a volunteer who has exhibited the finest qualities of bravery and audacity under all circumstances." This medal, the highest a noncommissioned officer could receive and the fifth to be awarded a member of the Escadrille Américaine in as many months, was in recognition of Prince's victories on 23 August and 9 September.[31]

Prince and Lufbery were able to fly on 4 October, but the flight was interrupted when Lufbery's machine gun jammed just as he was beginning an attack on a German airplane. To make matters worse, he began swearing and striking the faulty mechanism, only to see a piece fly off and strike the propeller, shattering it. He barely made it back to a small field at Fontaine for repairs.[32]

Bad weather again moved in on the fifth and continued until the ninth, when a temporary break allowed de Laage and Lufbery to search out the enemy. They became separated and lost contact with one another, de Laage to continue his two-hour fruitless search over the lines, and Lufbery to fly to the German aerodrome at Habsheim, where he found a lone Fokker. Lufbery attacked from above and behind, the best tactic against a single-seater, but the German pilot turned deftly out of his line of fire.

The first pass convinced me that I was in the presence of a master [Lufbery wrote]. This was no laughing matter. Banking my aeroplane, I saw him about fifty meters below me. He pulled up in order to bait me into making a loop, which would have left him a in a good position to fire a volley but I countered with a half reverse to the right. It was now my turn and I attacked him a second time but without result.[33]

In ten minutes of intensive combat, neither man could gain a decisive advantage. Each would have been happy to let the other go his way, but with fuel and ammunition still available, honor would not permit it. At this point, however, French antiaircraft fire signalled the presence of a German airplane over French territory, and Lufbery broke away, only too happy to use this "excellent excuse to abandon the conflict in an honorable manner." His opponent understood perfectly, and in passing for the last time, the two pilots waved to each other.[34]

Lufbery found the cause of the disturbance, a two-place machine painted, white, over Belfort. Delighted to find a suitable victim over French territory—the first time that this had ever happened to Lufbery—and eager for a kill, he threw caution to the winds and dove to the attack. In an approach reminiscent of Kiffin Rockwell, he withheld his fire until the last possible moment, but in vain. His aim had failed, and as he turned away for a second pass, his own motor suddenly quit. Three German bullets had given it a *"blessure mortalle."*[35]

Without power, Lufbery established a glide towards Fontaine. The German pilot declined to follow, but in passing, his gunner sent an accurate stream of machine gun fire in Lufbery's direction that cut the Nieuport's stabilizer, pierced the gas tank, and left numerous holes in the wings and fuselage. One bullet ripped through Lufbery's flying suit, grazing his chest, while another tore open his left boot.[36]

Lufbery nursed his machine back to Fontaine only to find that a mist partially obscured the field. He misjudged the landing, and both man and machine ended up in a tree. The Nieuport, shot up and broken up, was junked as being beyond repair.[37] Lufbery the Miraculous wasn't even scratched, but all in all it had been a bad day.

### The Great Oberndorf Bombing Raid

Meanwhile, even as these events were taking place, the reason for the move of the N-124 to Luxeuil was at last made clear to the men of the squadron. For some time, plans for a combined British and French bomber offensive, the first of its kind, had been under preparation, with the intention of launching the offensive against munitions centers in Southeastern Germany around 1 July 1916. Luxeuil, because of its proximity to the proposed munitions and industrial targets, was chosen as the staging area.[38] The N-124 was to be part of the protective or covering force for this impressive effort, which by its success or failure would certainly affect the future of aerial bombardment for the remainder of the war.

Supply difficulties and failure to meet aircraft production goals delayed the offensive, as did the severe drain on British resources after the opening of the massive Somme campaign on 1 July. Thus, it was early October before the offensive could be launched. A feeble attempt had been made to bomb the gasoline storage areas at Mulheim on 30 July but only nine airplanes had participated in this ineffective raid. The first big effort, aimed at Oberndorf, was scheduled for 12 October.[39]

The exact date of the mission was a closely guarded secret, for the British and French counted heavily on the element of surprise. In early October, when Thenault approached Captain Happe (who would have overall command) about the matter, the "Corsair Rouge" admitted that he did not know the date, but considering the weather and warning needed, did not expect it in the immediate future. Thus assured, Thenault went on leave.[40]

On 11 October, with Thenault vacationing in southern France and with the field at Luxeuil covered with fog, the word came down. The big event, involving more than sixty airplanes, would take place the next morning.[41] The target; the Mauser arms works at Oberndorf.

Despite a maximum effort it was early afternoon of the 12th before the formations took to the air. The fifteen Sopwith one-and-one-half Strutters, bombers of the Royal Navy, were the first to depart, followed by the Farmans and Breguets of the French, sixteen in number. Six British fighters, also Sopwiths, made up part of the protective escort, with the remainder composed of Nieuports assigned to French squadrons. Four pilots of the Escadrille Américaine took part, the honors falling to de Laage, Prince, Masson, and Lufbery.[42]

The mission helped to set a pattern that would be followed well into World War II. The bombers first made a diversionary feint to St. Die to confuse the Germans, and then proceeded to Oberndorf. Since the flight was more than three hundred kilometers one way, the fighters could not offer protection all the way to and from the target. Near Ettenheim on the Rhine River, the fighter escort turned back to refuel and await the appointed hour when they would rendezvous with the bombers on their return journey.[43]

For the fighters, the first part of the mission passed without serious incident, but the bombers encountered heavy antiaircraft fire between Colmar and Neu-Breisach. After that, there was almost continuous opposition from German fighters and although the bombers reached the target, they paid a heavy price. Before picking up protection back at Wittenheim, three British bombers and six French had fallen. The beautiful formations that began the trip had dissolved into widely scattered groups of airplanes, huddled together for what protection they could offer one another. In this condition they met and welcomed their escort fighters.[44]

In the dogfights that followed the reunion, at least six German single-seaters fell, three of them credited to the Escadrille Américaine pilots. Prince and Lufbery attacked a group of four Fokkers, and Prince shot one down for his third confirmed victory. Lufbery engaged the other three, which, operating as a team, attempted to bait him into following two of them in a wild plunge to the ground so that the third might catch him from behind. Lufbery was not deceived, however, and instead of chasing the two who seemed to be frightened and running away, he quickly turned and approached the third head on. It was this one that fell that day over the city of Schlestadt.[45]

Meanwhile, Masson had won a spectacular victory that stands as one of the most remarkable feats of the war. An excellent pilot, he had a Fokker at a decided disadvantage when his engine suddenly quit. In his excitement, he had failed to keep watch on his fuel supply, a seemingly disastrous blunder, for his engine was now dead, and there was no hope of reviving it. Moreover, he was over German territory with barely enough altitude to make it back to the French lines— provided of course, that he lived that long.[46]

The German pilot, recognizing the sudden change of affairs, transformed himself from the attacked into the attacker. He began shooting up the Nieuport almost at will, for Masson could ill afford abrupt maneuvers which cost him altitude. But with all the advantages, the German became confident to the point of carelessness, and dived under the Nieuport, pulling up in front to begin another pass. This maneuver cost him his life, for Masson suddenly banked his airplane and caught the German full fair with the top-mounted Lewis gun.[47]

Masson continued his gentle glide, passing so low over the German lines that German infantrymen nearly shot him down. His airplane was hit several times, but he came through unscathed, and expertly landed his machine just behind the first French trenches. A few moments after Masson had rushed to safety, German artillery blew the plane to bits.[48]

It was a really remarkable accomplishment. As one airman, himself an ace, put it : "Masson had accomplished the impossible. In a motorless glide, helpless to maneuver, he had not only escaped the almost certain death for which he had been fated, but in addition he had gotten his man. It was one of the greatest feats performed during the war, for it was against an enemy who held all the advantage."[49]

## The Death of Norman Prince

Darkness was coming on when de Laage, Prince, and Lufbery, having completed their mission, turned toward home. To avoid the dangerous thrill of landing a swift little fighter on a small, unlighted field at night, de Laage hastened to Plombieres, while Lufbery and Prince elected to go to Corcieux. De Laage and Lufbery made it in without incident, although Lufbery, unfamiliar with Corcieux and influenced by the gathering darkness, barely avoided an accident. Fifteen minutes later Prince, having stayed out until the last possible moment, came in. Like Lufbery, he was not familiar with the field, and it was too dark for him to notice the high tension line strung between a row of trees bordering the landing area. As Lufbery and others watched, unable to warn him, Prince's undercarriage caught this cable, breaking the glide of the airplane and sending it cartwheeling through the air. As it smashed into the ground, the seat belt broke and Prince was hurled out.[50]

Both of Prince's legs were broken and he had undetermined internal injuries. He did not lose consciousness, however, and as men came running to his aid, he smiled and called attention to the sound of an airplane overhead. "Hurry and light the flares," he said, "so that another fellow won't come down and break himself up as I have done." Then, according to Lufbery,

> I placed him in an ambulance, urging the driver to hurry him to the hospital at Gerardmer. Throughout the trip, Norman did not cease to talk and chat with the good humor that was one of his charming characteristics. . . . He spoke of his desire to be back with the squadron soon. But in the meantime, he began to suffer horribly and at times his face would be distorted with pain. His hand, which I was holding between my own, was wet with sweat. His endurance was remarkable and when the pain became so intense that he grew faint, he sang to keep from losing consciousness. My own heart was torn to see the struggle within him.[51]

At first, the doctors at Gerardmer had hopes for Prince's recovery, but the day following the accident, a blod clot formed on his brain and pressed him into unconsciousness. He never recovered and was unaware of the ceremony around his bedside on 14 October in which Captains Happe and Thenault, acting for General Joffre, commissioned him a *sous-lieutenant* and decorated him with the Chevalier of the Legion of Honor.[52] He died quietly the next morning, Sunday, 15 October 1916.

A few days later Prince was given a military burial at Luxeuil that paralleled the one given Kiffin Rockwell only three weeks before. The body, resting on a caisson, was draped in American and French flags and the ceremony was attended by high French and British officers, the entire N-124 and scores of men from other escadrilles. Prince was interred in a chapel in Luxeuil although the body was later moved several times by his father and finally laid to rest in a memorial chapel in Washington, D.C.[53]

The pilots of the Escadrille Américaine naturally regarded Prince's death as a great personal loss. "The nobility of his character had endeared him to all who knew him," his commanding officer wrote, and McConnell, who seems to have had a remarkably sound view of his fellow pilots and their activity, added, "He never let his own spirits drop, and was always on hand with encouragement for the others. I do not think Prince minded going. He wanted to do his part before being killed, and he had more than done it."[54]

The combined bomber offensive continued from Luxeuil, but on a greatly reduced scale. On 23 October, thirteen bombers attacked the Thyssen Works at Hagendingen, and on 10 and 11 November the steel works at Volklingen were hit. Two raids against the iron works at Dillingen were carried out in November and December.[55] None of these missions, however, approached the magnitude or importance of the Oberndorf strike, which had prompted Colonel Bares, the director of the French Air Service, to wire the participants as follows: "Lt. Col. Bares sends to all the French and British pilots who took part in the Oberndorf expedition, his most sincere felicitations for the courage displayed and the results obtained."[56]

The N-124 did not participate in these later raids. As a fighter squadron it was subject to constant change of station to meet or pose some threat. Thus, just two days after Prince's death, it suddenly received orders transferring it to Cachy. The stay at Luxeuil, less than a month in duration, was over. It had been a costly and not very satisfying time; days of waiting with only four men privileged to take part in the great raid; two of the best men and pilots in the squadron dead. No one seemed to mind that Cachy was in the Somme sector, where heavy fighting had been going on since the first of July and where the new center of the war was located. As Thenault put it, "We were eager for a change."[57]

## The Somme

The great Battle of the Somme grew out of Allied offensive strategy for 1916. It had its roots in an inter-Allied meeting held in December 1915 at Joffre's Chantilly headquarters, at which time it was decided to launch massive and roughly simultaneous attacks on all major fronts. As worked out by the military leaders, the campaign in the west called for an impressive effort the following spring by some forty French and twenty-five British divisions hitting astride the Somme River.

The area had little strategic value, being chosen primarily because it was the meeting place between French and British forces, neither of whom had sufficient power to go it alone. Besides, this battle, unlike the campaigns of 1915, was not designed with a breakthrough in mind.

This possibility naturally remained a fond hope, particularly after the British effort became dominant, and massive artillery had shown its frightful effectiveness at Verdun. Nevertheless, in the planning phase, Joffre emphasized the attritional aspect, declaring that it would be of "prolonged duration," and that it would be "premature" to set immediate objectives beyond the enemy's "first positions."[58]

The Battle of Verdun, having absorbed so much French strength, naturally altered the coming campaign, forcing both a postponement and a drastic scaling down. The idea was never abandoned, however. The Allies realized only too well that they could never hope to win the war without carrying the fight to the enemy, without applying so much pressure that Germany could not concentrate on knocking Russia out of the war. Besides, there was now a compelling need to take the pressure off the French at Verdun. Thus, although the French could spare only five divisions for the initial assault instead of the forty once planned, the offensive was launched on 1 July 1916, after a tremendous seven-day artillery bombardment.

The Allies, led by Generals Joffre and Haig, then sent the British Third Army and part of the Fourth, along with the French Sixth Army, head on against the German Second Army on a twenty-two-mile front. As was to be expected, the German lines bent under the pressure, yielding some ground. Nevertheless they held firm, even as both sides rushed in reinforcements to feed the conflagration. Thus, the campaign became a series of battles as thrust was followed by counterthrust. Day after day, week after week, the pounding match went on until eventually more than six hundred thousand men on each side of the lines had made the casualty rosters.[59]

In the air, the Battle of the Somme followed a pattern only indirectly related to affairs on the ground. The inability to maneuver, the nightmare of military leaders and the very foundations of the deadlock itself, was not denied the airmen. Moreover, for the first time in the history of military aviation, "air supremacy" came to be recognized as a prerequisite to proper air support of ground troops. As a result, a regular air war took place, which theoretically at least was but a preliminary to optimum use of the air weapon.

At the beginning of the Somme campaign, the Allies enjoyed almost unchallenged mastery of the air. This mastery, however, was by no means complete. As his famous "Future Policy in the Air" memorandum of September 1916 makes clear, Trenchard understood what it meant and how to achieve it, but this can be said of few other men. Moreover, as Trenchard pointed out in his memorandum: "It is impossible for aeroplanes, however skillful and vigilant their pilots, however powerful their engines, however mobile their machines, and however numerous their formations, to prevent hostile aircraft from crossing the line if they have the initiative and determination to do so."[60] Thus, it was quite possible for German machines to concentrate before the Battle of the Somme, cross the lines, and take note of the offensive buildup, as indeed they did. Nevertheless, the Allies had things pretty much their own way. In the SE 2 and the Nieuport, they had fighters clearly superior to the once-dreaded Fokker, and in total airplanes available, they outnumbered the Germans 386 to 129, a comfortable ratio of nearly three to one.[61] Also, as of May 1916, the Allies had a synchronizing system for machine guns, although not all fighters were so equipped when the Allies began the Somme offensive.

Finally, it should be noted that the Germans still clung to the defensive system, which when matched against the "offensive spirit" of the Allies, left the latter able to fly only regular reconnaissance and artillery ranging missions across the lines. Such missions, it will be recalled, were still the primary function of airpower and hence scored all the points. Thus, early in the campaign, General von Stein, the German commander of the XIV Reserve Corps wrote, "The foe unquestionably has mastery of the air. It increases the effectiveness of his artillery and decreases ours." Cuneo enlarges upon this situation as follows: "As August drew to a close the air situation at the Somme seemed black for the German Air Service. It had been swept into the rear areas and was unable to render the slightest assistance to the ground forces. The latter lost faith in them, but worse than that, its own faith in itself was shaken. It was a highly critical moment in the history of the German air weapon."[62]

Since nothing pointed out the importance of air supremacy more than the conspicuous lack of it, the Germans set about changing this dismal situation. Following in the wake of General von Falkenhayn's dismissal as Chief of the General Staff in late August 1916 and his replacement by General von Hindenburg, with General Ludendorff as Quartermaster General, the German Air Service on the western front underwent a thorough overhaul. In aircraft as well as manpower, the "sausage grinder at Verdun" lost its priority, and machines were withdrawn from that sector. By mid-October, fully 60 percent of all German air strength on the western front was concentrated in the Somme area. At the same time, newer and better fighters were brought in, among them the superb Albatros D-II and the Fokker biplane, both of which carried twin machine guns synchronized to fire through the propeller arc.[63] Once again the Germans could deliver a firepower that the Allies could not match.

The German Air Service also underwent drastic changes in organization and doctrine. The fighters were concentrated into powerful units called *Jagdstaffeln*, even as the great Oswald Boelke was brought up from Verdun to replace the fallen Max Immelmann as leader of the aerial offensive. "The formation of these pursuit squadrons," the British aero historian H. A. Jones later wrote, "was to have a profound influence on the whole future air war on the Western Front."[64] Equally important, however, the German fighter pilots were sent out in groups of three or more with instructions to carry the fight to the enemy.[65]

The result was a sensational comeback in German air strength and effectiveness. In September 1916, they claimed 123 victories compared to only 27 losses, a ratio of 88 to 12 in October, although one of the twelve was Boelke himself.[66] These figures may be open to question, but the implication is clear enough. By mid-October, just as the N-124 was ordered to Cachy in the Somme sector, the Allies no longer held air supremacy. In the seesaw struggle that followed, the American volunteers were privileged to play a part.

## End of the War Deluxe

Thenault, Masson, and Lufbery, the only pilots with machines capable of making the trip, flew to Cachy on 18 October, while the others followed by train. The latter soon took over airplanes left by another squadron, and by the twenty-third of the month, all were in place, ready to play a role in the great Battle of the Somme. As fate would have it, though, that role was destined to be a minor one.

At Cachy, the Americans found that their squadron was to be part of the newly formed Groupe de Combat 13, which consisted of the N-124, the N-65 (Nungesser's old squadron), the N-84, the N-15, and the N-88. This was something new for the Americans, although the French, in order to combine maximum hitting power with mobility, had begun concentrating their fighters into groups as early as June 1916. This change had done much to insure Allied air supremacy during the first weeks of the Somme campaign, although to the American airmen coming later, it meant only that henceforth they would be transferred and committed to action as part of Groupe de Combat 13. It also meant a reunion of sorts, for the new group commander was Commandant Philippe Féquant—later a full general and commander-in-chief of the French Air Forces—an old friend from Verdun days who thought very highly of the American volunteers.[67]

It should be noted, however, that the French grouping of fighters at the Somme was largely offset by the French ground forces' reaction to the resurgence of German airpower noted above. Under the German threat, these ground forces began to call long and loud for direct protection from enemy airplanes; by and by, the authorities yielded to the pressure. An order dated 25 October 1916 established a procedure for regular high- and medium-level patrols across the front of the Sixth Army, regardless of the presence or absence of enemy aircraft.[68] The French, in effect, turned to a partial defensive system even as the struggle for mastery of the air, itself predicated on offensive doctrine, reached its peak. Indeed, it is not too much to say that this false step, together with that recurring individualism among French fliers, once officially encouraged but now detrimental to effective teamwork, did much to convince the Germans that the British, rather than the French, were now the principal enemy in the air.

Meanwhile the pampered life that characterized the Escadrille Américaine at Luxeuil and Behomme also came to an end at the Somme.

> We had . . . come to believe that we would wage only a deluxe war [McConnell wrote], and were unprepared for any other sort of campaign. The introduction to the Somme was a rude awakening. Instead of being quartered in a villa or hotel, the pilots were directed to a portable barracks newly erected in a sea of mud.
>
> It was set in a cluster of similar barns nine miles from the nearest town. A sieve was a water-tight compartment in comparison with that elongated shed. The damp cold penetrated through every crack, chilling one to the bone. There were no blankets and until they were procured, the pilots had to curl up in their flying clothes.[69]

Moreover, no arrangements had been made for a squadron mess, a minor catastrophe for men nurtured on good living, and for several days, the squadron lived on the generosity of neighboring French escadrilles, particularly the famous N-3 (Storks) and the N-67. In desperation, Thaw and Masson journeyed to Paris where they met with Dr. Gros and secured the money to purchase the necessary stoves, cooking utensils, etc.[70]

Now equipped to withstand almost anything, the Americans set to work making the place liveable. The elongated shed was divided up into cubicles to provide some privacy. Portions of it were set aside for a briefing room, a reading room, a writing room and, of course the mess, which, with the aid of a chef who had once been employed in embassies, soon gained a measure of its former reputation.[71]

Eight squadrons shared the generally miserable conditions at Cachy, of which the barracks were only a part. Everything seemed temporary, from the large canvas hangars to the small bath house where "one may go and freeze while a tiny stream of hot water trickles down one's shivering form."[72] Moreover, Cachy lay in the valley of the Somme, where bitter cold and heavy mists prevailed during late fall and the winter months. The buildings at Cachy were simply no match for the weather, and the men lived and fought in an atmosphere of numbing cold.

At Bar-le-Duc the seeming endless movement of men and equipment was the main indication of the gigantic struggle going on at Verdun, but at Cachy one had only to go to the barracks door on a clear day to see the rows of observation balloons and now and then antiaircraft bursts signalling the presence of an aerial invader. And at just about any hour of any day there was the almost constant rumble of heavy artillery.[73]

At the time of the move to Cachy, a total of seventeen Americans had made the roster of the now famous Escadrille Américaine. Three of the seventeen, however, had given their lives, and two were in the hospital. Cowdin had been allowed to resign from the service and Bert Hall had become so unpopular that he had been asked to leave the Escadrille. Rumsey, too, had made his last flight with the squadron. Thus, with only eleven effective men, counting the two French officers, the N-124 was still well below its authorized figure of fifteen to twenty pilots.

During the transfer to Cachy and shortly thereafter, four Americans were brought in to bring the squadron up to strength. The first to arrive was Emil A. Marshall, from Brooklyn, New York, a gentle fellow who had come to France in 1914 because his brothers accused him of being a sissy and because he wanted to prove himself. Playing up his French ancestry, he bullied his way into the 356th Infantry Regiment of the regular army.[74]

In the line of duty, Marshall met James McConnell, who was then driving ambulances, and Paul Rockwell, a member of the Foreign Legion. Later on, after the Escadrille Américaine was organized, these two men, now either in the squadron or closely associated with it, arranged for Marshall's transfer to aviation. But there was a mixup somewhere, and Marshall was sent directly to Luxeuil on 15 October 1916 supposedly as a full-fledged pilot, although he had never been in an airplane.[75]

Marshall was a brave man, strongly devoted to the cause he had elected to serve, and the squadron would have liked to put him on its roster of pilots. In an effort to do so, Thenault arranged for him to enter flight training in November 1916. The French doctors at Buc soon discovered that Marshall had only one good eye—the other had been blind from birth—and he was sent back to the N-124 as nonflying personnel.[76]

Marshall rejected the role of a noncombatant and arranged for his own transfer back to the infantry, where he admirably distinguished himself. His departure left a gap in the squadron, for the Americans had lost a friend whom they had come to admire and appreciate. As one acquaintance put it, "His courage and determination in going back to the trenches just as the winter season was starting was admired tremendously by his comrades in the Escadrille."[77]

Since he never flew with the Escadrille Américaine, Marshall never made its roster of pilots. But he won a place for himself, and he, along with Paul Rockwell, was one of the very few men that the N-124 pilots always treated like full-fledged members of that august brotherhood.

A week after Marshall's arrival and just as the squadron was getting established at Cachy, Frederick H. Prince, Jr., joined the unit. Well educated and from a very wealthy family, he had come to France to fly alongside his brother Norman, one of the original members of the Escadrille Américaine.[78]

Frederick Prince's motives were much the same as those that brought his brother to France in January 1915: close ties with France, a great fondness for the country, and a desire to make a positive contribution to a worthwhile cause. While he would not hope to take the place of his popular brother, who possessed an almost overpowering personality, "Freddy" was deliberately jeopardizing a life of leisure and luxury—strong evidence of the integrity and courage of any man.[79]

Willis B. Haviland, who accompanied Prince to Cachy, hailed from Chicago. Like many other members of the N-124, he came from an excellent family. His father had been dead for some time, however, and Haviland eventually left home to enlist in the United States navy.[80]

Haviland was a qualified electrician, a skill that he had picked up in the navy, but he was attracted to the war in Europe. In early 1915 he went to France to drive ambulances. He found the job unsatisfying, however, and in November of that year, he enlisted in the Foreign Legion for transfer to aviation. By nature a faithful and conscientious soldier, he was a welcome addition to the Escadrille Américaine.[81]

The last of the trio to join the N-124 on 22 October was Robert Soubiran, who gave his residence as New York City. Like Masson and Lufbery, Soubiran had been born in France. His father had immigrated to America when Robert was still a child, but the family always retained strong ties with the mother country.[82]

Life was hard for the Soubiran family in America, and Robert was one of the few members of the famous Lafayette Escadrille who had the childhood experience of selling newspapers on the street corner. He leaned toward mechanics, however, and by the time he entered his twenties, he was an expert, and had serviced and driven racing automobiles. The outbreak of the war brought young Soubiran back to France. He enlisted in the Foreign Legion in August 1914, but his mechanical ability stood in the way of his desire to serve at the front. He spent the fall of 1914 driving a combine, harvesting the wheat that had been abandoned in the war zone.[83]

Soubiran entered the trenches early the following year and saw considerable action, including the Champagne offensive, where he was wounded in the left knee. After four months in the hospital, his transfer to aviation was effected by Kiffin Rockwell and William Thaw. Robert Soubiran proved an excellent pilot and a welcome addition to the squadron. Speaking French like a native, he not only flew and fought well but did much to create good will and understanding between the Americans and the neighboring French people.[84]

*What's in a Name:*

Meanwhile, with the activities of the Escadrille Américaine attracting considerable attention in the American press, the subject of the aviator volunteers again came up for diplomatic discussion. The basis for this revival of official interest was a protest lodged with the American State Department by Count Bernstorff, the German ambassador to the United States. In this document the ambassador charged that the American squadron not only had a "national character," a clear violation of the Hague Convention, but had actually bombed American citizens residing in Germany.[85]

The Bernstorff protest jolted the State Department. In late October 1916, Secretary of State Lansing met with Jules Jusserand, the French ambassador, to discuss the matter of the American aviators. The meeting must have been a spirited one, for each man had a different conception of just what the problem was. And neither viewed it like Count Bernstorff.

Jusserand apparently feared that the American government might take action to curb the American aviators. This could put his country in an awkward position, since it had allowed the formation of the unit. Feeling that the honor of his country was at stake, he took great care to point out that to the best of his knowledge Germany had never rejected a single volunteer, including the lone American who entered German aviation. For his part, Lansing viewed the problem as one of semantics. The United States was in something of an embarrassing position, to be sure, but he seemed to consider the term *Escadrille Américaine* and not the presence of the volunteers per se to be the point of contention.[86]

The American newspapers following the issue of the aviators largely agreed with Lansing and one even went so far as to suggest the name of Legion Américaine, apparently on the assumption that the word *legion* did more to indicate a lack of national character than the word *escadrille*. But this proposal came to naught when it was learned that the American government had earlier protested the use of the name by a contingent of the British army.[87]

At this point, the problem was almost solved by William Thaw, back home in Pittsburgh for a short leave. Since he was a member of the unit, the press naturally asked him what the real name of the outfit was, and Thaw cleverly replied that only newspapermen called it the Escadrille Américaine. The squadron, he said, had no official name other than the Nieuport-124. "The publicity given to these statements," Jusserand wired home, "may assist me in maintaining the status quo."[88]

The status quo could not be maintained, however. In France, the news that Secretary of State Lansing objected to the use of *Escadrille Américaine* forced the issue to the ministerial level, and after some discussion, the minister of war announced on 16 November 1916, "Hereafter, when squadrons are not designated by their number . . . the N-124 will be called the name *Escadrille des Volontaires*."[89]

At this point, someone, perhaps Dr. Gros or a member of the French Embassy in the United States, suggested calling the squadron the Escadrille Lafayette.[90] The brilliance of this suggestion was only too obvious. The new name suggested volunteers while implying a connection with America. In short, it was an almost perfect name and everyone was happy with it, except, of course, the Germans who were forced to watch the unit grow stronger and more famous every day.

The pilots of the N-124 were not unaware of the dust being thrown up around them, and many were originally opposed to dropping the word *Américaine*, a logical outlook considering their views on American neutrality.[91] But they were forced to bow to the inevitable when on 9 December 1916 an official order directing the change in name reached the squadron. It read as follows: "The Minister of War announced that in order to satisfy a demand emanating from the United States, he has decided that the Escadrille des 'VOLONTAIRES' shall hence forth be designated the Escadrille 'LAFAYETTE.' "[92] With the official adoption of the title *Lafayette Escadrille*, all other designations faded out of the picture. As Captain Thenault put it, "Henceforth we were never known by any other name."[93]

## The N-124 in the Somme Sector

When Thenault, Lufbery and Masson flew to Cachy on 18 October, foul weather forced them to fly all the way just above the treetops. All agreed that it was a miserable trip, but apparently none realized that it was the herald of things to come. In the Somme sector, low clouds, rain, fog, and generally bad weather were the order of the day during the fall and winter months.[94]

Because of the weather, the air activity in the Somme had already passed through the most bitter part of the struggle for air supremacy by the time the Lafayette Escadrille joined in. There was considerable airpower concentrated in the area, but after the advent of seasonal bad weather in October 1916 (somewhat earlier than usual), there were days at a time when flying was impossible. Even when one could fly, contact with the enemy was comparatively rare. It was a most disagreeable time and place, for the discomforts, which were legion, could not be offset by a significant feeling of accomplishment.

Had it not been for the weather, which affected both sides equally, the Lafayette Escadrille might well have made an outstanding showing at Cachy. The French, again recognizing the potential of the squadron and giving it some priority, began replacing the Nieuport 17 with the new and very effective SPAD VII, a machine that matched anything the Germans had in the air. Sturdy, flat-winged, and heavy, the SPAD mounted a 140 hp Hispano-Suiza water-cooled engine that gave it a top speed of around 120 mph. Designed to make its kill in a swift dive, it could not climb as fast as the Nieuport and was not as maneuverable. It was very effective, however, when used properly, and its structural strength allowed it to absorb considerable punishment and withstand stress and strain that would have torn a Nieuport apart.[95] Some Lafayette pilots still preferred the maneuverable Nieuport, however, and throughout its history, the squadron was rarely without at least two or three in its inventory.

The SPAD became one of the great weapons of the war, although most pilots disliked it at first. When its engine died it seemed to have the flight characteristics of a streamlined brick, and an accident in it almost always resulted in a fatality. Also, the machine gun synchronization system was tied directly to the camshaft that turned the propeller. This was a fine idea, except if the gun jammed, the pilot was completely disarmed, since the engine had to be partly dismantled to clear the breach.[96]

Had circumstances been more favorable in the Somme sector, the Americans might have matched their earlier performance at Verdun. But the weather would not allow it, and almost all the success among the Americans in the Somme fell to Lufbery, who, according to his comrades, now had the uncanny ability to locate German airplanes where "there just weren't any."[97]

From the last week of October and throughout November, generally bad weather prevailed. During that period, the squadron flew nearly a hundred combat sorties, mostly patrol work, but all activity was concentrated into fifteen days of flying. On only five occasions was there any contact with the enemy. Thenault, who now found more and more of his time taken up with administrative duties, finally brought down a

German airplane on 31 October near Villers Carbonnel, but it was not confirmed.[98] The only other significant engagement was a one-sided combat between Lufbery and a German pilot named Lieutenant Guerther near Busigny on the afternoon of 10 November. Guerther, flying a Halberstadt, attempted to hide in a cloud bank, but Lufbery, catching periodic glimpses of a contrail (the white, threadlike cloud created by airplanes under certain atmospheric conditions) correctly guessed where and when he could make his exit. Lufbery caught him by surprise from behind and below. The Halberstadt "rolled up like a shot rabbit" and fell, a dead pilot at the controls.[99]

December was much like the preceding month. Only one of the first ten days was suitable for flying, and although the squadron took advantage of this opportunity to go out en masse, there was no contact with the enemy. The period was not without its excitement, however. The Germans, taking advantage of the fact that the weather often improved during the night hours, began regular night bombing raids. Several times the Gothas hit the airfield at Cachy, and several times too they bombed the city of Amiens.[100]

The Germans had little to lose from this undertaking. By December 1916 night bombardment was something of an art, and both the Allies and the Central Powers practiced it. The ability to intercept these airplanes, on the other hand, was still a thing of the future. It was virtually impossible to locate enemy planes at night, let alone shoot them down. Besides, upon his return, the fighter pilot faced the extremely dangerous task of landing on a short field lighted only by gasoline flares. As one pilot put it, "Of all the hazardous missions developed in aviation during the war, night pursuit was one of the most perilous. Landing spies, trench strafing, balloon hopping and day bombardment all had their moments but they were hardly to be compared with flying *avions de chasse* in blackest night."[101]

Paul Pavelka, who had already lived through the terrifying experience of riding a flaming airplane to the ground, also learned about night flying the hard way. During the night of 9 December 1916, several Gothas bombed the airfield at Cachy, setting fire to one of the hangars and destroying several airplanes. After moving his own Nieuport to safety, Pavelka decided to avenge the indignity of the raid and, with bombs still dropping on the field, he climbed into his machine and took off.[102]

His airplane was equipped with a set of lights to identify it as a

French machine, and there was some cockpit lighting for his meager instruments. Shortly after takeoff, however, an electrical connection failed and all his lights went out. An immediate landing, even with lights, would have been difficult indeed, for the field was still under attack and there was no way of locating the bomb craters in advance. To make matters worse, Pavelka had no way of indicating his friendly intentions, and in the darkness was taken for one of the enemy. Under fire by gunners on the ground who aimed their weapons by the sound of his motor, he elected to try his luck elsewhere.

Pavelka first sought to establish himself between Cachy and the German lines in the hope of intercepting the bombers on the return journey. Meeting with no success, he turned toward Amiens, ordinarily an easy spot to locate. His approach was noted, however, and the French, thinking him to be an enemy, blacked out the city. It was now even too late to use the burning hangar at Cachy as a beacon.

Unable to read his compass or distinguish landmarks through the thickening haze below, Pavelka could no longer be certain of his position. He was lost above a sea of fog, with little idea as to the direction of his flight or the location of the enemy lines. To attempt a landing under such blind conditions was almost certain suicide, and besides, every time he flew low ground personnel attempted to shoot him down.

With approximately an hour and a half of fuel remaining, he elected to remain aloft, hoping against hope that he could hold out until the first light of dawn. Reducing power as much as possible to conserve fuel, he began the long and agonizing wait.

There were faint traces of light in the east when his engine drank the last drops of fuel, coughed and died. There was no longer any choice. For better or worse, he settled rapidly into the mist below. By a phenominal stroke of luck, Pavelka came down over a suitable landing field with barely sufficient visibility to enable him to partially level off the machine before he struck the ground. Both pilot and plane came through the ordeal intact.

Pavelka found himself in the British lines at Martainville, nearly forty miles from his point of departure. He was entertained royally by a group of British officers in a nearby château, but it was two days before he could get a call through to his squadron—which feared him dead or captured—and four days before the fog lifted sufficiently for him to fly back to Cachy.

Despite the terror of this unique experience, Pavelka did not give up night flying. Aptly described by his comrades as a man who laughed at danger, he joined with the courageous de Laage in making more than twenty such sorties. They never met the enemy, but they always returned safely, which is some measure of success. It was a courageous thing to do, for they were among the first to try it and anticipated by almost a year the time when night pursuit could become relatively common.

While Pavelka was enjoying British hospitality near Martainville and his fellow pilots in the SPA-124 were worrying about his safety, Ronald Wood Hoskier, a brilliant young man from South Orange, New Jersey, joined the squadron. Hoskier, who had shown considerable promise during his school days at Harvard, seemed destined for a literary career. He had experimented with aviation, however, and in the fall of 1915 made up his mind to go to Europe and fight against the Germans, even though, according to his father, "there probably never was a soul more averse to cruelty or killing." With the permission of his parents, who also came to Europe (his father to work with the American Ambulance Corps and his mother as a nurse in a French hospital), he joined the Foreign Legion in February 1916 for duty with the Service Aéronautique.[103]

Hoskier was a delightful addition to the SPA-124. Gentle and obviously refined, he was thoroughly dedicated to the cause he had come to serve. He fit to the letter an observation made by one of his comrades in training: "His eyes are so fearless and honest that one knows with absolute certainty that he is a man to be trusted in any sort of emergency."[104]

Lufbery, the one to educate any new pilot coming into the unit, was absent when Hoskier came to the Lafayette Escadrille. Lufbery had long suffered from rheumatism, an ailment that wore him down during the bitter winter on the Somme. In early December, Thenault sent him on a recuperation leave to southern France, but by the middle of the month he was back, thirsting for action. He found it, in an impressive and indeed extraordinary performance on the afternoon of 27 December.

On that eventful day, Lufbery took on an Aviatik southeast of Chaulnes. The combat was short, lasting all of ten seconds, but in that length of time the German pilot sent four bullets into Lufbery's machine. Nevertheless it was Lieutenant Leffers, the German pilot, who fell to his death moments later, a tribute to Lufbery's skill and marksmanship. Unfortunately, there is no detailed account of this battle, but it must have been a good one, for Leffers, a German ace and a holder of the renowned Pour le Merité, had nine confirmed victories to his credit.[105] At any rate, Lufbery regarded it as just another victory, apparently because he never learned the identity of his victim. As one who thrived on vengeance, it would heartened him greatly had he known.

The miserable weather that hovered over the Somme sector during November and December lasted on through January. Ten flying days and sixty missions was the score for the month, with only eight combats reported, two of them by James McConnell, who had succeeded in getting away from the hospital for a few days. Lufbery had three of the eight, although he was continually plagued by rheumatism, and spent the period from the 9th to the 22d of the month on convalescent leave.[106] Two days after his return, he was again back in business. On the morning of the 24th he met one Lieutenant Erdmann in an Aviatik between Chaulnes and Peronne, and after a brief engagement, sent both plane and pilot to a fiery death. Then, three-quarters of an hour later, he repeated the performance north of Chaulnes. Only the first victory was confirmed, however, for although both victories were seen and reported, credit for the latter one was given to a French pilot from another squadron who claimed to have administered the coup de grâce.[107]

Lufbery's victory on 24 January 1917 was the last combat between a pilot of the Lafayette Escadrille and a German airman during the stay at Cachy. Two days later, with bad weather hanging over the field as a reminder of days gone by, the Groupe de Combat 13 departed for Ravenel, a field about fifty kilometers to the southeast. All save Pavelka made the move without incident. Pavelka, at his own request, was transferred to another squadron (the N-391), preparatory to a pending transfer to the Orient. It was but another move in his continuing effort to see new places, bringing him closer to his tragic and ironic death. On 11 November 1917, while serving on the Salonika front, Pavelka, an excellent horseman, rode a particularly spirited animal belonging to a British cavalry officer. The horse fell on Pavelka, causing internal injuries that proved fatal. Thus ended the "Skipper's" spectacular and adventurous career.[108]

The men of the SPA-124 were glad to leave Cachy. For them, the

Battle of the Somme had comparatively little meaning. The bitter struggle for mastery of the air, an outgrowth of the now-recognized importance of air supremacy, had largely come and gone before they arrived on the scene. The weather alone had seen to that. Moreover, from their position on the firing line, the men were unable to recognize and appreciate the advances made in air organization and doctrine. They might well remember the two hundred sorties flown by the squadron, the fifteen-odd combats and Lufbery's impressive record. But they also remembered the boredom of waiting days on end for the weather to clear, and the wet, numbing cold which no one, it seems, who fought on the front during the winter of 1916–17 will ever forget.

# 5

# From St. Just
# to Chaudun

January – July 1917

The move to Ravenel was uneventful, in large part because the new field was only forty miles from Cachy, less than thirty minutes' flying time. Also, the men were already thoroughly acquainted with the area. Indeed, the most unusual aspect of the trip, other than the strategy behind the move, of course, was the participation of two new men who had joined the squadron just before the transfer. These men, both destined for future renown, were Edwin C. Parsons and Edmond C. Genêt.

"Ted" Parsons was a direct descendent of Cornet Parsons, one of the founders of Springfield, Massachusetts, and his family was reasonably well-do-do and influential. He had been well educated in public and private schools in Springfield, at Exeter Academy, and the University of Pennsylvania, but there was trouble at home when he refused to enter his father's prosperous insurance business. Unable to reach a reconciliation with his father, he left home and traveled west, trying his hand at ranching, mining, and marriage. Failing in all three ventures, he went to Los Angeles, where he worked at odd jobs in the movies. After a chance meeting with Glen L. Martin, the pioneer aircraft manufacturer, he learned to fly.[1]

In 1913 Parsons and a friend named Jean de Villa were hired by Pancho Villa to come to Mexico and train some of Villa's officers to fly. For eleven months the two Americans attempted to cope with a basic unwillingness on the part of the Mexican candidates to set foot in an airplane, while living through the most hectic adventures. These included accidents, which Pancho Villa could neither understand nor forgive. Finally, warned by a friendly German agent that Villa would soon be starting something that would involve the United States and take the eyes of the American people off the war in Europe, Parsons returned to the States, ostensibly to get some parts for the planes. He just kept on going.[2]

In Philadelphia, a newspaper reporter told Parsons about the Escadrille Américaine. Intrigued, he worked his way across the Atlantic as an assistant veterinarian on a ship carrying horses. Instead of immediate acceptance into aviation, however, he was told to expect a period in the trenches. The prospect displeased him, so he enlisted in the Ambulance Corps, where his boundless energy and conspicuous leadership ability soon earned him a position of responsibility. Finally in April 1916 he found the way open to aviation. He began training that same month, earning his brevet in the Caudron the following August. After further training in the Nieuport, he joined the SPA-124 on 25 January 1917.[3]

Edmond Charles Clinton Genêt, from Ossining, New York, was a direct descendent of Charles Clinton, the famed early governor of New York State. He was also the great-great-grandson of Citizen Genêt, whom the Revolutionary Government of France had sent to the United States in 1792. He had a normal if thorough education in his youth, but seemed unduly attracted to the sea, at one point barely missing an appointment to Annapolis. Failing in this endeavor, which had dominated him since he was nine, he joined the navy by lying about his age. He was not yet eighteen.[4]

A few months later the war broke out, and Genêt's ancestry, idealism, and desire to make a positive contribution moved him to make a momentous decision. He deserted the navy, taking care to inform his mother (his father had died two years previously) only after the event. "I have done nothing wrong, nothing to be ashamed of," he told his distressed family. But neither tears nor prayers moved him; he sailed for France aboard the *Rochambeau* in January 1915.[5]

Genêt left the United States guilty of desertion, and while he always stood firm in his decision—he turned down several opportunities to come home and clear himself—the blot on his record haunted him throughout his short life. "If anything should happen to me over here," he once wrote his mother, "it would be easier to meet if I knew I was O.K. with my own beloved country." And, as his industry and devotion to duty won praise from his comrades, he twisted in anguish. "Every time an article comes out . . . it cuts me like a knife," he wrote home, later adding, "What would they think if they knew?"[6]

Since Norman Prince was aboard the *Rochambeau,* Genêt heard of his plans for an all-American volunteer squadron, but while he liked the idea, he could not wait for it to become a reality. Two weeks after his arrival in France, he was a common *soldat* in the Foreign Legion.[7]

Despite an excellent record, Genêt was not happy in the trenches. He could take the mud and the lice, but he was too young to grow a mustache, the trademark of every Legionnaire. His hardened comrades, while appreciating his courage, taunted him for looking like a "little boy playing soldier." After fifteen months in the trenches, he applied for and won a transfer to aviation, still as serious and determined as ever.[8]

Genêt viewed aviation as a "sport with all the fascination and excitement and sporting chances any live fellow could wish for." With such enthusiasm, together with an idealism that did not shrink from any task, he made a significant addition to the Lafayette Escadrille. The fact that he "didn't look a day over fourteen" and had a "peach-bloom complexion" did not bother his comrades in the least. A brand of maverick themselves, they appreciated his desertion when they later learned of it.[9] They greatly respected the boy who could never do quite enough, and who suffered such anguish when one of his comrades fell in battle. To quote Parsons, "From the moment of his arrival at the Escadrille, no pilot in the air did more or better work than little Genêt. . . . He never hesitated to fly or fight in any kind of weather and against any odds. During his short career, he was one of the Escadrille's greatest assets."[10]

## Life at Ravenel

Since Ravenel was only forty miles from Cachy, it was largely governed by the same miserable weather system which haunted the Somme sector during the fall and winter months. Nevertheless, a higher purpose dictated the move, its roots lying in the then-critical situation of the Allies. Russia was on the way out, heralding the certain buildup of German strength on the western front. Britain was growing stronger despite the staggering losses on the Somme, but France had almost reached her breaking point. The idea that America might soon be entering the war on the side of the Allies, while heartening in the extreme, did not dispel the fear that the aid in quantity might come too late. In early 1917 Joffre himself, the man with the "olympian calm," admitted that France had sufficient strength for only one more great battle. After that, French manpower could no longer compensate for losses and a "progressive decline" must necessarily take place.[11] Thus the French logically turned to what people in peril like most to hear—an optimistic voice, claiming to possess the key that would turn the specter of defeat into visions of victory.

The voice belonged to Robert Nivelle, a young general who had masterminded a brilliant counterattack at Verdun, resulting in the recapture of Fort Douaumont. Claiming to have discovered the secret for success at Verdun, Nivelle intended to expand his formula on a grand scale. Essentially this consisted of a devastating artillery barrage, skillfully employed so as to wipe out virtually all opposition, coupled with what he called the effectiveness of "violence, of brutality, and of rapidity." This key, Nivelle, insisted, would break open the deadlock in forty-eight hours.[12]

Nivelle encountered considerable opposition from various sources, for although the Allies wanted success, they could ill afford a fiasco. Eventually Nivelle won out, and amongst other assurances, received a promise from the British to conform to his plan. There was one condition, however. If, contrary to his expectations, the deadlock was not broken "in depth in forty-eight hours," he was to call off the offensive.[13]

Nivelle went ahead with his plans for a British drive near Aaras to fix German reserves, and a large-scale French offensive between Reims and Soissons. Buried among the details was an order to move the Groupe de Combat 13 to Ravenel as part of the general buildup around Montdidier.[14]

Naturally the men of the SPA-124 were not privy to the workings of higher strategy. They knew of the coming offensive—Nivelle advertised it so openly that military men are still aghast at his lack of security—but their role in it was kept a secret for the present. Defensive patrols remained a part of the regular responsibility, but the Groupe itself was told not to advertise its presence to the Germans.[15]

Upon arrival at Ravenel, the Americans found living conditions even worse than at Cachy. Lacking barracks, they slept the first week on the dirt floors of underground bomb shelters, fully clothed as protection against the numbing cold. "We suffered agonies in the arctic temperature," one pilot recalled. "Despite three pairs of socks and fur-lined flying boots, I froze a toe and was unable to walk for a week." As for flying, "During the next two months our regular patrols were carried on under the most harrowing of weather conditions. All the oil had to be heated by inserting red hot rods into the crankcase before each patrol so it wouldn't congeal before the motors were started. With such temperatures on the ground, flying above ten thousand feet was pure agony."[16]

Because of the weather, the squadron flew only fifty patrols on twelve flying days during the month of February. SPA-124 pilots periodically saw but did not engage the enemy, in keeping with the order to keep their presence a secret. Nevertheless, the period was not without its moments of excitement. *Pannes du moteurs* were common, and in one instance, Parsons found himself alone in a sea of clouds, "never being sure whether or not I was right side up or in what direction I was heading." The terrible cold had first cracked his compass plate and then frozen solid the only instrument he had for indicating direction. Parsons came through the experience in good shape by finding a hole in the clouds and spiraling down to a safe landing he knew not where. Nor could he be certain of the nationality of the figures hurrying to his side. "One of the greatest thrills I ever had," he later reported, "was . . . hearing a soft voice . . . at my elbow say, 'Hi there, old chap. I s'y, wot's the matter?' "[17]

Such incidents during that dark month of February were events to be laughed at later when the conversation lagged. At the time, they were very real parts of the deadly game the Americans were playing; the truly stimulating topic of conversation was the rupture of diplomatic relations between Germany and the United States.

This news was most welcome to the American volunteers, for they had strong opinions about what their country's position ought to be. "I surrender—unconditionally and in profound disgust," Genêt wrote home after learning of Wilson's reelection on the slogan, "He kept us out of war." Later, on 3 February 1917, having learned of Germany's intention to resume unrestricted warfare but unaware of Wilson's reply, he vented his anger and frustration in another letter.

If the U.S. accepts this latest extraordinary dictation from Germany, which is in to-day's papers . . . I can't see that any genuine self-respecting American should feel justified in holding his head up any more. It's abominable and goes fully beyond all bounds of patience. . . . It's simply dictation and nothing more, and no self-respecting nation can stand it. Will ours? Damn the Boches! I hope and pray that I may live long enough to make them realize there's one American who refused to be neutral in the face of their confounded audacities.[18]

Learning of the severence of diplomatic relations on 3 February, the American volunteers felt certain that "the tiny thread keeping the two powers from actual hostilities will certainly break soon."[19] They would then no longer be mavericks, in the dubious position of trying to uphold the honor of their country at the risk of losing their cherished citizenship for doing so.

## Death of James McConnell

In early March, anticipating the coming offensive, the Germans countered with a strategic withdrawal to the famous Hindenburg Line. This move, while not cancelling Allied plans for the offensive, nonetheless dispelled the need for "hiding" certain forces. The flying restrictions for those escadrilles in reserve were suddenly lifted. The pilots were ordered to go out as often as possible to harass the enemy and bring back much needed information on their movements and troop concentrations. Thus on 1 March even as Lufbery was receiving the Cross of the Legion of Honor at the hands of Commandant Féquant—the latter without a hat because Whiskey had just made a meal of it—Haviland, Parsons, and Johnson were on patrol. Genêt too was to have gone, but crashed on takeoff without injury to himself. The stepped-up activity continued throughout the month of March. The squadron journal is filled with reports of combats with enemy airplanes, forced landings, attacks on balloons, accidents, and contact with ground troops from "very low altitude." In nineteen flying days, they flew 148 sorties.[20]

The American pilots won considerable praise for their activity during the German retreat. Thaw won a citation for the "intelligent initiative" of landing near some advancing troops and giving them some important information he had just picked up. Later on when Commandant Féquant was drawing up the memorandum proposing the SPA-124 for a unit citation, he mentioned the "active role" played by the squadron during the retreat, emphasizing how "the long distance reconnaissance made by its pilots kept the French command in close touch with the enemy."[21] This well-deserved recognition, however, was not won without a price in blood. On 19 March, James

McConnell, one of the original members of the Escadrille, was killed near Jussy.

Actually, it was McConnell's own courage and devotion that led him to his death. At the beginning of the German retreat, he was hospitalized far from the front, with every indication that his wrenched back and nagging rheumatism would keep him bedridden for some time. But learning of the coming push up north (an indication of how well General Nivelle advertised his offensive) and determined to take part in it, he left the hospital by the back door and returned to his squadron. He insisted that he was now all right and perfectly capable of taking his place on the patrol rosters, although he still needed help to dress and had to be lifted bodily into the airplane. Thus it came about that he joined Genêt on a morning patrol on 19 March. Parsons was to have gone along, which might have made a difference, but his engine overheated because of a fouled oil line and he crash-landed two kilometers from his starting place.[22]

Genêt and McConnell continued on alone. Near Jussy, in a sky partially obscured by clouds and haze, they encountered two German airplanes. The Germans, with the advantage of altitude, "bounced" the two Americans, who attempted to meet the assault head on. In the ensuing engagement, brief as it was, Genêt and McConnell lost contact with each other. Genêt, a relatively inexperienced pilot, soon found himself in considerable difficulty. His opponent flew a two-place machine—probably an Albatros—which allowed the gunner to continue firing even in a tight turn. Genêt, on the other hand, had to have his machine aimed towards his adversary before he could fire effectively. Moreover, the German gunner was a real marksman, and with the first volley he shot away one of the Nieuport's upper wing supports. Another shot severed the guiding rod for the left aileron control, a piece of which struck Genêt in the left cheek, leaving a deep gash.[23]

Though stunned and flying a damaged airplane, Genêt refused to retreat. "I thought I had him on fire for one instant," he wrote, "as I saw—or supposed I did—flames on his fuselage. Everything passed in a few seconds and we swung past each other in opposite directions at scarcely twenty five meters . . . the Boche beating off toward the North and I immediately dived down in the opposite direction wondering every second whether the broken wing spar would hold together or not." Genêt remained in the area for another fifteen minutes, attempting to locate and join up with his friend, but McConnell was nowhere to be seen. Assuming that "Mac" had returned home, Genêt flew back to Ravenel.[24]

McConnell, however, had not returned. Bad weather prevented an air search, and the squadron waited in vain for word of a forced landing or the customary note from the Germans that he had been taken prisoner. Late at night on 23 March Commandant Féquant received a telephone call announcing that a cavalry patrol had just discovered the wreckage of Nieuport No. 2055, about 2 kilometers south of Jussy, and near it, a dead pilot. There were no identifying papers on the body; the retreating Germans had stripped it clean.[25] It did not take long to identify Nieuport 2055 as the machine McConnell had been flying. The following day, therefore, Thenault and several members of the squadron drove to the site of the disaster. McConnell's body, they discovered, had several bullet holes in it, any one of which could have caused his death.[26] At least he had been spared the agony of a conscious fall.

They buried McConnell where he fell, without fanfare and without ceremony, for that was the way he had wanted it. A letter written by him and addressed to the other pilots, to be opened in the event of his death, ended with the following words: "My burial is of no import. Make it as easy as possible for yourselves. I have no religion and do not care for any service. If the omission would embarass you, I presume I could stand the performance. Good luck to the rest of you. God damn Germany and *vive la France.*"[27]

A short time later, a peasant woman was found who claimed to have witnessed the fatal combat. According to her, the Nieuport pilot had been attacked from behind by a German machine while he himself was attacking another one. If true, McConnell's physical condition may have contributed to his death. Unable to move his head from side to side, he was also unable to comply with one of the cardinal rules of aerial combat: never commence an attack without first checking the area behind you. The airmen regarded it as axiomatic that "you can perhaps shoot down an aeroplane that you see; those that you do not see can shoot you down."[28]

## Changing the Guard

During its two month stay at Ravenel, the Lafayette Escadrille lost two men, one of them James McConnell. The other was Frederick H. Prince, Jr., who had been with the squadron only four months. Though young Prince wanted desperately to avenge the death of his brother, his father, Frederick H. Prince, Sr., was unwilling to risk his only remaining son. He thus had him pulled out of the squadron and sent to Pau as a flying instructor. For young Prince, this transfer from the front, like the death of Norman, was a tragedy of the first magnitude.[29] The seven men picked up during this brief period, however, easily compensated for the losses. Most of the newcomers were college graduates and most of them went on to win well-deserved recognition with the Lafayette Escadrille.

The first to arrive was Stephen Bigelow. A bright but not too energetic son of a wealthy and influential Boston family, he was something of a playboy, although he had picked up a good education at Groton and Harvard.[30] In early 1916, having learned from the Boston newspapers that an all-American squadron of volunteers was being formed, Bigelow hurried to France. He signed his enlistment papers on 12 April, just one week before the unit became a reality. He received his *brevet* in the Bleriot the following September, and after further training in gunnery and acrobatics, was sent to the SPA-102. He remained with this escadrille for only three weeks, however, taking his place with the already famous Lafayette squadron on 8 February 1917.[31]

While Bigelow's record was a mediocre one at best, he had sufficient courage to win mention in the Aeronautical Orders of the Day in August for holding off six German airplanes at once. But he lacked the enthusiasm that marked many of his comrades, and this, coupled with the fact that he was often ill—which eventually forced his retirement from aviation—left him generally recognized as a quiet and ineffectual member of the Lafayette Escadrille.[32]

Bigelow was followed by Walter Lovell, who hailed from Newton, Massachusetts. Lovell too came from a fine family background, and like Bigelow, had a degree from Harvard. Very early in he war he had grown concerned about the world situation. Feeling that he personally ought to do something about it, he went to France in February 1915 and enlisted with the American Ambulance Corps. There he earned a citation for "proof of a noteworthy spirit," and setting "an example of courage to the other drivers," along with a promotion to assistant section leader. He was also one of the few to win a medal (the croix de guerre with star) for driving ambulances.[33]

Partly because of his contact with Dr. Gros, who had important connections, and partly because he wanted to become an active combatant, Lovell entered the Service Aéronautique in May 1916. He completed his schooling the following February and was assigned to the Lafayette Escadrille the 24th of that month. Lovell's leadership ability carried over into his work with the SPA-124. In a remarkably short time he was patrol leader, guiding men who had been at the front considerably longer than he.[34]

Harold Buckley Willis joined the Lafayette Escadrille on 1 March. From an old Bostonian family that dated back to colonial times, he had excelled at Harvard, earning a letter on the crew and a degree in architecture in 1912. Brilliant, idealistic, and full of energy, Willis went to France in early 1915 to drive ambulances. Again he excelled, winning a citation for "courage and daring of the highest order." After driving ambulances for more than a year, Willis entered aviation in May 1916 and was breveted in the Bleriot the following October. He came to the Lafayette Escadrille nearly four months later, after having gone through training in gunnery and acrobatics.[35]

Willis's courage and intelligence were a valuable asset to the squadron, particularly during the German retreat. Captain Thenault wrote: "With his trained and intelligent brain he always brought back from trips information that was greatly prized by the High Command. It is very hard to make good observations from a single seater. Willis had made a specialty of it and thanks to the speed of his machine, he was able to go places where the slower two-seaters could not have ventured without being brought down."[36]

The fourth American to join the Lafayette Escadrille during its sojourn at Ravenel was Edward Foote Hinkle, who came from a well-known and respected family in Detroit. Hinkle, who was already more than thirty-eight years of age when the war began, had earned a B.A. at Yale (class of 1899) and had undertaken some graduate work at the University of Pennsylvania before going to Paris to continue his studies at the École des Beaux-Arts. A very promising artist who had studied under Pierre Vignal, he felt himself obliged to give up his studies and go to war.[37]

Although Hinkle was well over the age limit when he applied for military service, through the influence of Ambassador Jusserand, a close friend of his father, he was allowed to enlist in the Foreign Legion in July 1916, with the stipulation that he be sent to aviation.[38] After a creditable record in the schools, he was sent to the Lafayette Escadrille, effective 1 March 1917.

Hinkle's combat career with the SPA-124 was good, but unfortunately short. Before an attack of pneumonia left him with chronic bronchitis, "Pop" Hinkle could claim two unconfirmed victories and several harrowing experiences. Since flying at altitude only aggravated his malady, Hinkle was forced to leave the squadron. But for all his troubles, his conscientiousness had made a lasting impression. "He was a courageous fellow," one acquaintance told me, "and in extending the 'glad hand' did much for the squadron."[39]

On 30 March, the last of the men to join the Lafayette Escadrille during its stay at Ravenel arrived. Three in number, they were each as distinctive as the unit they were entering.

Wiliam E. Dugan, Jr., was the son of a prominent Rochester, New York, shoe manufacturer. After graduating from Rochester University, he took a position with the United Fruit Company and for a time served as assistant manager of a banana plantation in Central America.[40] A young man who could not reconcile his sense of responsibility with a position of neutrality, he hurried to France in August 1914, enlisting in the Foreign Legion the following month.

A small but very dedicated man, he fought well with the Legion through every battle from September 1914 to May 1916, including the first months of the Battle of Verdun. Dugan had his eyes on the sky, however, and wanted to enter aviation and become a part of the then-proposed American squadron. Unfortunately, his officers in the Legion, not convinced that the unit would ever become a reality, made no effort to assist him. Then, in May 1916 he was wounded in the arms and shoulder by shell fragments and sent to a hospital at St. Etienne where he came in contact with Dr. Gros. By the time he was released from the hospital the following month, Dr. Gros had made the necessary arrangements and Dugan entered aviation. With the SPA-124, Dugan was as valuable as he had been in the trenches. His idealism and reliability were well matched by his courage and endurance under fire.[41]

Kenneth Marr was born in San Francisco, but to his comrades, he was a genuine "sourdough" from Alaska. At least, he was living like one in late 1914 when a French agent hired him to bring some dog teams to France for use in the Vosges Mountains. This job complete, he drove ambulances with the American Ambulance Corps for a year before transferring to aviation in July 1916.[42]

Called "Si" by his comrades, a contraction of *Siwash*, the name of an Alaskan tribe with which he reportedly spent some time, Marr proved a particularly valuable addition to the Lafayette Escadrille when he joined it on 30 March. Acquainted with hardship and extremely friendly, he did much to cement good relations between the American pilots and the neighboring French people. According to two men who knew him well, he "knew intimately half the personnel of the French Air Service from the Commandants down to the *popote* orderlies." Other friends spoke of his courage and leadership ability.[43]

The seventh and last man to join the squadron during its stay at Ravenel was Thomas M. Hewitt, Jr. Hewitt came from a respectable family of Westchester County, New York, and seemed to have a promising future before he came to France in 1915 to drive ambulances. He enlisted in aviation without particular difficulty, although his service record shows that he was twice punished during training for going into town without permission and for being late to formation. Unfortunately, Hewitt did not have the temperament to be a good fighter pilot. Moreover, he came into the squadron at an inauspicious time. Combats were daily occurrences, and it was his misfortune to run into some solid opposition his first trip across the lines. The strain proved too much—not such an uncommon occurrence as one might think—and he henceforth avoided flying, incurring thereby the enmity of his comrades, who expected every man to do his duty and who were severe critics of those who failed to do so.[44]

## The Sioux Insignia

Meanwhile, in mid 1916, when the Escadrille Américaine was flying and fighting in the Verdun sector, squadrons up and down the front began adopting distinctive insignia which were painted in striking colors on all squadron aircraft. Some followed the humorous vein, others the menacing, and still others the artistic. At first the Escadrille Américaine used the American flag, but after Bernstorff's protest to the U.S. State Department a new insignia, as unique as the squadron itself, was devised.

The idea stemmed from a gift by Robert Chandler, Victor Chapman's uncle, of a dozen Browning shotguns. Chandler intended the men of the squadron to use these weapons when their own Lewis guns jammed, as often happened. The shotguns were naturally ineffective in the air, however, and the pilots ended up using them on a skeet range and to poach partridges. Remington Arms Company had emblazoned the head of a Seminole Indian on their cases of shotgun shells, and this gave the pilots the idea for their insignia. It was colorful, distinctive, and thoroughly American. The Seminole Indian head insignia was adopted by the SPA-124 shortly after the move to Cachy. With the arrival of Harold Willis, who had trained as an architect, and Edward Hinkle, a skilled artist, however, the insignia was due for a change. To their exacting eyes it appeared "anemic" and "not a bit war-like."[45]

Willis and Hinkle wanted to replace the docile Seminole with a sketch of a yelling Sioux brave in full war regalia. This design, when worked out and presented to the others, was simple enough to be recognized at a distance. It was also very colorful, for its designers had used the French and United States national colors. There was certainly no mistaking it for the insignia of any other squadron, anywhere.[46]

## Unlucky Ham

By the first week of April 1917 the systematic retreat of the Germans to the heavily fortified Hindenburg Line had left the home field of Groupe de Combat 13 more than forty miles behind the defensive patrols. The entire unit was thus hurriedly moved on 7 April to a field near the village of Ham, a field still smoldering from fires set by the vacating German airmen.

This move signaled the beginning of a period of intense activity for the men of the Lafayette Escadrille. Three days previous, the British had begun the heavy artillery bombardment and aerial offensive preliminary to a ground assault near Aaras on 9 April. To the southeast, Gen. Georges Nivelle was massing his Fifth and Sixth Armies for the main punch in the Chemin des Dames area of the Aisne sector. This assault was scheduled for 14 April but did not get underway until the 16th. The Lafayette Escadrille at Ham sat almost midway between the two major assault areas, its mission associated with a secondary holding attack by the French Third Army east of St. Quentin.[47]

In this cauldron of trouble boiling all along the front from the Verdun sector to Flanders, the area near Ham had its share of air activity. The day following the move to Ham, for example, every available pilot of the Lafayette Escadrille flew *chasse* (offensive) patrols, barrage patrols, or protective missions for Allied reconnaissance aircraft. Lufbery, on one of the protective sorties, took on three enemy airplanes, sending one down in flames east of St. Quentin, while de Laage relieved the pressure on a group of British bombers by shooting down two German fighters, a feat that earned him the highly prized Legion of Honor.[48] All in all, it was the beginning of a period of intense aerial activity, a period as rewarding, as vicious, and as costly as any yet experienced by the men of the Lafayette Escadrille.

## The Death of Edmond Genêt

Despite the heartening performance on 8 April, the Americans soon came to regard Ham as an unlucky place. Like virtually all World War I airmen, their survival seemed to depend in large part on the whims of chance. It was natural that they should seek out signs of good luck or omens of misfortune.

One such omen occurred two days after their arrival at Ham. A Maurice Farman aircraft, burning like a torch, suddenly appeared out of the morning mist and crashed onto the field, burning its occupants to death. The men never learned where the plane came from or what ill wind brought it to Ham. Then, too, some of the men were concerend when Edmond Genêt, with characteristic compassion, adopted a scrawny, partially paralyzed pup named Archie. "It was a fatal mistake," one pilot wrote. "Archie promptly put the curse on him."[49]

On the morning of 16 April, exactly one week after the mysterious Farman crashed at Ham, Edmond Genêt and Raoul Lufbery left on a morning patrol. The flight was uneventful, and after an hour and fifteen minutes in the air, both men returned to the field. Genêt suddenly announced that he wasn't feeling well and went to bed, hoping the rest would make him feel better for another patrol scheduled for two-thirty that afternoon. Willis Haviland urged Genêt to stay in bed and offered to take his place, since his own plane was out of commission. Genêt, however, would not hear of it. Insisting that he was all right, he took to the air as scheduled and again in company with Lufbery, flew under a heavy layer of clouds towards the patrol area between St. Quentin and La Fere.[50]

The two men came under antiaircraft fire as they crossed the lines. Lufbery saw several shells burst near Genêt's plane, but he was not particularly concerned about so common an occurrence. Nor was he particularly disturbed when he noticed Genêt suddenly turn back toward the French lines. "I followed him for three or four minutes to make sure he was taking the right direction," he later reported. "After that I went back to the lines to finish my patrol duty."[51]

But Genêt did not return. Later that afternoon they found his broken body about five kilometers from the front lines and only a few hundred meters from where McConnell had fallen four weeks earlier. For lack of eyewitnesses to the tragedy, the men of the Escadrille could only speculate as to what had happened. It appeared that Genêt's machine had been hit by an antiaircraft shell and that Genêt had either fainted or been knocked unconscious by the explosion. The plane was obviously out of control when it hit the ground and there was evidence the motor was going full speed at the moment of impact. "I have never seen a more complete wreck," Parsons wrote. "He had dug a hole five feet deep in the hard packed road. The tank was a flat piece of metal, the wheels were ribbons, and there wasn't a piece of wing or framework bigger than a match. Every bone in his body was broken and his features were completely gone."[52]

Genêt's death was a devastating blow to his comrades, for they had come to love and respect the peach-blossomed boy of twenty whom they called "Smiler." "I have lost a very dear friend and a courageous comrade of combat; the squadron lost one of the most conscientious pilots that it has ever had or ever will have," was Walter Lovell's comment. Captain Thenault paid him one of the highest compliments when he wrote that Genêt "was one of our best pilots, the type of man who always had to be restrained rather than encouraged."[53]

Genêt's death also had an effect reaching far beyond the front lines. Intense, idealistic and very dedicated, it was the fate of this young man, still posted as a deserter by the U.S. Navy, to be the first American to fall in combat after his beloved country entered the war. As indicated earlier, the stain haunted him and perhaps helps explain why, sometime before his death, he had told his fellow pilots, "If I die, wrap me in the French flag, but place the two colors together upon my grave, to show that I died for the two countries." It was no mere coincidence that the soldiers who prepared him for burial found that "Smiler" carried an American flag wrapped around his body.[54]

Such a tragic and touching tale was bound to affect Frenchmen and Americans alike. The French ambassador to the United States sent the

Genêt family a note of sympathy, as did President Woodrow Wilson. But as gratifying as these might be, none was more welcome than the one from the secretary of the navy, Josephus Daniels. In part, it read as follows:

There has but recently been brought to my attention a story full of interest to me, a story glorified by the unselfish patriotism and final sacrifice of an American lad. . . . Edmond Charles Clinton Genêt, having honorably terminated an enlistment with an ally, since he died on the field of battle . . . the offence [of desertion] is nullified by his conduct in the common cause under the flag of our ally. I myself am honored in having the privilege of deciding the record of Edmond Charles Clinton Genêt, ordinary seaman, United States Navy, shall be considered in every respect an honorable one.[55]

## The Jinx Continues: Death of Hoskier and Dressy

For six days following Genêt's funeral, the Lafayette Escadrille was out in force, for this was the period of the French offensive east of St. Quentin. Besides several forced landings and jammed machine guns, there were half-a-dozen combats with enemy pilots, numerous patrols, reconnaissance missions, and even a few attacks on enemy balloons. Few flights came back without something important to report.[56]

On Monday, 23 April, the Lafayette Escadrille flew no less than eighteen sorties, one of them a reconnaissance mission in a two-place Morane Saulnier, an outdated airplane kept by the squadron for training purposes. This ship was to be sent to the rear the next day, but Hoskier, who was particularly fond of it, asked to fly it for the last time. Dressy, de Laage's orderly and faithful friend, asked to go along as an observer. South of St. Quentin, Hoskier and Dressy encountered a group of three German Albatroses. A savage fight developed, in which Dressy fired every available bullet. He put one fighter out of action, but the remaining two soon overwhelmed their adversary. The stricken Morane, with Hoskier either dead or severely wounded, fell in an uncontrolled spin, crashing in an exposed area just within the French lines. Because of heavy German artillery fire, the bodies could not be recovered until after dark.[57]

The pilots of the Lafayette Escadrille shared the intense grief of Hoskier's parents, who, living in France, were able to come to the funeral. They also grieved for Dressy and for de Laage. De Laage seemed utterly overcome at the loss of the orderly, who had served him since the beginning of the war and who had once carried his wounded patron to safety while under heavy German fire. As he and Edwin Parsons drove to Compiègne to pick up Hoskier's parents at the train station, the courageous officer "cried . . . like a little child all the way there." "It was the first time I had ever seen the gentle, cultivated officer break and give play to his emotions," Parsons later wrote.[58]

The double funeral at Ham on the morning of 25 April was simple but impressive. The two broken bodies, laid out in plain pine boxes, were covered with spring flowers. For Dressy there was a citation, praising him as a devoted and courageous orderly; for Hoskier, a similar token describing him as "the very soul of bravery and self-sacrifice." For the men of the Lafayette Escadrille there was the loss of another fine comrade in arms, and the grim reminder that it was the kindhearted Hoskier who had fallen heir to "Archie" after Genêt was killed. The poor dog was now a regular pariah, but de Laage, scorning the idea of a jinx, took him in.[59]

Meanwhile, the squadron continued its activity with only brief pauses to pay tribute to those who fell. On 24 April, the day after Hoskier's death, the squadron flew twenty-two sorties. Thaw went out four times, Lufbery, Soubiran, and Campbell three, and several others twice. Lufbery happily scored another victory while escorting a French reconnaissance machine. Spying a German fighter maneuvering into position to attack the reconnaissance craft, Lufbery baited his adversary by pretending not to notice him. Then just as the German pilot, one Lieutenant Schmidt, had gotten his Rumpler into position, Lufbery plunged down. Warned by the first streaks of machine-gun fire, Schmidt tried to break away and race for his lines, but Lufbery, anticipating this move, stayed with him and sent him crashing to his death north of Noy, not far from where Hoskier and Dressy had fallen the day before.[60]

While none of the other Lafayette pilots could match Lufbery's seemingly phenomenal ability to search out enemy airplanes and his equally impressive ability to finish them off, they too had their moments of combat, and, for a few, the reward of success. On 16 April, Chouteau Johnson gained his first victory over a German biplane near St. Quentin. A few minutes later, Thaw joined with Haviland in bringing down an enemy ship, which, they explained in their report, had been in a vulnerable position to a SPAD from another squadron which refused to attack it.[61]

The bitter aerial activity that characterized April 1917 grew even more intense the following month. The *Journal de Marche* reveals that the squadron flew more than 350 sorties during May. Some days every available pilot was in the air; certain of them flew as many as four missions in a ten-hour period. They fought thirty-four aerial duels with enemy airmen and made several attacks on balloons, utilizing for this purpose one of the airplanes mounting a 20mm cannon and firing incendiary bullets.[62]

It is worth noting, however, that in this period of bitter fighting and seemingly endless flying, the squadron did not log a single victory. Even the great Lufbery, pushing himself to the limit, accounting for more than half the combats of the entire squadron and at times taking on as many as four enemy airplanes at once, could only report after one hectic engagement that one of his adversaries "apparently" sustained "serious damage" and "seemed" to be coming apart in the air.[63]

The fighting was not so intense, however, that there could not be the customary time out, as in all wars, for ceremonies and awards. On 10 May, for example, a delegation of the SPA-124 journeyed to Paris to be guests of honor at a special banquet given by the famed French Aero Club. At this assembly, Lufbery received the club's Grand Gold Medal, a signal honor, for the award was a rare one. In another ceremony ten days later, Lufbery received the British Military Medal. This decoration, common among British airmen, was special in that Lufbery was the first American to receive it in the Great War.[64]

### The Loss of Lieutenant de Laage

One of the purposes of the "visit" to Paris on 10 May was to pick up the first of the new SPAD 13s, an advanced model of that famous airplane. Boasting a 200 hp Hispano Suiza engine, this machine could reach 250 kilometers per hour in level flight, just the sort of toy, as Lufbery put it, "to play hide and seek with the enemy."[65]

As its foremost flier, Lufbery was naturally the first of the Lafayette Escadrille to receive this new aircraft, and de Laage, a man who liked to fly as well as command, was the second. Thus it came about that on the evening of 23 May, de Laage, delighted with the new plane, decided to try it out.

Shortly after takeoff, de Laage began a *chandelle*, a common maneuver calling for a tight 180° climbing turn. Purposely sacrificing airspeed for altitude, this maneuver had great utility, particularly in combat, but it left the airplane hanging on its prop, as it were, with a very narrow margin of safety should the engine fail. It was a particularly risky maneuver in the heavy SPAD, whose flat wing gave it a steep glide angle.

At about 150 meters altitude, de Laage's motor suddenly sputtered and stopped. As one eyewitness carefully—and sadly—noted in his diary that evening: "I saw . . . [de Laage] start in a spiral, made about one turn, motor off, kept plunging earthward, and when about 50 metres from ground he seemed as though he would redress but did not have time. He struck the ground with a crash about 200 metres from the hangar, his motor on. Died immediately. Just one month today that Dressy was killed."[66]

The impact of de Laage's death on the squadron can hardly be exaggerated. To the American members of the Lafayette Escadrille, he was "the man" of the French army, a fearless and cultivated officer possessing great leadership ability. The Americans often turned to him instead of the aloof Thenault and he had won the respect and admiration of the commander and the men alike. Moreover, better than most Frenchmen perhaps, he appreciated and genuinely liked his American comrades. He made mention of these heartfelt sentiments in his last will and testament, a handwritten document penned shortly before his death. "Since the formation of the American Escadrille, I have tried to exhalt the beauty of the ideal which brought my American comrades to fight for France. I thank them for the friendship and confidence they always showed me. If I die, do not weep for me. It is not good that a soldier should let himself give way to sorrow, and now, 'Vive la France!' "[67]

## The Replacements

The stay at Ham had proven costly to the Lafayette Escadrille, although in confirmed victories alone it had taken a better toll of the enemy than it had yielded in return. To make up the losses, however, additional men were brought in without delay.[68]

The first of the newcomers was Andrew Courtney Campbell, a handsome and impetuous young man from Chicago. After spending some time at the University of Virginia, he had worked as a professional dancer. But on his enlistment papers for the Foreign Legion he listed his occupation as "aviator."[69] Brave but reckless to the point of foolishness, he quickly made an impression on men already accustomed to danger. On patrol, for instance, he delighted in seeing how close he could fly to a comrade without actually hitting him. "He was a pain in the neck on patrols," one pilot recalled. "Many times when I was leading a patrol, I came back with the leaping jitters if he had been behind me, for he kept his whirling propeller not three feet from my tail. I'd spend more time trying to keep out of his way than I would looking for Boches. It was impossible to shake him off and no amount of pleadings, coercion, or threats of physical retaliation was sufficient to make him desist from his distressing tactics in the air."[70]

Though a pain in the neck, at least on patrols, Campbell was everywhere recognized as a good pilot and a useful companion in case of trouble. And although he acted like a wild Indian in the air—and sometimes on the ground as well—his unfailing good humor proved a delightful tonic to men worn down physically and mentally with the rigors of combat. "We admired him as a pilot," Hall and Nordhoff wrote of him, "for, despite his furious fun at his own expense, he never failed a comrade in combat and was a skillful and courageous fighter."[71]

After Campbell came Ray Claffin Bridgman, who hailed from Lake Forest, Illinois, and whose father was a professor and headmaster of a prep school. In a way, the quiet, scholarly Bridgman, who was Phi Beta Kappa from Yale, was the complete opposite of Campbell. He hated war with his whole being and was led to fly and fight for France by an idealism as intense as that of Kiffin Rockwell and Victor Chapman. As a result, he never spared himself in the slightest, putting his heart and soul into a job that was repugnant to him. Though a skillful pilot, he never had the good fortune to win a confirmed victory, but his comrades preferred not to rate him by this criterion. As Hall and Nordhoff put it, "It is difficult to speak with restraint of his service to the Allied cause. It was so immeasureably fine in kind. One must have known him intimately, in the *popote*, on patrol, in combat. No American has tried harder to live up to an ideal duty. It was an almost impossible task because of the loftiness of the ideal. In his own opinion, no doubt, he failed, but it was a failure that most men would call splendid success."[72] Bridgman was far from being a spectacular fighter pilot but his lofty idealism earned him the distinction of becoming one of the few men at the front to win a citation without some special and courageous accomplishment to back it up. In October 1917 a citation signed by the commanding general of the Sixth French Army described him as a "combat pilot, skillful, modest and conscientious; has always fulfilled with greatest keenness the missions which have been entrusted to him." Citations speaking of skill and courage were so common at the front that they lost much of their intended value; however, in Bridgman's case, the description was accurate.[73]

John Armstrong Drexel, whose home was Philadelphia but whose parents were then living in London, followed Bridgman into the Lafayette Escadrille by some nine days. His family was very wealthy, and he spent much of his youth in England. Drexel was one of the few to enjoy prewar aviation experience, flying the famed Bleriot as early as 1909. Indeed, like Thaw, he had something of a reputation in aviation. At one point he held the altitude record for the Bleriot. In another instance, he won a remarkable competition calling for the most exquisite flying skills. Known as a "turtle race," the flight took place in a strong wind, and the idea was to "slow-flight" the machine barely above the critical stall speed. Since the air speed was less than the wind, the idea was to lose a maximum amount of distance in a given time.[74]

Drexel, a "very superior personage" to his comrades in the SPA-124, was immediately thrown into the maelstrom of aerial activity. He served honorably and well, but his tenure with the squadron was brief. The American Air Service was setting up its headquarters in Paris, and perhaps under pressure from Drexel's parents, requisitioned the young pilot to act as a liaison officer between the British and American forces. The following December, he was dropped from the rolls of the Service Aéronautique and commissioned a major in the American Air Service. He had served with the Lafayette Escadrille a total of one month and five days.[75]

Charles ("Carl") H. Dolan II, another bright and impressive young man, arrived at Ham the same day as Drexel. One of Dolan's grandfathers had lost a leg in the Civil War and another had been killed with Custer at the Battle of the Little Big Horn, but young Dolan was from Boston and had studied electrical engineering at the Massachusetts Institute of Technology. Thus, he was not only an educated man but seemed to be well on his way to a quiet future of professional and financial success. At the outbreak of the war, however, he hurried to England, where he quickly became a chief inspector in a munitions works. He later transferred to the Sperry Gyroscope Company as an installing engineer of auto pilots, a job that took him to Paris. One day at Buc airfield Dolan met some of the Lafayette pilots. He instantly liked what he saw and heard. So patriotic himself that, in his own words, "I was in Coventry when Wilson said 'We are too proud to fight,' and I had to lick nine Englishmen to prove that we all didn't feel the same way,"[76] he had felt all along that Americans should take an active part in the war. Thus, when the volunteer fliers suggested that he join French aviation and eventually become part of the famed Lafayette Escadrille, the offer was too good to turn down.[77]

Dolan was an immediate success with his comrades, who had good reason to appreciate his presence. A good pilot and a firm self-disciplinarian, he was also full of compassion and understanding for those who lacked his self-control. A complete teetotaler, for example, he kept liquor in his locker for those instances where certain pilots had a real need for it, just as, in later life, he was the one that best understood and hence helped the so-called derelicts of the war. Moreover, he put his engineering knowledge to good use. As a direct result, the average number of aircraft "out of commission" for maintenance dropped to a new low for the squadron. At the same time, the confidence of the pilots in the reliability of their machines—a factor that must not be underestimated—soared to a new high.[78] Thus blessed with a sense of duty that marked his work on the ground and in the air with a painstaking thoroughness, he was a good man to have around.

Henry Sweet Jones, who came from an old and respected family from Hartford, Pennsylvania, joined the squadron along with Dolan and Drexel. Educated at Lehigh University and heir to a proud tradition of service to his country, Jones had a humorous, almost playful approach to life. At one time he seemed headed for a career in the U.S. Navy but he was expelled from the Naval Academy for smoking, and he refused to use family influence (one of his uncles was an admiral) to get reinstated. In 1916 he went to France to drive ambulances in the Battle of Verdun, but the heart of this easygoing and pleasant youth was in the air. In November 1916, he enlisted in the French Foreign Legion for immediate transfer to the Service Aéronautique.[79].

Jones came into the squadron with something of a legend behind him. While in flying training at Buc, he one day felt supremely confident in his ability to fly and somehow managed to nurse his "Grasshopper," a clipped-wing airplane used only for learning to taxi, into the air. He not only got it off the ground, but put on a dazzling display of spontaneous acrobatics. "There have been some magnificent crashes at

Buc," Hall and Nordhoff wrote of the result, "but never a better one than this." Jones agreed. "The instructors were angry," he later told me, "that I wasn't killed."[80]

The last of the arrivals to join the SPA-124 at Ham was Lt. Arneux de Maison-Rouge, who came in as a replacement for de Laage. The son of a distinguished French general, de Maison-Rouge had served with the cavalry at the beginning of the war, but as that service slowly lost its importance, he transferred to aviation. He served with the SPA-67 for several months before coming to the Lafayette Escadrille.[81]

Maison-Rouge was a typical French professional officer: courageous, dignified, and dedicated. But at the same time, he was nervous and aloof, and he found himself in the difficult position of replacing the gallant de Laage, a man so beloved by the Americans that almost any replacement would have paled by comparison. Maison-Rouge's personality gave him a bad start with the Americans, and although there was some improvement in relations as each began to acknowledge the courage and ability of the other, the Americans never really warmed up to him. For his part, he could never reconcile himself to the antics of the Americans, who, in his eyes, often seemed crude and childlike. Indeed, in his opinion some of them were nothing less than "les sauvages."[82]

Ham had proven to be a good place for the new airmen to get acquainted not only with themselves but the Germans as well. Some, such as Hewitt, had proven themselves relatively ineffective, but anyone doing his duty and living through the hectic weeks could properly consider himself a real fighter pilot and a seasoned veteran. Nevertheless, even though there was plenty of aerial activity in the area—the squadron flew some fifteen combat sorties and experienced two combats the same day it left Ham—strategic considerations prompted a move.[83]

The Nivelle offensive, once a beacon of hope, had turned into a nightmare of despair. The German lines had withstood the onslaught, while the French had lost another 100,000 men. At this point French troops, their confidence in their military leaders and their government undermined by years of seemingly senseless effort and sacrifice, cracked under the strain. The first mass mutinies in modern military history began in the Champagne sector, spreading until more than sixteen army corps were measurably affected. Not all troops were openly rebellious, of course, but the rot was so widespread that one

French official later insisted that only two loyal divisions stood between the German armies and Paris.[84] The situation could hardly have been more critical. If the Germans were to learn the extent of the French troubles, victory was possibly hers. A well-timed offensive would have cracked the western front wide open.

Naturally the French made monumental efforts to keep the mutinies a secret. Very few people, even among the highest levels of the Allied civil and military structure, were allowed knowledge of the scope and magnitude of the danger. The British obligingly continued their Aaras offensive in order to keep pressure on the Germans. For their part, the French brought in General Henri Pétain to replace the disgraced Nivelle. A man of recognized caution and ability, Pétain had the overwhelming task of shoring up the sagging French morale.[85] In a monumental display of leadership, he slowly revitalized the armies, balancing firmness with compassionate concern for the just grievances of the downcast troops. Many other steps, some great, some small, were also taken, among them the transfer of the SPA-124. On 3 June the Groupe de Combat 13 was suddenly yanked from its station at Ham and sent to Chaudun, a field near the Chemin des Dames area of the Aisne sector. It was here that the Nivelle offensive had recently come to its tragic conclusion.

# 6

# From Chaudun to the End at La Noblette

## July 1917 – February 1918

At Chaudun, the primary mission of the Lafayette Escadrille, now known officially as the SPA-124 because it flew the SPAD almost exclusively, was to assist in the protection of five French reconnaissance squadrons.[1] Ordinarily this mission would have been routine, one of the less glamorous aspects of *avion de chasse*, but these were not ordinary circumstances. The danger inherent in the French mutinies made it supremely important to keep the enemy from learning of them and taking advantage of an opportunity unparalleled in the Great War. In part, this meant shielding French positions from prying eyes in the sky. It also called for an extensive offensive operation into enemy territory, the idea being to force them into protecting themselves in the air behind their own lines.

The SPA-124 was by no means new to this type of operation. Over the months it had flown hundreds of such missions, winning in the process an enviable reputation for a particularly successful ability to ward off German fighters or force them to stay their distance. "In all our protection missions," one pilot later recalled, "we lost only one bomber." Perhaps this explains why Thenault once wrote: "For this work, no fighting escadrille was more sought after than our own. This was very complimentary. The sheep were always delighted with their watchdogs, particularly when there were so many wolves about."[2]

Unfortunately the move to Chaudun was not without mishap. Hewitt, whose flying is said to have left much to be desired, crashed his new SPAD on a prominent irrigation ditch bordering the field. Furious at what seemed to be a display of poor airmanship—all pilots had been warned about the obstruction—Thenault sent Hewitt back to Ham to pick up Soubiran's SPAD, since Soubiran was on leave at the time. This proved a mistake, for on the return flight, Hewitt displayed consistency if not skill; he crashed Soubiran's SPAD into the very same ditch, not ten feet from where he had wrecked his own the day before. For this feat, the hapless pilot picked up the nickname of "Useless" Hewitt.[3]

The field at Chaudun was both large and smooth, fully capable of handling the sixty-odd aircraft that would be operating from it. But although the Aisne sector was comparatively quiet on the ground, the mission of the Lafayette Escadrille and the other fighter squadrons of Groupe de Combat 13 was by no means an easy one. Besides the protection of the observation craft, which called for flights of varying duration at altitudes up to 18,000 feet, each fighter squadron also had its own sector to patrol. The purpose of these blockade patrols was to deny the enemy aerial observation behind the French lines.

The sector of the SPA-124 ran between Soissons and Rheims, a distance of more than fifty kilometers. It was too long for adequate coverage, particularly since there was no ground-to-air communication to direct the pilots should the Germans attempt a penetration. Yet to spread the patrol too thin was to invite disaster, for individual pilots would be simply overwhelmed by several enemy pilots flying as a team.

To offset this disadvantage, the pilots of the Lafayette Escadrille chose to fly in groups, yet maintain considerable mobility by means of a unique system set up in conjunction with the French antiaircraft batteries. They divided their sector into four parts, numbering them consecutively one through four. If a German aircraft crossed over the lines in a certain sector while the Lafayette patrol was in another, French ground troops telephoned the news to the antiaircraft batteries in the sector where the Lafayette was operating. A French battery then sent up one, two, three, or four shells to indicate by the number of bursts the sector in which the Germans were then flying, setting the shells to burst above or below the assigned altitude of the SPA-124, thereby giving the approximate altitude of the intruders. It was a good system, leading one pilot to remark, "We gave our Jerry pals quite a number of surprise parties, probably to their vast amazement, as they must have wondered how we could be on the job so quickly."[4]

Apart from their standing patrols and escort missions, SPA-124 pilots were often sent on fighter reconnaissance missions, usually over

sectors judged too dangerous for the clumsy observation craft. Moreover, those who were so inclined could sometimes wangle what they
called "free flight." These were voluntary "missions of opportunity"
on which they could seek out their own entertainment, provided they
took the necessary precaution of flying in groups of three or more.[5]

## Give and Take

Although the Aisne sector was considered a comparatively quiet
one now that there was no major ground battle going on, the area was of
great strategic importance, particularly in view of the recent mutinies.
The *Journal de Marche* reveals that during the 43 days the squadron
spent in this sector, its pilots flew 400 sorties and fought some 62
individual engagements with the enemy. They did not score heavily
against the Germans during this period, but the balance was in their
favor. A newcomer to the squadron by the name of James Norman Hall
was shot down and barely escaped with his life, but on the other side of
the ledger, the squadron had officially disposed of one German plane
and pilot and may have brought down another three or four.[6]

James Norman Hall, once an Iowa farm boy, had already seen
considerable service with the British army. In Wales when the war
broke out, he enlisted after some hesitation in the Royal Fusiliers of the
British army, eventually finding himself in Flanders. He served in the
trenches there from April 1915 to early the following year, when he
was wounded. After his release from the hospital and with the influence of some Boston friends, he secured permission to return to Iowa
and visit his ailing father. This leave ended with his release—again
because of his wound and his friends in Boston—from the British army.
Hall spent some months in the Boston area, lecturing on his experiences and writing *Kitchener's Mob*. He had in mind however, returning
to England and reenlisting, using his new position and experiences to
write a series of articles for the *Atlantic Monthly*.[7]

In late September 1916 Hall sailed for France, intending to do two or
three articles on the famous Lafayette Escadrille before rejoining the
British army. He came to Paris with a letter of introduction to Paul
Rockwell, whose position with the French government made him the
man to see. Rockwell listened to Hall's program, but thoroughly impressed with the man, gave advice as well as information. "Good

heavens man," he said, "You don't want to write about them. You want to fly with them." Thus James Norman Hall, whom one of his comrades would describe as "one of the most lovable men in the world,"[8] an energetic soul, quiet and retiring almost to the point of shyness, and withal a thorough idealist, joined the Lafayette Escadrille.

His initial sojourn with the squadron, however, was a short one. Hall flew his first sortie over the lines on the morning of 24 June 1917, in company with Harold Willis, at which time they attacked and drove away a German two place observation craft.[9] It looked like a good beginning, but only two days later, Hall stumbled into a situation that nearly cost him his life.

After the regularly scheduled patrols had already been flown by the SPA-124 on 26 June, it was decided to send up an exhibition patrol to impress a group of visiting American officers. Lufbery was designated the patrol leader, with orders to assemble his unit high over the reservoir, a prominent body of water near Chaudun, and patrol the lines till dark.[10] All eight of the pilots assigned to this patrol, with the exception of Hall, took off on schedule. The latter, whose position as the newest man in the squadron automatically earned him the oldest airplane, in this case a SPAD with a rebuilt engine, had trouble getting started. He was ten minutes late getting off the ground, and by the time he nursed his ailing machine up to the assigned altitude, the others, certain that he would not be making the trip, had gone on.

Hall had been warned to stay behind the forward balloon line if he missed the patrol, but he was impatient, and putting caution aside, crossed the lines alone. He soon spied a group of seven ships about five kilometers inside the German lines. Assuming that they were his lost comrades, he hurried to join up.

I counted seven machines [he later wrote], five of them well grouped, a sixth—that would be Lufbery—several hundred meters above the others, and a seventh several hundred below. I turned in their direction at once. It was getting dusk and as I approached, I lost sight of the pilot nearest down; he was approaching at exactly my altitude and it is difficult to see a plane in that position, particularly in fading light. Suddenly he loomed up directly in front of me, and he was firing as he came. His tracer bullets were going by my left side but he corrected his aim and my motor seemed to be eating them up. As I banked to the right, I felt a smashing blow in my left shoulder accompanied by a peculiar sensation as though it had been thrust through by a white-hot iron. My left arm seemed to be off, but it was still there although there was no more feeling in it. Blood was trickling into my eyes so that I could scarcely see and my flying goggles were hanging down over my ears in two parts; they had been cut at the nosepiece. . . . There followed a vacant period that I can't fill in but when it passed, I realized that I was falling a kind of half-vrille—spinning nose dive—with my motor going full speed.

Hall's pursuers, satisfied that they had dispatched their victim, did not follow him down. This no doubt saved his life. Half-conscious after falling several thousand feet, he mustered such lucidity as he could and succeeded in pulling out of the spin. Then, holding the joy stick between his knees, he reached across with his right hand and throttled back the engine, which suddenly quit altogether. In Hall's crippled condition he had no hope of restarting it; however he "didn't care much" at this point except for wondering in a "drowsy kind of way" whether he was on the French or German side of the lines. Hall came out of his spin only five hundred feet above the ground, near enough for him to see through the blood and gathering dusk that the terrain below was a "wicked looking place for a landing: trenches and shell holes everywhere." It was a momentary worry, however, for he again slipped into unconsciousness.

When Hall came to, he was lying on a stretcher. He remembered portions of his earlier predicament with clarity, but since he felt no pain, he felt certain that he had been crushed and was in shock. Some anxious experimentation, however, soon disclosed that he could move all his limbs except his left arm.

I accepted this miracle without trying to explain it [he continued], for I had something more important to wonder about: who had the handles of my stretcher? I opened my eyes but saw nothing at first but a red blur. I wiped them dry with my right sleeve and looked again. The broad back in front of me was covered with caked mud, but the shrapnel helmet on the man's head was French. I thought in the hospital later, that if I lived long enough to gather a few possessions and have a home of my own, I would have a bust length view portrait of a French *brancardier*, mud covered back and battered tin hat, as a souvenir of the war.

Hall had indeed been saved by a miracle of sorts. His SPAD had fallen astride a front line trench, the wings collapsing as they struck the sides of the parapet, thereby absorbing much of the shock. Moreover, since his machine had been in the act of turning when it hit, with another twenty feet of altitude Hall would have come down in no-man's land, drawing the artillery bombardment that immediately befell any such hapless aviator. As fate would have it, Hall was not only safe in a French dressing station, but doctors could find no mark whatever of the crash. All of his wounds had come at the hands of German gunners more than 14,000 feet in the air.[11]

Naturally Hall won some renown for his remarkable experience. Thenault notes that Hall's flight had ended in the Ravine of Ostel, where the Germans were conducting a violent offensive, and that the aviator's "gallant fight" had "brought forth cries of admiration from the French troops, themselves engaged in the bitter struggle against the enemy and contributed not a little to that day's victorious resistance. Indeed, Thenault proposed Hall for a citation, though when this impressive document finally appeared, carrying with it the Médaille Militaire—which had been earned separately—and the croix de guerre, the facts were a little mixed up. It properly mentioned Hall's "splendid courage and . . . purist spirit of self sacrifice," but it also suggested that he had "plunged down upon seven enemy aeroplanes by himself."[12] Actually, Hall was later to write in his autobiography, "I don't believe I fired a single shot."[13] Be that as it may, James Norman Hall was out of the war for some time.

The lone victory during the stay at Chaudun came on 12 June and fell, as usual, to Lufbery. While on one of the "free flights" east of Rheims, he spotted several German biplanes regulating artillery fire, protected by seven pursuit ships. Lufbery was above the German fighters and "up-sun" as well, but as he prepared to pick one of them off and take his chances with the rest, one of the Germans lagged behind his fellows, perhaps through carelessness or perhaps as a ruse. At any rate, it was a fatal error. Lufbery swooped down, sending both pilot and plane spiraling to earth with one well placed burst of machine-gun fire. The enemy airplane, as often happened, came apart in the air and crashed near Sapingnal in the first line French trenches.[14]

It later proved to be Lufbery's tenth confirmed victory, but for the moment, circumstances did not permit him to stay around for self-congratulations. He had stirred up a hornet's nest, and since his machine gun had jammed during the initital engagement, he was "cold meat" for anyone capable of taking advantage of him. He thus beat a hasty retreat back to Chaudun, where he found that the victory had already been confirmed, a most unusual happening.[15] It was a momentous occasion, for with ten kills, Lufbery had doubled the magic number required to be a certified ace. Henceforth he could glory in the very rare distinction of the "double ace." But even so, there was something missing. After almost three years of service, victories, medals, and citations galore, he was still an adjutant, while others less gifted had gained commissions in a fraction of the time. The reason, however, seemed clear, at least to Lufbery. It went back to a "ridiculous incident" which had taken place the previous August when Lufbery was saying goodbye to a friend in the train station at Chartres. "Luf" had gone out on the *quai* without the required ticket, which provoked a challenge by a station attendant. When the latter tried to bodily eject him, Lufbery countered with a "superb right to the mustache" which sent the attendant sprawling. Lufbery soon found himself before the military commissioner of the station, who promptly gave him fifteen days in the stockade, a punishment a reviewing authority increased to thirty days. It was the only blemish on an otherwise sterling record, but according to Lufbery, it was enough to delay "for several months my promotion to officer."[16]

Four days after he became a double ace, Lufbery and Robert Soubiran each sent an enemy aircraft spiralling down in what they described as an uncontrolled fall. Each asked for confirmation, but no ground witnesses appeared and so nothing came of their claims. The same thing happened nine days later, when Lufbery attacked and thought he shot down a two-place machine near Laffraux.[17]

Meanwhile, as a result of his tenth confirmed victory, Lufbery won another palm for his croix de geurre—his sixth—and another citation, this one praising him as a "marvelous pilot" and a veritable model of "audacity, of *sang-froid* and of devotion." This was followed on 21 June by an equally or perhaps even more important award. Lufbery was at last named *sous-lieutenant.*[18]

If Lufbery's recognition came at a time of considerable combat, it also coincided with another trial by ordeal. Recognized not only as the vanguard of American volunteers, but also as the foremost of those representing the United States, the squadron was plagued by visitors, coming from far and wide, who somehow wangled permission to visit the unit. For the most part, the men of the Lafayette Escadrille regarded these visitors as intruders, be they newsmen or American army brass. In view of their fame and status, however, they came to expect the interruptions, and some even seemed to enjoy it.

Such was the case on 7 July, when an impressive ceremony at Chaudun served to remind them of their position vis-à-vis their own country and their adopted France. The celebration had begun three days earlier, when the entire squadron was given forty-eight hours' leave to participate in a "glorious" commemoration of American Independence Day in Paris, one of the very few instances in the history of the squadron when ceremony was given precedence over front-line responsibility. In this instance, the pilots of the Lafayette Escadrille were the guests of honor, and no one, it seemed, American or French, would have it otherwise. The festivities supposedly climaxed on the 7th, when the squadron was honored by a parade at the home airfield. But the parade came only after ten morning missions had already been flown and before the eight afternoon missions were scheduled to depart. At any rate, the parade was an impressive one. Personnel from virtually all the French air squadrons in the sector formed a square, a battalion of *chasseurs à pied* presented arms, and Commandant du Peuty presented a silken American flag to the Lafayette Escadrille. The flag was hand made for the occassion by Mrs. William Gibbs Macadoo, the wife of the United States Secretary of the Treasury and a daughter of President Woodrow Wilson, along with some forty women employed by the Treasury Department. It proved a memorable scene. As one French observer wrote, "The Tricolor bowed before that starry banner, the bugles sounded 'au *Drapeau*,' and everyone felt that it was France saluting America."[19]

The ceremony made a deep impression on the American airmen, many of whom would recall it almost half a century later with emotion and exceptional clarity. But they also remembered 7 July 1917 for another reason. That morning, just before the flag ceremony, Andrew Courtney Campbell had one of the most memorable experiences of the war.

Returning from his morning patrol, Campbell could not resist the temptation to give the gathering visitors a display of daring acrobatics. At about 5,500 feet in the air, upside-down at the top of a loop-the-loop, the lower left wing of Campbell's Nieuport suddenly tore from the fuselage and fell fluttering away. Thus disabled, the plane seemed destined to fall off into a spin which would tear away the remaining wings. But somehow Campbell managed a half-roll out of the loop, and pulling back on his throttle, set up a slow and precarious glide. Descending past his fluttering wing, which fell into a dense forest and was never recovered, he managed to put his aircraft down safely in a beet field some ten kilometers from the home field. Except for the lost wing, both plane and pilot were in perfect shape. Campbell hadn't even blown a tire in the forced landing.[20]

By any standard, it was a spectacular bit of airmanship. Remaining true to form, Campbell was not in the least upset by his miraculous escape. Aviation experts, on the other hand, came from far and wide to examine the crippled machine. It seems that the model Nieuport Campbell was flying at the time had a nasty habit of shedding one of its lower wings. Authorities had been unable to pinpoint the exact cause since the incidents always resulted in a fatal accident with neither pilot nor plane in a condition to reveal the circumstances which produced it. Now, in Cambell's miraculous escape, they might have the answer.[21]

For his part, Campbell got a citation, his first. It was well earned.

## The Additions

The Lafayette Escadrille had not lost a pilot to combat or aircraft accident since de Laage's tragic death in May. But vacancies were created by other causes: Edward F. Hinkle had been forced to drop out because of ill health; Drexel had departed for liaison duty with the A.E.F. in Paris; and Lawrence Rumsey, still dominated by alcohol, had been released so that he might fulfill his promise to join the American army.[22] Thus two new men, each unique in his own way and each destined to make a name for himself, were brought into the squadron.

The first of the new men was David McKelvey Peterson, from Homesdale, Pennsylvania. The son of a physician, he stemmed from a distinguished family with a long military tradition. He held an engineering degree from Lehigh University, and unlike so many of the others, he came directly into aviation. Soon recognized as a "splendid fellow," the tall, slender, and phlegmatic Peterson was extremely conscientious and deeply devoted to the French cause.[23] Also, his coolness and balance made a deep impression on his fellows. Hall and Nordhoff described him in the following words:

> It may be said without any exaggeration that he is the only American who has never had a thrill from his adventures as an airman. No event of the war ever stirred the tranquil depths of his nature. He simply couldn't be elated or depressed, frightened or overjoyed. The first *tour de piste*, the first *Brevet* flight with the inevitable *planne de château*, the first *vrille* at the *École d'Acrobacy* at Pau, the first patrol over the lines, the first official victory—these events, so memorable in the lives of most pilots, he accepted with admirable placidity. For him, red-letter days had no existence.[24]

Douglas MacMonagle, the only son of a San Francisco physician who had died just before the war, also came into the Lafayette Escadrille at this time. MacMonagle, whose name betrayed his Scottish ancestry, came to France in 1916 to drive ambulances, a calling that eventually won him a citation for rescuing three wounded men under intense artillery fire. Coming to the Layfayette Escadrille in June 1917, he soon won a place of great respect among his fellow fliers, who described him as a "man's kind of man," one who hated pretense and who was a "born enemy of 'barracks flyers.' "[25] MacMonagle was also a skillful pilot who did not hesitate to meet the enemy at any time and any place. Unfortunately, he won his greatest laurels not in victories but in death.

James Norman Hall's sudden if somewhat spectacular exit from the SPA-124 created another vacancy. To fill this gap, James Ralph Doolittle (not to be confused with the later Lt. Gen. Jimmy Doolittle), who hailed from New York City and who listed his occupation as "student," was brought into the Lafayette Escadrille. Doolittle came from excellent stock. He was conscientious and most unsparing of himself, but through no fault of his own, he seemed plagued by bad luck. It began during his short stay at a reserve depot, preparatory to leaving for the front. His Nieuport stalled at low altitude, falling off into a spin and crashing to earth. Doolittle was badly cut up about the face, and since even his eyelids were damaged, he missed losing his eyesight by the narrowest of margins. Yet after eight weeks in the hospital, he was again ready for action.[26]

On 2 July Doolittle was brought into the SPA-124, taking his place on the regular patrols at a time when combats were a regular occurrence. Like most newcomers, he was at first restrained from becoming a prime partner in these engagements, but even in his short combat career, he lived up to the best traditions of the squadron.[27] But that, of course, came after 17 July, when the squadron was suddenly withdrawn from the Aisne sector and sent to St. Pol-sur-Mer in the Flanders Sector, a small village on the Channel coast, located some two miles south and west of Dunkirk.

## Over Flanders Fields

Fully aware of the intense activity around Chaudun, the move naturally came as a surprise. The pilots of the SPA-124 did not know that the

British were preparing a powerful offensive in the Flanders sector, an offensive so large that it included the French First Army under General Antoine. Under his command were three groups of French aviation, including one combat group, the thirteenth, of which the Lafayette Escadrille was a part.[28]

This great offensive, known to military historians as the Third Battle of Ypres and to laymen and the men who fought in it as the Battle of Passchendaele, was the brainchild of Sir Douglas Haig, the commander in chief of the British armies in France. Aside from the preliminaries, which included the famous and successful assault on the Messines Ridge, and an air assault, launched on 11 July and designed to gain mastery of the air, the offensive anticipated a breakthrough in the vicinity of Ypres. Through the gap the troops would storm the ridge between Staden and Passchendaele and cut the rail between Roulers and Thourout, thereby threatening the German defenses in the north. The enemy would have no choice but to withdraw, thus paving the way for an even more important objective, an amphibious landing on the Flemish coast, outflanking the German position in Belgium. This stroke, strongly supported by the British admiralty, was considered an essential one if the German U-boats, which were then playing such havoc with British shipping, were to be deprived of their submarine pens at Ostend and Seebrugge.[29]

In this great offensive the French army had been delegated a role, not so much because the Allies had pooled their efforts as because the ill-fated Nivelle offensive of April 1917 had almost proved the undoing of the French forces. At the time, it was felt some display of offensive spirit by select French forces was needed, even as the others were getting back on their feet. Among those forces called upon to make an offensive show were the American pilots of the Lafayette Escadrille.

On the flight to St. Pol-sur-Mer, made on the evening of 17 July, the pilots of the LaFayette Escadrille ran into considerable trouble. They had no maps, but had been given simple instructions by Thenault to follow the front lines to the sea, turn left, and land. But unfortunately the weather was bad, with low clouds and mist all the way. The flight was a shambles. Haviland crashed north east of St. Pol; Peterson cracked up attempting an emergency landing at a British field; Parsons and Willis almost ran into a British balloon obscured by mist; Masson had motor failure at one point but got his ship down safely; and poor Doolittle got lost and came out over a German aviation field.[30] Unaware of his location, he was on the point of landing and asking for directions when a German machine gunner fired several bursts, warning Doolittle of his near-disastrous mistake. Naturally he beat a hasty retreat, taking refuge in some clouds while he tried to find the lines. As fate would have it, he emerged from his refuge just in time to witness a German airplane attack a British balloon which was receiving some protection from a British fighter. Not one to shirk his duty, Doolittle joined in and gave chase to the now fleeing German. It was something of a trap, however, for the German suddenly turned back on his pursuer and proceeded to make Doolittle's first real combat with the enemy also his last one. Before it was over, the engine of his SPAD had been shot up and one bullet had passed through the calf of his left leg. Doolittle managed to keep the airplane under control until it reached the ground, but upon landing in the rough terrain just behind the front lines, the machine turned over. In the ensuing crash, Doolittle's old face wounds were reopened. For J. Ralph Doolittle the war was over.[31]

At St. Pol-sur-Mer the Lafayette Escadrille received a new type of assignment. Since the struggle for mastery of the air—the type of activity for which these men had been trained—had already been decided for the most part, the squadron received orders to await the day of the assault, now scheduled for 31 July. Their mission then would be to swoop down low over the enemy airfields in their assigned sector and bomb and machine-gun the enemy airplanes on the ground.[32]

Such strike missions were virtually unknown in 1917. Raleigh and Jones list it as a new development even for the British, who surpassed all the Allies in this sort of thing.[33] At any rate, it was certainly new to the pilots of the Lafayette Escadrille, who now found most of their pre-assault time devoted to practice missions, flights which did not sit well with the American pilots. As one participant explained it: "To begin with, the Spad was a flat-winged ship of great speed but small lift. . . . It was tough enough with a full load of gas and such a short run to get them off the ground without hitting the sea wall. Adding a couple of heavy liquid bombs seemed like suicide." There were also other difficulties.

Sighting the bombs had been figured out by our armament officer, a gentle-man of Polish extraction named Ciecomski, in which he used as aids a broken slide rule and a dream book. That seems to be the only feasible explanation for his instructions were to go to a thousand meters, fly straight until the objective disappeared beneath your lower wing, pique (dive) at a forty five degree angle for five hundred meters, straighten out, count ten and let fly.[34]

Meanwhile, on 31 July, the great offensive of Third Ypres, which would go down in history as a veritable blood bath and haunt soldiers and statesmen for years to come, got underway after four days of artillery preparations which used up 4½ million rounds. On the first day, the assault proved deceptively successful, for the Germans had adopted a new flexible defense system, tested earlier at Aaras, in which lightly manned outpost zones cushioned the enemy shock in front of a main line of resistance some distance back. It was intended that the line would consequently bend but not break under the force of the assault.

Surprisingly enough, this great battle began with almost no air activity. After six weeks of excellent weather during the preparatory phase, a veritable deluge of rain poured down on Flanders on 31 July, making life utterly miserable for the unfortunate soldiers on the ground and bringing air operations on both sides of the lines to a virtual halt. On this fateful day, the SPA-124 mounted only five missions, not a one of which lasted longer than an hour. For three days following, rain and low clouds kept the airmen out of the sky, while on the ground the rain and the mud sapped strength from the assault. As important as it was to maintain pressure, the Allies had no choice but to await better weather.[36]

But the weather did not break, at least not for very long. On 4 August the SPA-124 flew eight missions and twice mixed it up with German aircraft, which seemed to be out in force. The next day twelve missions were flown by the squadron and again the returning pilots reported considerable enemy air activity, including four combats. After another two days of inactivity due to weather, the squadron flew four missions. On the ninth, they flew no less than fourteen sorties, fighting four wild combats in which, in every case, the Vickers machine gun jammed.[37]

Surprisingly enough, two volunteer missions following that hectic day marked the end of air activity for the Lafayette Escadrille in the great Battle of Third Ypres. On the ground the first phase of the battle had ended in the usual deadlock, and in the air only marginal value had been gained from the 500-odd Allied airplanes in the sector. Indeed, in the journal of the SPA-124 and in the records kept by the American pilots during this period, one finds uncommon reference to practical jokes, baseball games, barracks lounging, etc. It was to have been one of the greatest aerial campaigns of the war from the very beginning, with the top pilots on both sides engaged in the bitter struggle. But bad weather had proved the deciding factor. There would be plenty of air activity later, of course, but with the first phase over and ended in the usual deadlock, the French, disillusioned with the results of the campaign, withdrew the Groupe de Combat 13 along with other aviation units from the battle.[38] The Lafayette Escadrille and its sister squadrons in the unit were sent to Senard, in the Verdun sector, where it came under the French Second Army, now under the command of General Guillaumat.

## Senard

Senard was a small village lying on the southern edge of the Argonne Forest, some 250 miles from the station at St. Pol-sur-Mer. At the time, the Verdun sector was comparatively quiet, and had been for some time, but now that he had successfully restored the confidence of the badly sagging French armies, General Pétain decided on a limited offensive in the symbolic Verdun area. He hoped to give the French army a feeling of accomplishment by restoring the French line to where it had been before the famous German assault of 21 February 1916.[39]

Pétain began his preliminary bombardment on 17 August, two days before the infantry assault. As usual, the struggle in the air focused on attempts to get intelligence information or prevent others from getting it. Of critical importance, however, was the struggle for control of the air, which, like a three-ring circus, involved French fighters against German reconnaissance and artillery-ranging machines, German fighters against French reconnaissance and artillery-ranging aircraft, and, of course, fighter against fighter. This "battle in the air," which began well before the ground offensive, was full blown when the Lafayette Escadrille arrived. Indeed, while the overall campaign was small compared to the colossal battles of Verdun, the Somme, and Third Ypres the pilots now found "some really intensive air work, the most exhausting of all our campaigns."[40]

The SPA-124 did not spring forthwith into action after their arrival at Senard. There were always several days of preparation and reorganization after a move, and during this particular interval the squadron came in for a signal honor indeed. Some months before, it seems, Commandant Féquant, a man who had learned to know and appreciate the American pilots at the great battle of Verdun, had proposed the squadron for a unit citation. Now this citation, as rare as individual citations were common, was to be presented. Signed by Pétain, the general-in-chief of all the French armies, it proved a glowing tribute to the men of the SPA-124. In part, it read as follows:[41]

An escadrille composed of volunteer Americans who have come to fight for France in the spirit of purest sacrifice. Under the command of Captain Thenault, who formed it, it has maintained without ceasing an ardent struggle against our enemies. In exceedingly difficult combats and at the price of severe losses, which, far from discouraging it, have exhalted its morale, has brought down twenty eight officially confirmed planes of the enemy. It has excited the profound admiration of the officers who have had it under their command and of the French Escadrilles who, fighting by its side, have striven to vie with it in valorous deeds.

Pétain

The squadron flew its first combat mission from Senard on the evening of 16 August, but sighted no German aircraft. The following day, however, they flew nineteen sorties, recording no less than eleven different combats, more than they had experienced during their entire stay at St. Pol-sur-Mer.[42] For the pilots of the SPA-124, their second great air battle over Verdun had begun in earnest.

The next day, several planes and pilots from the SPA-124 were assigned the mission of escorting a group of bombers attacking Dun-sur-Meuse. About forty-five minutes after takeoff, the formation was attacked by a flock of German fighters. A general melee followed, in which Walter Lovell sent a German down in flames, and Willis, the dedicated young architect from Boston, dispatched another, who was attacking one of his comrades. But he in turn became the focal point of a deadly crossfire.

I did all sorts of stunts to avoid fire on the line of flight. The enemy flew well. We missed collisions twice by inches. I was badly raked by crossfire; music of bullets striking motor and cables. Towards the end, my windshield was shattered and my goggles broken by a ball, which slightly stunned me. I had an awful feeling of despair at the thought of the inevitable landing in Germany. As I neared the ground, I had an instant's desire to dive into it—saw a wood in front of me, jumped it, and landed instinctively on the crest of a hill. One of the Germans flew over me, waved his hand, turned and landed, followed by his two comrades.

All saluted very politely as they came up—young chaps, perfectly correct. My machine was a wreck; thirty bullets in the fuselage, motor and radiator, exactly half the cables cut, tires punctured, and wings riddled. It was a beautiful machine and had always served me well. Too bad![43]

Harold Willis was a prisoner, the first of the Lafayette Escadrille to achieve that dubious distinction. But he was by no means an ordinary prisoner of war. On this particular day, he had taken to the air wearing green striped pajamas and a brown sweater under his flying suit. Also, he carried no identification papers of any kind. Since the Germans had no way of immediately checking his identity, Willis quickly sized up the situation and promoted himself to *sous-lieutenant*. It was a time-honored guarantee of better treatment, at least for a time. Besides, he had been proposed for officer rank anyway.[44]

After three anxious days, the squadron learned through the Red Cross that "Lieutenant Willis" was a prisoner. Parsons, also following a time-honored procedure, flew over the lines and dropped a bundle of clothes, cigarettes, and money carefully addressed to the new officer. The ploy worked for several days before Willis received the inevitable "demotion" and was moved out of the officers' compound.[45]

Meanwhile, throughout the remainder of August and well into September the air battle continued above what Thenault called "the hardest sector we had ever flown over."[46] With almost monotonous regularity, the men of the SPA-124 flew patrols up and down the lines, undertook reconnaissance missions when and where it was too dangerous to send the cumbersome observation craft, and now and then conducted strike missions against enemy ground targets.

It was on one of the escort missions toward the end of August 1917 that Stephen Bigelow, hastening to the aid of a hard-pressed Sopwith bomber, took on six German fighters at once. In the ensuing melee, he received a bullet wound in the face which sent him to the hospital for several weeks. This wound and failing health ended Bigelow's tour with the escadrille. On 24 December 1917 he was finally released from the service altogether.[47]

Shortly after Bigelow flew his last mission, Kenneth Marr, known to his comrades as "Si-wash," had one of those spectacular experiences that men still talk about. On this occasion he was on patrol with Henry Jones and Douglas MacMonagle when the trio ran into a flight of four German fighters. In the middle of the dogfight which followed, Marr suddenly found himself upside-down without his elevator control. The cables, it seems, had been cut by machine-gun fire. He could still use the ailerons on the wings and he had control of the rudder, but technically he had no longitudinal control. Taking the logical way out, he cut the throttle and dropped off on one wing, letting his machine slide into a steep dive. Jones saw that something was wrong and hurried to his friend's rescue. By giving the tenacious German pilot problems of his own, he allowed Marr to devote all his time and talent to getting on the ground in one piece.

Marr found that by alternately gunning and cutting his throttle, the air blast of the propeller and the increase in air speed forced the sagging elevators into a neutral position while the increased lift momentarily levelled the aircraft off, permitting him more or less to control his descent. In this way, he managed to bring his machine down to a shaky landing in the shell-torn forest of Hesse. Borrowing an infantry staff car from his rescuers he rushed back to Senard, picked up several mechanics and some spare cable, and several hours later, had the machine repaired. Marr then flew it out of the ruined forest himself, arriving back at home field just in time to take on a load of fuel and go out on another patrol.[48]

Marr's exciting experience had a happy ending, and even Bigelow's misfortune could have been much worse. But shortly thereafter, on 24 September 1917, fate proved particularly unkind, and the squadron lost Douglas MacMonagle in what Parsons calls a "most pathetic combination of circumstances." Suffering from combat fatigue, MacMonagle had taken a short leave two days earlier. He had a premonition that he would be killed, and after some heavy drinking, confided as much to Charles Dolan, who had accompanied him and who, with considerable effort, got him back to Senard. MacMonagle had a bad hangover when he returned and did not want to fly, but Thenault, who was firm on such matters, insisted on it.[49] Thus, MacMonagle was with Lufbery, Parsons, and Robert Rockwell when the group left for an early morning patrol along the west bank of the Meuse River.

About half an hour later, the quartet ran into a group of eight German fighters. Not liking the odds, Lufbery, as patrol leader, elected to turn back and get both altitude and the up-sun position before returning and attacking. Parsons and Rockwell followed the leader, but MacMonagle, for some reason, headed "straight for the Boches." It proved a fatal mistake; the enemy opposite were members of Baron von Richtofen's deadly "Flying Circus." MacMonagle never had a chance against such odds. Before his astonished comrades could come to his aid, two machine-gun bullets had crashed through his head, killing him instantly. As Lufbery, Parsons and Rockwell watched helplessly,

"Mac's" SPAD twisted and fell to earth, crashing into the same forest of Hesse where Marr had landed only days before.[50]

The fully irony of this tragedy, however, had not yet unfolded. Even as MacMonagle took to the air that fateful morning, his mother, who lived in Paris and worked for the Red Cross, arrived at the rail station serving Senard. "Mac" was to have met her, and she waited in growing uncertainty until Charles Dolan arrived with the news that her son had been killed only minutes before.[51]

Mrs. MacMonagle stayed for the funeral, where, according to eye-witnesses, she showed "admirable fortitude." But her presence only heightened what was a saddening loss for the whole squadron. When James Norman Hall, then flying with the SPA-112 because of a mistake in his orders, dropped in on his old squadron for a quick visit, he found Lufbery "inconsolable" and the whole unit a "picture of dumb grief." Later, after rejoining the squadron, he wrote that "with Mac gone, it doesn't seem like the old crowd."[52] It was a sentiment shared by all.

Since the Lafayette Escadrille was flying mostly patrol missions during this period, the pilots had relatively few opportunities to brawl freely with their German opponents. Even so, they took a toll of their adversaries sufficient to more than make up for Bigelow's wound, Willis's capture, and MacMonagle's death. On 4 September, for example, a day marked by six different patrols, twenty-seven sorties and no less than twelve individual combats, Parsons tangled with two German pilots, sending one of them falling out of control. He did not see it crash, but its fall was observed by ground forces near Neuvilly, giving this budding ace his first confirmed victory. A few hours later, Lufbery, on the second of his four flights that day, found an unfortunate German pilot by the name of Winger near Vaquois-Cheppy. Winger succeeded in putting three bullets into Lufbery's machine, but it was he who died when his airplane, badly shot up, came apart in the air and crashed to earth.[53] It was Lufbery's eleventh official kill.

After a fortnight's interval, another German fell victim to a Lafayette pilot, this time at the hands of David Peterson, who, like Parsons, was destined to be an ace before the war ended. After dealing his opponent a death blow in the air, however, Peterson followed him down. Over-anxious to confirm the kill, he came so low that his own machine was damaged by rifle fire from the ground. His daring paid off; upon his return, he reported that his victim had "crashed to earth between Trory and Montfaucon, behind a woods and next to a road."[54]

Three days later Lufbery, who seems to have had some trouble mastering the techniques of patrol engagements (a necessary tactic, since the Germans now flew and fought in groups), brought down his twelfth confirmed victim, a Lieutenant Ruppertz. Taking on two of the enemy at once, Lufbery almost simultaneously sent Ruppertz to his death and forced the other enemy pilot to "dive vertically for his own lines."[55] Since Ruppertz fell into no man's land, his fall was quickly recorded. This was Lufbery's second victory for the month. Obviously he was back in good form.

Time at Senard was running out. It had been a bitter period, marked by intense fighting and tragic losses. The pilots would long remember the fatique and the sadness of it all. But they would also remember with gladness the time Lufbery and Thaw set up a machine gun on the field and blasted away at some German bombers making a night raid on the air station. The next morning, finding a map from a German airplane and a German flying helmet covered with blood, they filed claim for a victory.[56] Also, the men would long talk of the time a German two-place aircraft landed at Senard, out of gas. The pilot, apparently new to combat but certainly arrogant about it, not only refused to surrender but would talk only with the ranking officer. He demanded fuel and an unhampered return to his own lines, and when this was denied him, he asked for fuel and a five-minutes' head start, offering to take his chances with a single fighter the French could send up after him. "Of course," Parsons wrote, "he got the horse cackle from everyone and was taken away, sadly shaking his head over the unsportsmanlike conduct of his enemies."[57]

In late September the SPA-124 suddenly received the news that it was moving again, this time back to its old field at Chaudun in the Aisne sector. In a way, this was a welcome reprieve; bad weather would soon set in, and the stay at Senard had taxed the physical and mental endurance of the American pilots. In six weeks, they logged more than 420 combat sorties, and on no less than 150 of these missions they matched their skill with German pilots and gunners. They had not come out of it unscathed—Bigelow in the hospital, Willis a prisoner, and MacMonagle dead—but they had given more than they got. Official records credit them with killing five German pilots during this hectic period and with destroying at least as many airplanes, quite apart from the satisfaction of carrying out their assigned patrols and their escort and reconnaissance missions.

*Interlude at Chaudun*

The transfer of the Lafayette Escadrille and its sister squadrons in the Groupe de Combat 13 to Chaudun took place on 18 September, almost a month before a French assault was scheduled at Malmaison. For the first time, it seemed, the Lafayette Escadrille would play a prominent part in a French bid for pre-assault mastery of the air.

Like the recent Verdun campaign, the Malmaison or Third Aisne offensive, as it was officially called, was strictly limited in scope, the assault force comprising only seven divisions of the French Sixth Army. Compared to some of the other great battles, it was not a big offensive, but its limited objectives were very important ones: to test, as at Verdun, the mettle of the revitalized French army, and to clear the Germans from the heights of the Aisne between Allemont and Malmaison, where for three years they had held firm against two other major attacks. Also, if the French were to improve their defensive posture and pave the way for future offensives in the area, it was vital that the Germans be moved back across the Aisne River.[58]

General Maistre, the commander of the French Sixth Army, planned his campaign with great care, paying particular attention to the standard procedure of a heavy preliminary artillery barrage. This included concentrated fire upon known enemy artillery positions in order to prevent the Germans from "counter preparation." This was the usual practice by both sides when aware of a coming assault, and involved concentrating one's artillery fire in the forward area just before the troops went "over the top." Designed to take the heart out of the attacking infantry, it was usually a most unnerving experience.

Because of the paramount importance of artillery, the spotting of enemy gun positions received comparable emphasis. It is not surprising that the pre-assault phase of the Malmaison offensive found the Lafayette Escadrille, already well known for its ability in protective assignments, usually flying cover for photographic and observation missions.

At first the Germans did not maintain an air offensive of their own, a significant change from their aggressive showing at the Somme. Allied aircraft entering German air space could expect trouble, of course, but often those patrols which ran up and down the lines reported "rien à signalier," or perhaps the sighting of German aircraft well behind their lines.[59]

Combats were still relatively common, however. The pilots of the SPA-124 found plenty of opposition on escort missions across the lines, and of course they were looking for trouble on their "free flights." Sometimes, as on 1 October, even a regular patrol could run into trouble.

On this occasion, Henry Jones and Courtney Campbell were on "high patrol" between Craonne and Berry-au-Bac, just inside the German lines, when they suddenly found themselves involved with four German Albatroses. In the scramble, Jones managed to fight his way clear, but just as he nursed his damaged aircraft back across the lines, he glanced back to find Campbell absent from his customary place, his propeller two or three feet from his friend's rudder. Instead he was a mere speck in the distance. Apparently the "Wild Indian," in one of his wildest escapades, had decided to take on four German Albatrosses single handedly.[60]

It was the last that was ever heard or seen of Andrew Courtney Campbell until long after the war. The Germans did not report him as dead or a prisoner and his body was never found. It was the last act of a brave, eccentric, and incredibly lucky career. Besides his famous exploits of having a wing fall off and putting his wheels through the upper wing of de Maison-Rouge's SPAD, Campbell had also lived through a bad landing accident, in which a returning bomber crashed into his machine as he was taxiing across the runway. One propeller cut through the top wing less than a foot from Campbell's head, and his machine was rolled over and over until it was demolished. Actually, Campbell was at fault, since he had been instructed to taxi to the end of the field before attempting to turn off the landing strip, but this bothered him no more than the accident. Unperturbed, without a scratch on him, he "looked [the wreck] over nonchalantly, lit a cigarette and calmly continued to stroll across traffic to the hangar on foot." Now his luck had run out. As one of his comrades put it, "He had wooed the capricious lady and wooed her well but she finally tired of him. . . . He mysteriously died as he had lived, recklessly and foolishly brave to the end.[61]

Campbell's death—the French officially listed him as dead on the 8th of February 1918—was the last such tragedy to be suffered by the Lafayette Escadrille while in the French service.[62] Some of those still flying with the squadron would yet die in combat, but when their time came, they would be in American uniform.

## The Additions and Subtractions

Less than a week after Campbell's death, de Maison-Rouge left the squadron. An able officer, he had not been happy with the unit, partly because he never completely reconciled himself to the antics of "les sauvages." Campbell, in particular, had proved a trial for him. No member of the Escadrille denied his courage and he, in turn, returned the compliment. But there had always been a coolness between the Americans and the man who had the misfortune to replace the popular and beloved de Laage de Meux. Because of this strain and his own failing health, de Maison-Rouge felt it was time to move on. On 6 October, at his own request, he was transferred to SPA-78.[63]

De Maison-Rouge's replacement was a gallant French officer by the name of Louis Verdier-Fauverty, who, like de Laage, had served in the cavalry in 1914. He came to the SPA-124 from a sister squadron in Groupe de Combat 13, the famed SPA-65, and most of the older men of the Lafayette Escadrille knew him well. Reportedly there was great joy in the squadron when the men learned of Verdier-Fauverty's assignment as second-in-command, for as one acquaintance put it in a letter to a friend, "He is one of the finest Frenchmen I have ever met, and is so cheery and self-possessed at all times, that one is ashamed to mope in his presence. We do a little too much of this sometimes. . . . I notice that all of the men are keen to have his good opinion. He keeps us up to the mark, and he does it without word either of praise or blame."[64]

Verdier-Fauverty also had a reputation for impressive courage. This was something the men of the Lafayette Escadrille could appreciate, particularly now that they were in the hazardous business of strafing trenches and roadways from low altitudes. Also, he seemed to have unusually good luck, a relationship with fortune that most airmen took very seriously. It was common knowledge that in August 1917 Verdier and Lieutenant Ciecomski, the group armament officer, had collided in midair while engaged in a furious dogfight eleven thousand feet above the ground. For the first two thousand feet the stricken machines fell locked together. Then, Ciecomski, with some control over his aircraft, managed to set up a long motorless glide that ended in a fairly soft crash into some high tension wires. He suffered only a broken collar bone. Verdier's aircraft, on the other hand, had been shattered in the collision and was uncontrollable. He had no choice but to ride the stricken machine the two long miles to certain death on the ground below. But fate proved particularly kind to Verdier-Fauverty. His SPAD, a heavy machine noted for fatal accidents, fell into a dense forest and the trees absorbed most of the shattering impact. The SPAD was a total wreck, but the pilot came through the terrifying experience with nothing more than a bruised forehead and a split lip.[65]

About a month after Verdier-Fauverty joined the Lafayette Escadrille, and after James Norman Hall had returned to the SPA-124 from his temporary assignment with the SPA-112, the squadron received its newest and last American pilot. The new man was one Christopher Ford, who listed New York City as his residence and his occupation as "student." Before coming to France, however, he had been an accountant and a reporter for the *Wall Street Journal.* He had a background in aviation, having learned to fly at the Eddie Stinson Flying School in San Antonio.[66]

Ford dutifully went through the preliminary flying school for military aviators but somehow missed being sent to the school for combat acrobatics at Pau. It was his misfortune to come to the front and learn the all-important tricks of getting into a fight and the equally important ones of getting out of it, in the "school of hard knocks."[67] He learned well, however, and this quiet and retiring person, the last American to make the roster of the Lafayette Escadrille, was soon a full-fledged member of the combat team.

## The Lafayette Escadrille in the Malmaison Offensive

Meanwhile, in the air offensive preceeding the campaign on the ground, the Lafayette Escadrille found itself playing a prominent role. The air activity at first seemed mild compared to the terrible days at Verdun. On all but five or six days when the weather would not allow it, the squadron flew its scheduled patrols and escort missions, strafed trenches, and indulged in the highly popular free flights. But as the day of the offensive neared, the tempo increased, particularly after the preliminary artillery bombardment began on 17 October.

The many sorties were not without compensatory successes, and as usual, Lufbery led the pack. On 15 October, while out on one of those volunteer patrols in which he specialized, he mixed it up with two German airplanes near Anziny. Although his own machine was damaged in the process, he reported that both his opponents appeared "seriously hit." The following day, on another free flight, he attacked a two-place German observation craft near Vaucillion, "moving in very close," as he put it, he sent it down in flames along with its occupants, Lieutenant Keyne and Gefreiter Heimer. It was his thirteenth official victory.[68]

On Wednesday, 23 October, the opening day of the assault, bad weather prevailed; predawn drizzle started it off, and fog and low-broken clouds persisted throughout the day. The next day was a different story. The weather cleared and the Germans, alarmed at the 2¼-mile advance of the French the day before, launched a heavy counterattack. In response to this threat, the SPA-124 was called upon for twenty-one missions, most of them regular patrols, although Lufbery was able to work in one of his preferred "free flights." Combats were common and more than one Lafayette pilot returned with holes in his machine to tell of some bitter two-man struggle high above the holocaust below. But it was reserved for Lufbery to put on one of his most formidable performances. On the first flight of the day, beginning at 6:40 A.M. and lasting an hour and twenty-five minutes, he fought two separate combats and, according to his comrades, gained two solid victories. After a twenty-minute refueling and rearmament stop, he again took to the air, this time to meet three German airmen in succession and to send two of them spiralling to earth. Just before midday, on his third sortie, he once more encountered two German planes and downed them both, the last one falling shortly after noon.[69]

Six victories in as many hours! While such displays of airmanship were not unknown during the war, Lufbery's performance on 24 October 1917 nonetheless seems so incredible that one is tempted to pass it off as another of these exaggerated claims for "our man," claims which always seem tragically common in wartime. In Lufbery's case, however, there is at least an even chance that all six of the victories were genuine ones. The squadron *Journal de Marche* records the time and place of each combat, and Lufbery, who was never inclined to exaggerate, reported that all six victims appeared "seriously damaged." His commanding officer maintained to the end that Lufbery brought down six machines, noting somewhat sorrowfully that "only one was confirmed as the infantry was in full movement and the control services were naturally . . . disorganized in consequence." Thenault was not an eyewitness, of course, but he credits "several French aviators" with "unofficial confirmation."[71]

Naturally there was another citation—his tenth—this one praising him as a "remarkable pilot, an outstanding example of bravery, energy and audacity." Significantly enough, the citation went on to mention how, on 24 October, he fought seven engagements, "shooting down his fourteenth victim and driving away five other German machines."[72]

The Third Battle of the Aisne ended officially on 2 November 1917 when General Boehn, the commander of the German Seventh Army, withdrew his hard-pressed forces behind the Ailette River. The struggle in the air also died down, in part because of the comparative inactivity on the ground, but mostly because winter was setting in. There were still daily patrols to be flown, as the *Journal de Marche* makes clear, but there were no outstanding losses or victories except for another superior performance by Lufbery on 2 December, one which gave him "intense satisfaction."

On the first of two free flights for the day, Lufbery attacked a German pursuit ship near Ailles and sent the pilot racing for his lines. "Luf" pressed the attack, however, until his victim fell in a flaming spiral from which there could be no recovery. An hour and a half later, on his second sortie, he found a two-place machine registering artillery near Laval. Suspicious that there might be fighter protection lurking above, Lufbery cautiously maneuvered himself into position, cleared his rear and then swooped in for a quick kill. As the machine fell, trailing black smoke, Lufbery followed it all the way down, anxious to make certain of the crash.[73]

It was a great day for the American ace. Both victories, his fifteenth and sixteenth, were confirmed. Captain Thenault suggested that it was a fitting commemoration for the anniversary of the Battle of Austerlitz, but Lufbery had a more personal purpose in mind. "Just think," he wrote to a friend, "It was three years to the day that Marc Pourpe fell on the field of honor. Each anniversary I have made an effort to avenge him. I want to dedicate the victims to him. . . . Our great friend should be satisfied with the manner in which I honor his memory although never on God's green earth will he receive all the honor he deserves."[74]

## The Departure of the Pets

One loss sustained in the final days at Chaudun cut deeply into the hearts of the Lafayette Pilots. Comm. Philippe Féquant, the commander of Groupe de Combat 13, peremptorily ordered that Whiskey and Soda, the squadron pets and mascots, were to go. Given what had happened, not much of a defense could be made out, either for Soda, the innocent party, or Whiskey, the culprit. It seems that the commandant, on his way to an important ceremony, encountered Whiskey, who was allowed to roam about the camp. For Whiskey, who liked to chew on bright things, it seemed a splendid opportunity; he playfully knocked the commandant down in the mud and then methodically chewed up the gold braid on his uniform, finishing off his meal with the patent leather visor of the cap. The commandant greatly respected and appreciated his American friends, but this was more than he could tolerate. He first ordered the lions to be shot; then he softened his attitude and spared them on the condition that they be sent to a zoo.[75]

It was a sad day indeed when the two pets were placed in an open touring car and taken to the zoological garden in Paris, where hasty arrangements had been made for their keeping. Soda, it is reported, fell into a "furious passion." The airmen didn't mind seeing her go, but when the time came for parting at the zoo and poor Whiskey realized that he was being left, his forlorn look nearly broke the hearts of his masters. The members of the squadron continued to visit him from time to time when they were in Paris, and Whiskey rejoiced at their coming. Obviously weakening under his unaccustomed inactivity and suffering from rheumatism picked up during the terrible winter at the Somme, he welcomed each in a pathetic sort of way, sucking the extended hand like a baby.[76]

Thus the lions passed out of the daily life of the Lafayette Escadrille. They had added much to the fame of the unit, but their greatest contribution was unquestionably the endless hours of delight and amusement they gave the men in combat. Parsons paid them and all the menagerie of squadron pets a great compliment when he wrote: "To all those dumb friends of ours, I, for one, am deeply grateful. They deserved a citation every bit as much as we humans for they were our constant companions and comforts in all the black hours and endured every hardship with us cheerfully and uncomplainingly. Knowing that we loved and appreciated them, may their souls rest peacefully in the animal heaven."[77]

## The Finale at La Noblette

With the conclusions of the Third Aisne offensive and the advent of winter weather, the Lafayette Escadrille was ready for its final assignment. On 7 December, the unit was moved to La Noblette in the Champagne sector where camouflage preparations by the Germans hinted of a possible offensive.[78]

The anticipated German attack did not materialize and the Lafayette Escadrille and her sister squadrons of Groupe de Combat 13 entered a period of relatively little opposition. There were patrols to be flown, and the squadron *Journal de Marche* shows numerous flights and some combat between the 9th and the 16th of December. After that, however, no combat is recorded and the flights dropped off dramatically. Only seven patrols were flown by the Americans before Christmas. After the holiday, some new French names appear on the *Journal de Marche* before the entry on 7 January, but no American ones.[79]

While the squadron would not officially pass out of existence until 18 February, the combat operations of the unit for all practical purposes had ceased to exist. There were solid reasons for this, the main one being the "standing-down" of the squadron preparatory to the transfer of its members to the American Air Serivce. This had proven a long and difficult process, taxing some of the energy and much of the patience of the volunteers. For this reason, the transfer is also an integral part of the history of the Lafayette Escadrille.

# 7

# The Transfer

The entrance of the United States into the World War on 6 April 1917 delighted the American airmen. In the innocence of youth, they had come to regard the struggle as a clear case of good versus evil, with no doubt as to which was which. Knowing little and caring less for high-level politics and diplomacy, the path of duty seemed obvious, and they deplored what appeared to be timidity and weakness on the part of the American nation. After all, they were willing to risk their all for the "most noble of all causes," as Kiffin Rockwell termed it, and for the most part they were hard put to see why their countrymen would not do the same. "Where has all the genuine honor and patriotism and humane feelings of our countrymen gone?" Genêt wrote his sister. "Oh, it's a bitter, bitter subject with everyone of us Americans over here."[1]

America's entry into the war changed all that. Young Genêt, destined to be the first American to fall after his beloved country entered the war, put it as follows in a letter to his mother.

I think that the United States coming in with the Allies has really been the crowning assurance for all of a sure and complete victory. I got to Paris a few days after war was declared, and what a change I found there. American flags were flying everywhere among those of the Allies and everybody was feeling far brighter and more cheerful than I have ever seen them before. It was fine to see Old Glory waving everywhere, Mother. We've waited so long for it to fly over here and all Americans have had to be restrained before. Now it's entirely changed and all are happy and contented and hopeful. One can see that it has made a big moral impression on the French soldiers.[2]

And the American fliers in the Lafayette Escadrille, joyfully hoisting the Stars and Stripes over their headquarters at Ham, jokingly told Captain

Thenault, "Captain, you're going to be replaced. You will soon be no longer the Commander-in-Chief of the Americans—an American General is coming soon to succeed you in your high office."[3]

The fact that the United States was now officially at war with Germany naturally brought up the question of the status of the American pilots. And once again it was a matter for discussion at the very highest levels, beyond the control of those men on the firing line, who, ignorant of the factors involved, were not likely to understand the problem. In the first wave of enthusiasm, they tended to see themselves as the vanguard of the American army, just as they had been the vanguard of American volunteers for France. Obviously their hard-won knowledge and skill could and would be put to use in the very near future. They seemed unconcerned with such intricate problems as grade, pay, discipline, and materiel that a transfer would naturally bring to the fore. On the other hand, if they were naive about these matters, so too were the high French and American officials who turned their attention to the transfer.

## The French Take the Initiative

The French in particular were extremely anxious to get the airmen into American uniform, for the obvious reasons of morale and high diplomacy. On 6 April, the same day America declared war on Germany, Jules Jusserand, the French ambassador to Washington, on his own initiative, cabled a request to his home office that the Lafayette Escadrille be transferred to the American Air Service as soon as possible. "From the point of view of the effect of the transfer both here and abroad, it is highly desirable that this suggestion, if possible, be accepted. It is of great importance that the American flag be engaged in the conflict without delay."[4]

Jusserand apparently looked upon the transfer as a simple matter. While there is some evidence that the French military attaché had talked the matter over with Brig. Gen. George Squier, the commanding general of the Signal Corps, and received his endorsement, the ambassador referred to the transfer almost as if it were a unilateral thing, unhampered by such weighty matters as changes in rank, pay, etc. Judging by his wire, he seems to have thought it sufficient to bring together all American pilots, group them together into Lafayette Escadrilles number 1, 2, and so on, and change the uniform and the flag.[5]

Ambassador Jusserand's request apparently struck a most responsive chord at the Quai d'Orsay. Within four days the matter had been discussed at the very top echelons of the French civil and military structure and a significant decision reached. In a wire to the grand quarterier général, dated 10 April, the French minister of war announced, "With the approval of the Premier and the Minister of Foreign Affairs, I have decided that henceforth, from this day forward, all flying and non flying personnel attached to the Lafayette Escadrille will fight in the uniform and under the flag of the United States."[6]

Even as the French authorities were searching for American army uniforms in which to dress some of their own nationals, as well as the pilots assigned to the Lafayette Escadrille, the news passed down through channels to the squadron. The men, however, were never made aware of it. Upon receiving the message, apparently given in the form of an order, Thenault sat down and wrote a long letter to the général commandant en chef, dated 17 April, in which he pointed out some of the intricacies of the transfer the higher-ups had overlooked. The American pilots, he suggested, had taken an oath to serve under the French colors "for the duration of the war," implying that they would need to be formally released from this oath before they could be transferred to the American army. "It is not enough merely to change flags," he wrote.[7]

Thenault also brought up the delicate question of rank, pointing out that if the men were transferred with their present French ranks of *caporal, sergent, adjutant, sous-lieutenant,* etc., they would immediately be out of harmony with their comrades in the American Air Service, all of whom were officers. Yet to give them officer status commensurate with the policy of the American army while they were still part of the French military structure—as they obviously would be for several months to come—would disrupt the French system. The same was true of the pay scale.[8]

Finally, Captain Thenault brought up the matter of compensation for changing uniforms, since the men would be forced to buy them themselves. He ended his communication with the significant announcement that if the feelings of the men were to be considered, the name of the Lafayette Escadrille should by all means be retained to indicate the voluntary nature of their enlistment.[9]

Captain Thenault's letter apparently had the effect of throwing the whole program into reverse. Heretofore, it seems, no one had seen the individual trees for the forest. Now the commander of the SP A-124 had pointed out some of the more conspicuous ones, pointing to the obvious conclusion that the issue was a delicate one and could only be resolved by intensive coordination between the two countries involved. And this took time.

## America: Willing but Unable

Actually, the American authorities committed the same mistake as their French counterparts. In his conversations with the French military attaché in Washington, General Squier had given his endorsement, although at this point he could not speak "officially" for the U.S. government. This, however, was apparently enough for the French, who announced to the press on 11 April that the Lafayette Escadrille would soon pass into the American army. The French announcement, in turn, brought the issue to the attention of the United States War Department, where the secretary of war, Newton Baker, side-stepped the problem, indicating that while his government had not officially sanctioned the plan, they would do nothing to oppose it. Indeed, Baker and his subordinates added fuel to the fire by announcing that the Americans would definitely not be brought home to become part of the national military establishment, since they were doing more important work at the front than they could do at home.[10]

The American military authorities soon became aware of the problems inherent in the transfer. As a result, they also backed off until such time as the American Air Service was ready to receive the new squadron. The "compelling" reasons to get the squadron into American uniform were still present, of course, but when and where the Air Service would be ready to receive it was an open question. In view of the faltering advance of that fledgling service, fast becoming committed by overeager airmen and politicians to a program far beyond its ability to complete, it was obvious that this would take considerable time.

Thus the movement for an early transfer came to be an abortive one. Aside from the lost political and psychological advantages, whatever they might have been, the greatest victims of this hasty advance and equally hasty retreat were the airmen themselves. The news of the transfer in the press, and their own world fame—brought to their attention again and again—led them to believe that they would indeed be America's advance element, and soon. Most of them, it is true, had grown attached to their French comrades and felt grateful to the French nation for the training they received. They would leave the Service Aéronautique reluctantly, but they nonetheless felt that it was their duty to help their native country now that it was at war. The French naturally agreed, ruling that the very entrance of America into the war and the "democratic nature of the French constitution," required that the Americans be given their release if they demanded it.[11]

Now, however, after a whirlwind courtship conducted in an atmosphere of great enthusiasm, the airmen were left waiting at the altar. Unfortunately, no one told them of the broken engagement, nor were they informed of the reasons for the delay which now set in. As one angry pilot put it,

Almost daily we waited word from Paris, expecting that, with our experience, we would be called on to help the United States form a real aviation corps. Then we would fight for our own country in our own uniforms. We who had gone through the mill and survived would be enabled to give our countrymen the benefit of our hard-won knowledge. Alas for our great hopes and expectations! They were but idle dreams but they were such nice dreams until we were rudely awakened.[12]

The feeling of anguish and then anger that came over the pilots of the Lafayette Escadrille stemmed from what seemed to them an endless and inexcusable delay. In a way, it was the story of the founding of the unit all over again. Having little or no knowledge of the background, they were at a loss to understand it. They viewed the war as men on the firing line naturally would, as a bitter contest between opposing forces, with the issue to be decided where they stood. From their particular vantage point, delays and shortages were obviously the result of incompetence and neglect on the part of someone back home. What they did not realize was that the delay itself was foreordained.

America, it will be recalled, had entered in war in a woeful state of unpreparedness. The Wilson administration's campaign to maintain strict neutrality had been carried to the questionable point of refusing to plan for the possible entrance of America into the war, on the grounds that the planning itself might produce the result. Thus in April 1917, when America at last found herself caught up in the holocaust, she had less than 200,000 men in her army, and her air service, still considered an "insignificant" segment of the Signal Corps, despite the emphasis placed on aviation by the belligerents, numbered 131 officers, most of whom were pilots or in pilot training, and 1,087 enlisted men. It had fewer than 250 airplanes, not one of which could be considered as worthy of combat.[13] Indeed, in appropriations of money expended for military aviation—one of the primary causes of these early woes—the nation stood fourteenth among the world powers, well behind such nations as Bulgaria and Greece. Little wonder that General Pershing later wrote, "The situation at that time as to aviation was such that every American ought to feel mortified to hear it mentioned."[14]

Yet it was in aviation that America, with supposedly endless resources and vast manpower, was expected to make its greatest contribution, apparently because the Allies felt it was here the American contribution could be quickest. The various military missions which made their appearance in Washington shortly after America declared war drummed this point home, thereby attempting to channel American enthusiasm in this direction.[15] Thus the way was paved, in part at least, for Premier Ribot's famous telegram of 24 May 1917, urging the United States to have at the front by June 1918 a "flying corps" of 4,500 planes, 5,000 pilots and 50,000 mechanics.[16]

This remarkable telegram was accepted by Congress and the American people, but not the General Staff. As interpreted by overzealous Signal Corps officers, it provided for not less than 22,625 aircraft, including 12,000 of the latest models and a suitable training program capable of producing 6,210 pilots.[17] In short, what the French were asking for and the Americans more than willing to give was an air force considerably larger than France herself had brought into being in nearly three years of total mobilization and war.

Since Congress authorized $640 million for this ambitious undertaking, America now not only had a program of the first magnitude, it also had money for it, and, of course, plenty of enthusiasm. But this was not enough. The whole program was hopelessly out of proportion to America's ability to produce within the specified time limit; the country had only a dozen companies capable of manufacturing aircraft, and that in meager quantity. Moreover, the experience of the Allies had shown that it took about ten months after the design and testing of a particular machine had been completed before production in quantity was possible. At the same time, no amount of facilities and hardware (which were also lacking) could make up for the conspicuous absence of technical know-how and for the even more critical shortage of trained personnel. As one discerning critic observed, "No amount of money will buy time. Even the most generous preparations do not open up the years that have passed and enable us carefully to lay the foundation of a great industry and a great aerial army."[18]

The point is obvious. The United States was soon struggling with an overwhelming program well beyond its ability to meet the schedule; the General Staff was swamped with problems of the first magnitude; and military aeronautics, which would soon be running the affair, did not even have a firm doctrine for employment of its airplanes, let alone the ability to wage large-scale war. In view of these staggering problems on the home front, problems which involved hundreds of millions of dollars, the mobilization and training of millions of men, and basic decisions affecting the whole war effort, it is not at all surprising that the authorities did not pause to straighten out the question of the Lafayette Escadrille. It was a matter of first things first, the basic and governing fact being that the transfer of the SPA-124 could not take place until the American Air Service was ready to receive the squadron. Considering the hectic period immediately following the American delcaration of war, by any reasonable calculation that was months away.

It was nonetheless an annoyance and a disappointment for the men of the Lafayette Escadrille. After all, France and the United States had hastened to propose a marriage of convenience and then backed off without bothering to explain why. Conditioned by their position on the firing line and without knowledge of the trials and tribulations back home, the men of the squadron were incapable of figuring it out for themselves. As a result, they were led to what seemed an inescapable conclusion. They were not acceptable because, for some reason, they were not wanted.

It is easy enough to follow their line of reasoning. As they read in the newspapers that individuals back home with little or no military training were receiving commissions of captain, major, and above, they were hard put to understand why they were being passed over when they had proven themselves in combat time and again. Moreover, the contribution they could make was so obvious as to be acknowledged by all. Yet instead of being allowed to make this contribution, they were being treated with contemptuous silence, even as those who might some day command them were being picked out of the unproven.

## Commandant Féquant Proposes

The result was just what one might expect. In May 1917 Comman-

dant Féquant, the commander of Groupe de Combat 13, had proposed
the squadron for the much sought-after unit citation, praising the Americans for their "purest spirit of sacrifice" and for having "roused the
deep admiration of their chiefs . . . and of French escadrilles which,
fighting beside it, have wished to rival it in courage."[19] The following
September he was writing to the officer in charge of aviation at G.Q.G.,
complaining of a "certain ill air" among the men of the Lafayette
Escadrille. This letter, which reveals deep insight into the nature of the
problem as well as the attitudes of the Americans, deserves to be
quoted at some length.

> Whereas all the Lafayette pilots once rivaled each other in their ardour to
> maintain at a high level the reputation of their unit, a certain number now appear
> to have lost interest. Only the better ones continue to be moved by the noble
> sentiment of the past.
>
> The cause lies in the uncertain future of the squadron. How long will it
> continue to exist? What will happen to the pilots who belong to it? Will the
> American Army give credit for the voluntary service rendered the French Army?
> And will the French Army give due credit for the sentiment which prompted
> them to serve with us?
>
> The only answers to these questions are rumors spread from mouth to mouth
> and surely deformed in the process.
>
> Generally speaking, the Americans now serving France are, for reasons of
> sentiment, inclined to continue to serve under our flag but they feel it would be
> to their interest to transfer to the American Army. They ask themselves, for
> example, what are their chances of becoming officers if they remain with us,
> chances that appear to them minimal. On the other hand, they are receiving at
> present some 200 francs monthly from the Committee which helped create the
> squadron, a stipend which renders their situation an enviable one even as
> non-commissioned officers. This stipend will no doubt come to an end as soon as
> the first American aviation units are formed. Thus, if they remain with us but do
> not become officers, their material situation will be very inferior to what it is at
> the moment.
>
> In summary, the Lafayette Escadrille seems to be in the process of liquidation
> at the moment and, as in all cases such as this, the energy of the participants is no
> longer bent towards making a future success of the unit.[20]

Féquant greatly admired his American friends, and like so many of
his countrymen, he deeply cherished the motivation behind the squadron of volunteers. As a result, he offered a radical solution to the problem, one unquestionably designed to preserve its good name. "Under
the circumstances, I respectfully propose that the Lafayette Escadrille
cease to exist under its present name and that the greater part of its pilots

be assigned to other French combat squadrons. The vacancies would then be filled with French pilots."[21]

The Grand Quartier Général naturally would have none of this suggestion. In a reply to Féquant, General Duval, the Chef du Service Aéronautique, emphasized what he called the "great importance" of maintaining the Lafayette Squadron as an American unit fighting under American colors. In this way, he announced, the squadron will be "called upon to render the American nation the most signal service."

In summing up, the general flatly declared that the Lafayette Escadrille would not be dissolved, particularly when "American units are being formed, preparatory to coming to the front. It will remain in Groupe de Combat 13 until American aviation units effectively enter the front lines. This is the desire of the French High Command, the Americans and, I might add, the Lafayette Squadron itself."[22]

General Duval's letter implies discussions of some sort or other between the French High Command and American authorities on the status of the Lafayette Escadrille. If so, there certainly was no agreement except to maintain the status quo. In point of fact, the matter was not settled at all, but was left in a state of flux with the future of the squadron still uncertain.

The main reason for this has already been explained, its foundations resting in the maelstrom of confusion and difficulties arising out of the sudden mushrooming of an insignificant section of the Signal Corps into a projected air armada of gigantic proportions. At the same time, however, it is safe to say that matters were not helped much by direct negotiations between French and American authorities in France, negotiations which were carried on with varying degrees of enthusiasm and intensity after General Pershing organized his air staff in August 1917.

## Franco-American Negotiations

Actually, there were American military personnel in France long before General Pershing arrived, but these early officers were members of military missions with no authority to deal with the French on such weighty matters. Most of these officers, it seems, visited the Lafayette Escadrille at one time or another, but they could give no indication of progress in the transfer. Indeed, it was not until after Pershing organized his air staff that anyone was specifically authorized to deal with

Allied air ministries on matters which included such things as the proposed transfer.

When Pershing set up his air staff, he divided the Air Service, American Expeditionary Force (A.E.F.), into two segments. The Zone of the Advance, comprising the yet unborn combat elements, was placed under the command of Col. William A. Mitchell, the ranking American pilot in France. The other segment, known as the Zone of the Interior or Lines of Communications, was placed under Col. Raynal C. Bolling. A chief of the Air Service in the person of Brig. Gen. William Kenly was to bridge the gap and provide the necessary coordination between the two segments.

Kenly was not an air officer, but he had some appreciation of the potential of the airplane. Bolling, on the other hand, knew how to fly but was really a businessman in uniform. He had left his position as general solicitor of the United States Steel Company to head the so-called Bolling Mission to France for the purpose of deciding just which foreign airplanes the Americans should build. It was in this capacity that he had been commissioned a major and sent to England and France in June 1917. He had stayed on in France after submitting his final report on the purchase of airplanes in August 1917, to be commissioned a colonel and take on the position of commander of the Zone of the Interior, Air Service, A.E.F.[23]

Though Colonel Bolling owed his commission and position to his business acumen rather than any military experience or background, he was the one designated to carry on the negotiations with the various air ministries of the Allies.[24] In this way, the negotiations leading to the transfer of the famed Lafayette Escadrille first came to be the responsibility of a lawyer and a businessman who knew very little of the military art and even less of aerial combat.

Colonel Bolling did a remarkable job considering the difficulties he had to face, and it is greatly to his credit that he recognized the importance of transferring the American pilots then flying for France into the American Air Service. Primarily through his insistence, orders were finally issued on 11 September 1917, creating a commission of three officers[25] to visit certain French aviation schools "for the purpose of [medically] examining Americans now enlisted in the French Army with the view of their transfer to the United States Army."[26]

This first step was a feeble one, to be sure, but it was deemed a necessary part of a pattern which would become more evident later on. This pattern had its foundations in the fact that the great glamour of aviation had led a surprisingly large number of American men to volunteer for flying duty with the American Air Service, so many in fact that even under the expanded program only half the applicants could be accepted.[27] As a result, the American authorities could afford to be highly selective.

One who is to fly three or four miles up in the air must have perfect heart and lungs; to master aerial navigation, reconnaissance, wireless and machine gunnery, he must have a clear mind; and to pick out and send down important information he must have judgment and a sense of responsibility. Many men have one, perhaps two, of these characteristics but only a limited number have all three.[28]

Besides that, to quote from a War Department bulletin:

The candidate should be naturally athletic and have a reputation for reliability, punctuality and honesty. He should have a cool head in emergencies, good eye for distance, keen ear for familiar sounds, steady hand and sound body with plenty of reserve; he should be quick witted, highly intelligent and tractable. Immature, high strung, over-confident, impatient candidates are not desired.[29]

These criteria seem as logical as they are understandable, but they indicated a clear lack of experience with the physical and especially the psychological realities of air combat. Also, in the case of the American flying on the front, it proved something of an injustice. A pilot who had flown long hours in an open cockpit and who had often heard the sound of gunfire might no longer have a "keen ear for familiar sounds," and the rigors of combat actually tended to leave the airmen "high strung." Indeed, it is obvious that the American authorities had not yet learned a basic fact about combat flying: some of the best pilots might be high-strung, daring, untractable, and overconfident, not to mention any number of other faults, yet be superb in combat. On the other hand, the intelligent, clear-headed, college-athlete type might very well be a decided liability once the chips were down.[30] In short, as every combat veteran knew, there was simply no way to tell in advance how each and every budding pilot would meet his personal trial by ordeal. The only sure criterion at the time was experience, something the men of the Lafayette Escadrille had in abundance. Bill Thaw put the matter squarely when he complained to one of the examining American physicians, "You haven't got an instrument in that bag that can measure the guts of a guy."[31]

Meanwhile, again at the instigation of Colonel Bolling, a second major step had been taken. On 1 October 1917, orders were issued by Headquarters A.E.F., creating a board of four officers to examine

such American citizens, now commissioned or enlisted in the French Aviation Service, as may desire to obtain their release from that Service for the purpose of entering the Service of the United States. The board will make specific recommendations in each case, covering suitability of the applicant for service in the Air Service, American Expeditionary Forces, and the grade in which he should be accepted at such time as it shall be agreeable to the French Government to release him.[32]

In accordance with this directive, the Board, comprised of Dr. Gros, Maj. George Goldthwaite, Maj. Robert Glendinning, and Maj. William W. Hoffman, visited French installations from Nancy to Dunkirk, interviewing the pilots, subjecting them to physical examinations, and consulting with their commanding officers. By mid October, their report, addressed to General Kenly, was ready.

According to the document itself, the conclusions and recommendations were based "upon reports from Escadrille commanders, group commanders, and from Plessis-Belleville (Instruction); also on personal impression and past history." In other words, the French commanders were given a prominent say in the evaluation of the Americans. On this basis, then, the Board proceeded to class each of the aviators into one of six categories:

1. Capable of commanding a squadron—rank, major.
2. Capable of commanding a flight of six aeroplanes—rank, captain.
3. Capable of command, but not to be commissioned as flight commander until later, owing to lack of present experience—rank, 1st lieutenant.
4. Capable of being pilots—rank, 1st lieutenant.
5. Capable of being an instructor, 1st Class—rank, captain.
6. Capable of being an instructor, 2nd Class—rank, 1st lieutenant.

In this evaluation, the men of the Lafayette Escadrille came out very well indeed, for the Board, with remarkable foresight, placed primary emphasis on experience. Except for the recent arrivals, most of the pilots of the SPA-124 were fully capable of commanding at least a flight of six airplanes; they had done it more than once. Thus in the recommendations for rank, which constituted the final evaluation, these men were recommended for majorities: Thaw (whose leadership

was in a class by itself and who had excelled in combat as well),
Lufbery (the master airman and an international hero), the war-hating
Bridgman, James Norman Hall, Dudley Hill, Kenneth Marr, David
Peterson, Robert Rockwell, and Robert Soubiran, all men with vast
experience who had long since proved their ability. The remainder—
Dolan, Dugan, Jones, and Chouteau Johnson—were recommended for
captaincies.[34] Not a man in the Lafayette Escadrille, in the view of the
Board, was deserving of responsiblity below that of flight commander
or senior instructor, or rank below that of captain.

Actually, these recommendations were even more impressive than
they appeared on paper, for according to the physical standards set up
by those responsible for the American aviation program, some of the
Lafayette pilots had no business flying. Lufbery, the master airman
who could "fly as the bird flies," could not walk a line backwards, a
failing certain to be regarded by some as a lack of perfect balance.
Besides, he was overage at thirty-two. Thaw, one of the really great
leaders and fighters, had defective vision in the left eye, defective
hearing, a recurring knee injury that limited his motion, and a crippled
elbow resulting from a combat wound. Walter Lovell was overage and
completely color blind; Henry Jones had flat feet. Charles Dolan had
mild defects in his vision, and Dudley Hill, who had flown many a
successful mission, was practically blind in his right eye.[35] As Parsons
put it, "After comprehensive physical examinations . . . we were put
through a long series of rather ridiculous physical demonstrations."
Then the awful truth came out. "In solemn, owlish conclave, the board
decided that not one of us, despite hundreds of hours in the air, most of
us aces, all thoroughly trained war pilots with many victories to our
credit, could ever be an aviator. Their tests definitely showed that . . .
we were unfit to be pilots."[36]

It is true that according to the prevailing physical standards for
accepting or rejecting potential pilots, the men of the Lafayette Escadrille were largely misfits, although it had not always been so and most
of their ailments could be traced directly to the rigors of combat. The
Board, however, took this factor into account. These men, the Board
felt, were fully capable of exercising command and fulfilling responsibility, an assumption later proven perfectly sound.[37]

In its report to General Kenly, the Board twice mentioned that they
were "much impressed by the class of the men examined, the fine

reports of their work given by their officers, and their great desire to serve under their own Colors." By way of conclusions and recommendations, the report went on to say:

The material is valuable as a nucleus of aviators, experienced at the Front, around whom can be grouped the less experienced pilots recently trained or undergoing training here. It is capital with which to build and should be preserved. . . . The Americans are not receiving any outside assistance which they have had hitherto, cannot live on French pay, and most have no independent source of income. It is the opinion of the Board and also of the French officers commanding these Americans, that their position should be settled as soon as possible; that they should be allowed to remain at the front until required by the A.E.F.; and that as soon as they are required they should immediately undertake the new duties assigned them.[38]

In passing this report to the French, who were directly concerned with its contents, Colonel Bolling added a few important details.

The commission is quite of the opinion that these men should be transferred immediately from the French into the American Air Service but that they be left where they are at present, until their services are needed and where they will be able to give effectual help to the American aviation. At present these men are in an abnormal situation. If, however, they could be assigned definitely by giving them grades in the American Service, they could be left where they are for the present until we have need of them. This is in conformity with the offer of the French Government to take trained French pilots in these squadrons. . . . The French having already made this proposal, there is no reason why the Americans, who should be thus transferred from the French to the American Service, should not remain in the French Aviation whilst we have no need of them, and it would appear particularly advisable to take them from the French Service only when we need them. All we desire is to give them a definite assignment, . . . leaving them with the French Army although at the same time considering them as in our service.[39]

From Colonel Bolling's letter, it is obvious that the French and Americans were at least close to an agreement about what to do with the American airmen. French authorities had insisted all along that the best thing would be to get the Americans in proper uniform but let them fly with the French. Now the Americans, after great delay and after reevaluating the men to make certain that they conformed to the "new" standards, were proposing virtually the same thing. Indeed, for the first time, things looked so promising that the Americans were advised to seek their releases from the Service Aéronautique, while the

Franco-American Committee asked the French to hurry matters along for the Americans.[40] Unfortunately, things again got fouled up.

The American airmen, and particularly the men of the Lafayette Escadrille—the latter, for the most part, had been in combat much longer than the others and hence had much more to offer in the way of experience—were naturally somewhat hesitant by now to accept promises of an immediate transfer. While there is every indication that they were both willing and ready to serve their own country, they felt obligated to the country that had trained them, and almost without exception, they were deeply attached to their French comrades and by no means anxious to get out of the French army. On the other hand, since they were inclined to be men of action, they were disquieted at the slowness with which the American army was being brought into combat. At the same time, they were afraid that they might be taken from the front and sent back to America to act as instructors.[41] They were not war lovers by any means, but this would have been one of the unkindest cuts of all.

Under the circumstances, many of the American pilots began to wonder whether they might not render best service to the Allied cause by remaining solidly with the French, at least until the mess had been cleared up and the American Air Service was obviously ready to receive them. They appreciated the argument that it was essential to get Americans fighting in their own uniform at the front as soon as possible, and no doubt there was great attraction in the traditional American longing to be first. By early November 1917, however, this idea, so popular in April, had lost much of its glamour. Some of the pilots definitely made up their minds to remain with the French, while others hung back for a time. In the end, according to one authority, it was necessary to bring "much outside pressure" on the Lafayette Escadrille to get it to offer its services as a unit.[42]

By early November, those airmen deciding to make the transfer had submitted their request for releases, a formal appeal which read as follows:

À Monsieur le Sous-Secretaire d'État de l'Aéronautique;
   Being an American citizen and having enlisted in the French Army as a [pilot or observer]. I respectfully request that I be released from my enlistment in order that I might pass into the Aviation portion of the American army.[43]

For their part, the French now seemed particularly slow in handling the releases. In a way this is understandable, for releases, except for ineptitude or physical disability, were new to the system. Despite the fact that Colonel Bolling and Major Gros, strongly supported by General Kenly, pushed the matter, and the French made a "special effort to hasten the process," it took plenty of time for the papers to work their way through the various offices. Although the French had long since acknowledged the right of the Americans to serve their own country should they desire to do so, it was 11 December before the French premier and minister of war announced categorically that Americans desiring releases could get them, provided, of course, they conformed to "certain criteria," such as getting a proper medical certificate and signing an enlistment with the American Air Service. The French were particularly firm on this last part. "The engagement which brought them into the French Army," the announcement read, "cannot be terminated until they have signed a new enlistment in their own national army."[44]

On 14 December, only three days after this announcement and before the news had reached the men on the line, Major Gros, realizing their anxiety, wrote the airmen as follows:

> Knowing how impatiently you must be waiting for the time of your release, I want to tell you everything is being done to hasten the delay, which is entirely due to slowness in the ministerial *Bureaux.* Your papers are now going through the *Bureau* of the Minister of War, and we expect that in a very few days your official release will be granted. At that time you will be notified, and asked to come in and take the oath of an officer of the American Expeditionary Forces. I want you to know that the delay in your transfer is entirely beyond my control, and that I am doing everything in the world to hasten these steps.[45]

Actually, Major Gros knew whereof he spoke, at least in part. In "a very few days"—on 25 December, to be exact—the French authorities announced that they were accepting the cancellation of enlistments of all American pilots asking for them.[46] All that remained, or so it seemed anyway, was for the Americans to be called in and given the prescribed oath for a commission in the American army. But already forces were in motion which made this impossible. In the weeks preceeding, some new and powerful officers had come into positions of authority in the American Air Service, and their views generated a drastic change in A.E.F. policy regarding the Lafayette pilots.

General Kenly, Colonel Bolling, and Major Gros, it will be recalled, were the officers most concerned and interested in the problem of the transfer. All were very anxious to see it brought about as soon as possible, and had they retained the controlling voices, it is safe to assume that the pilots might have been picked up by the American Air Service as early as December 1917. But in mid November, the whole structure of the Air Service, A.E.F., was suddenly thrown into a state of imbalance by the arrival of Brig. Gen. Benjamin Foulois and a large staff of officers.[47]

## The Foulois Faux Pas

Foulois, who arrived in France with almost no advance notice, had been directed by President Wilson to succeed General Kenly as chief of the Air Service, a move that was bound to cause some difficulty. Foulois was not personally at fault. An air officer with considerable experience, he had excellent credentials. But the move was handled in such a way that General Pershing, it is said, was much displeased with what he considered "interference" with his command, and warned Washington that he would resign if this sort of thing happened again.[48] Equally serious, however, was the fact that the personal connections with French authorities, so painstakingly established by General Kenly and his subordinates, were suddenly negated, with very little attempt made by the "newcomers" to capitalize on the work already done. Indeed, many of the officers in place were removed from their jobs in a rather brutal manner to make way for the officers General Foulois brought with him. Colonel Bolling, for example, was eased out of the Air Service altogether, a move that his biographer—and the colonel himself for that matter—blamed on personal jealousies.[49]

Without attempting to judge Colonel Bolling's case, there nonetheless appears considerable merit in his charge, for jealousy and bitter in-fighting were characteristic of the Air Service, A.E.F. at this time. The great mushrooming of the air arm had swept up into its whirlwind energetic airmen with exceptional ambition, but with very little command experience (Foulois himself had been a major only months before). Incoming personnel included old line officers who had exercised command—they already had rank and some place had to be found for them—but who had never been in an airplane and had little respect for its potential. A flood of regular and reserve officers also arrived in France, men who had been transferred out of the artillery or infantry and who also expected responsibility commensurate with their rank. Others included civilians who, like Colonel Bolling, were really "business men in uniform"; the so-called Ninety Day Wonders, young men hurried through a course of instruction and given commissions; new men fresh out of West Point, bound to have an exhalted view of their own potential; and finally, American airmen like the Lafayette Escadrille pilots, who had ample combat experience but little else.

Who was to lead? Unfortunately, this was largely an open question. It could hardly have been otherwise. At the time, there was no basic agreement on the potential of the airplane and hence no proper guidelines for the employment of the weapon. Indeed, lacking experience in such matters, even the most hardy advocates had insufficient evidence to make their own speculations sound logical, let alone convince others. Some central questions were these: Could only airmen, claiming that they alone understood the potential of the new weapon, guide aright? Or were these "rousing enthusiasts" to be dismissed as "dangerous upstarts"? Could the Ninety Day Wonders do the job, or should it be entrusted to line officers, or West Point graduates who had a theoretical acquaintance with such things as strategy and tactics, even if it was outdated? Or, if the real objective of the Air Service was to fly airplanes in combat, to bomb the enemy's resources and knock his fighters out of the air, should not precedence go to airmen with experience in this sort of thing? It was truly a vicious circle, for everyone wanted to be the leader and all too many were willing to elevate their own position by deliberately downgrading the others. Under the circumstances, one of the great misfortunes of the period was almost automatic; with the rapid changes in personnel came drastic and disruptive changes in policy.

In a way, this is what took place when General Foulois took command of the Air Service, A.E.F. Curiously enough, this airman, unlike his predecessor, did not regard the American pilots already flying for France as "capital with which to build," and hence was in no hurry to get them into American uniform. As Hall and Nordhoff, both of whom were involved, summed it up: "Very little interest was shown in the Lafayette Flying Corps, and although it was repeatedly brought to the attention of those responsible that serious complications would arise unless the men were commissioned as recommended by the Board, no heed was paid to the warning."[50]

Edmond C. Genêt.

Genêt's funeral, April 1917. *Courtesy of the United States Air Force.*

Hoskier and Dressy's funeral. *Courtesy of Charles H. Dolan II.*

The airfield at Ham, with Lufbery supervising the refueling of his SPAD VII.
*Courtesy of the United States Air Force.*

Chaudun, July 1917. *Front row, left to right:* Masson, Bigelow, Johnson, Thaw, Thenault, Parsons, Hewitt, Willis, Haviland. *Second row, left to right:* Bridgeman, Rockwell, Jones, Peterson, Dugan, MacMonagle, Lovell, de Maison Rouge.

Presentation of American flag to the Lafayette Escadrille, 7 July 1917. *Courtesy of the United States Air Force.*

Andrew Courtney Campbell, minus the lower left wing, 7 July 1917.

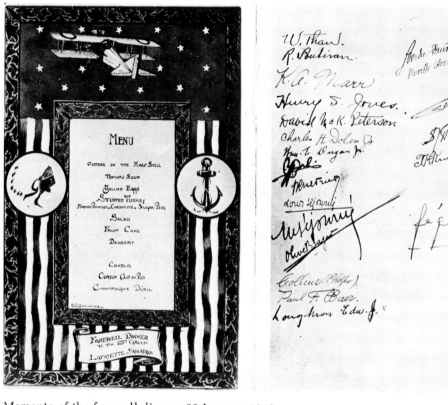

Memento of the farewell dinner, 22 January 1918.

Lafayette Escadrille Memorial. *Courtesy of Paul A. Rockwell.*

Crypt of the Lafayette Escadrille Memorial. *Courtesy of Paul A. Rockwell.*

Paul A. Rockwell and Charles H. Dolan II, France, July 1967. *Courtesy Ministère des Armées de l'Air.*

General Foulois was not particularly anxious or even willing to follow the recommendations of the Board, which had submitted its report more than a month before. Thus a letter which arrived from a French commander requesting that the recommended commission of a particular airman be revoked served as a pretext for bringing the whole report into question. As a result, the French commanders were again asked to evaluate the Americans serving under them, giving details on such matters as discipline, capabilities as a pilot, behavior at the front, and leadership potential.[51] According to Hall and Nordhoff, this was a "serious and absolutely unnecessary cause of delay, as in all cases, except [one], the new reports were found to correspond with the recommendations of the Board."[52]

This setback naturally delayed the scheduled transfer of the airmen, but the greatest misfortune was that it came at a time when the French were already releasing the Americans, as they had been urged to do by General Kenly and others. The result was chaos approaching disaster. The Americans technically had a release date when they could transfer, but only if the American Air Service could accept them. The Lafayette Escadrille itself was still an integral part of the Service Aéronautique. Its pilots had not been dropped from its roster, nor were they (or any of the other Americans flying for France, for that matter) free to leave the front. Their release being conditional upon their joining the American Air Service, the French were perfectly willing to charge with desertion anyone not living up to this obligation.[53] Those who attempted to hurry matters along by simply presenting themselves to the American authorities for acceptance met with ill success, as a frantic telegram from the American commander of the 6th A.I.C. to Dr. Gros clearly reveals.

The CO French school has asked me to let him know what to do with Americans that have been transferred from the French to the American Army here. They have no orders and I have not been instructed to take them over. Francis Gill, a pilot, has no orders and is not in uniform, but he is here as an officer. I request that I be notified as to what disposition to take of those who have already been transferred and are still here. French CO requests me to notify him.

At this point General Foulois made another serious mistake, which, in the words of Major Hoffman, one of the members of the Board, "led to great discontent and did more to harm progress than anything we know." Taking the recommendations of rank as outlined by the Board in October, the general reduced them by one grade in every case.[55]

This, of course, was a bombshell! However necessary it may have been in General Foulois's eyes, the fact remained that his predecessor had given the men to understand that they would receive certain grades, and on this basis they had requested their releases from the French. Now General Foulois, who had been a major himself only months before, was unwilling to honor that agreement, at a time when the releases from the French army had been requested and were being processed.[56] To the airmen, viewing the unsettled and indeed hectic condition of the American Air Service, where rank was being given freely to favorites of those in power, it seemed a most arbitrary and unfair decision. The "ill air" that Commandant Féquant had mentioned in September now gushed forth as a whirlwind of resentment and hostility. Wrote one embittered pilot to a close friend,

Yesterday they asked us to design American cockades for our machines and the row was on.—When the dust settled the Capitaine had discovered that the entire escadrille intended to fly under French colors as long as we are French—that they do not intend to lose their identity—that American officers now training are not going to take charge of us until they are worthy of the responsibility—and lastly that the escadrille remains French until the questions of machines, mechaniciens, grades and officers under French colors are satisfactory. They are not going to hang anything on us![57]

Men like Edwin C. Parsons in the SPA-124, Austin Crehore in the SPA-94, and Reginald Sinclaire in the SPA-68, who did not request releases from the French army for one reason or another, considered themselves fortunate. Those who did go through with the transfer would don the American uniform somewhat reluctantly, deeply hurt by what seemed to them truly "shabby treatment."[58]

General Foulois had not dropped the idea of the transfer, preferring to pursue the matter in his own way and at his own pace. He had committed some unfortunate errors in the process, none of them intentionally, but his name would henceforth be anathema to the Lafayette pilots and others. On the other hand, he did arrange for the Americans in "limbo" to be paid by the United States army, and he had formulated in his own mind the direction he wanted to take. Primarily, this involved the activation of a single squadron which would come under the American colors but which would continue to operate under French control. This latter point, in his view, demanded a written agreement between the two countries, outlining the exact status of the squadron as to supplies, control, discipline, etc. He had no intention of grouping the more than one hundred American pilots then flying for France into four or five squadrons as some had advocated. One would be enough to get the American flag in the air. The surplus airmen could be utilized in the Air Service elsewhere, "leavening of the lump," as it were.[59] Only the Lafayette Squadron, which had already created a great name for itself, would remain as a unit, thereby gaining the distinction of becoming America's first combat squadron at the front.

## The Agreement

At long last, after months of confusion and indecision, in January 1918, the American Air Service began to commission pilots into the U.S. Army. Some were sent off to work at some training center, or, as in the case of William Thaw and those who would be members of the new squadron, to prepare for the day of activation. At the same time, work was continuing on the written agreement, which first appeared in draft form in January 1918. There were numerous changes as objections were voiced here and there, but by 10 February, this too was ready.

In essence, it provided for an American squadron composed of eighteen pilots, commanded by William Thaw, and comprising all of the fourteen Americans then flying with the SPA-124 with the exception of Lufbery, whose new rank as major and whose skill as a fighter pilot brought him back to the training center at Issoudun. Also Edwin C. Parsons, a future ace, was not included. He flatly refused to leave the French. To fill these two gaps and bring the squadron up to strength, new men, gathered from among the pilots in other squadrons, were to be brought in.

The agreement, known officially as the "Conventions Concerning the Creation of American Escadrille, called 'Escadrille Lafayette,' " verified the fact that the old Lafayette squadron would be "considered" French until the actual time of the transfer. It then specified the exact terms under which the transfer could be effected. Captain Thenault would represent the French and Major Thaw the Americans in transferring the aircraft and in the actual changing of command; the French would provide spare parts and gasoline as well as the airplanes, but a careful reckoning was to be kept so that reimbursement could be made later on. The agreement also specified that the squadron would be composed entirely of American flying and nonflying personnel, although the French were willing to let French soldiers and mechanics remain and instruct their incoming American counterparts. Thaw, as commander of the squadron, would have no jurisdiction over these Frenchmen, they being the responsibility of the nearest French unit, to which they would technically be assigned. Thaw would "have with regard to the American personnel all the attributes and prerogatives of his rank, such as they are outlined in the regulations of the American Army," but the commander of Groupe de Combat 13, to which the squadron would be assigned, would have the same authority over the squadron in "tactical matters and in general discipline," as he had over his regular French escadrilles. Finally the right was reserved for the French Chief of Aeronautics, G.Q.G., to transfer the squadron to another group if he so desired, with all of these arrangements to come to an end as soon as the squadron was claimed by the American Air Service.[60]

When this "convention" was accepted by General Foulois on 14 February the way was open at last for the Lafayette Escadrille to become the first and only American combat squadron at the front. It was to keep that distinction for several months.

Thus, on 18 February 1918, the long-awaited marriage between the famed Lafayette Escadrille and the American Air Service was finally consummated. At the higher levels, both on the French and American sides, the transfer was considered largely a paper affair, and no formal ceremony between the two governments took place. There was, however, a brief exchange of command ceremony at a dinner given the American volunteers by Commandant Féquant and his fellow French officers of Groupe de Combat 13.

In the speeches delivered on that occasion, there may have been some fourth of July rhetoric. There usually is at such affairs. But there is no reason to doubt the sincerity of Féquant's and Thenault's heartfelt expressions of admiration for the men of the Lafayette Escadrille. The French would later demonstrate in a hundred ways the gratitude felt for these men who voluntarily risked their lives for a national cause not their own, and who made their squadron a veritable symbol of devotion to duty and self-sacrifice.

The dinner party was also a little bit sad. In submitting, the bride had forfeited her name and much of her identity. The Lafayette Escadrille of recent and happy memory became henceforth the 103d Pursuit Squadron.

# 8    The Legacy

For reasons almost too obvious to miss, the Lafayette Escadrille was legendary long before its formal existence came to an end with a brief ceremony and a dinner of oysters on the half shell. The uniqueness of the "vanguard of American volunteers," the initiative of individuals in volunteering to fly for France before their own country was involved in the war, and the unusually high caliber of most of its members easily set them apart. Then too, the glamour associated with aviation in the Great War, a consequence of the grim contest on the ground, high-lighted combat flying all out of proportion to its military value.

There is ample evidence that the members of the Lafayette Escadrille relished the recognition, but differed significantly with the public at large on the reasons for it. To the public, the glamour of World War aviation, with danger and daring the common denominators, was primary. The men of the Lafayette Escadrille, on the other hand, tended to judge the value of the squadron on the basis of their own motives for fighting. For most, and particularly for the early volunteers, the spirit of the Lafayette Escadrille was inseparably connected to their early perception of dangers, which to their view transcended national boun-daries. Thus, they fought not so much for the excitement and inevitable public recognition, but because their perceptions carried the moral obligation to fight. Their view coincided perfectly with that of General Henri Gouraud, Commander of the Front de Champagne, who had them in mind when he said, "When men who have no obligation to fight, who could not possibly be criticized if they did not fight, yet nonetheless decide upon their own individual initiative to risk their lives in defense of a cause they hold dear, then we are in the presence of true heroes. The young Americans who entered the *Légion Étrangére* and the *Escadrille Américaine* are in every sense heroes, and France owes them all the homage that word implies."[1]

The basic reasons for this remarkable disparity between the squadron's view of itself and the public perception of the unit are not hard to find. In general, the pilots stressed idealism, farsightedness, and moral courage, the same motives and characteristics that led so many of them to fight for France in the first place. And while not all Lafayette Escadrille pilots were idealists, all could appreciate the uniqueness of a squadron founded on such lofty motives. This is evident in the fact that the fliers invariably thought of themselves first and foremost as members of the special squadron and then as ordinary pilots flying for France.

On the other hand, except for the grateful French, the public by and large made little or no distinction between the Lafayette Escadrille and other aviation units. The unit was often mentioned in the lurid accounts of combat flying, not as a sterling vanguard of American volunteers or a group of idealists, but as a squadron of daring adventurers. Even then, the primary emphasis was on individuals rather than the squadron as a whole, in large part because only aviation provided the individual heroes so essential in wartime. Also, individuals, not units, made the best copy.

The same emphasis continued after the war when breathtaking drama and soaring sensationalism helped sell aviation books and articles. Moreover, the war discredited idealism, which, having helped elevate the war to the level of a crusade, was thought to have been an unwholesome spur to the now discredited war. Thus the survivors of the Lafayette Escadrille could not count on the public and the popular writers to preserve the tradition and spirit of the squadron. If the legacy of the squadron was to fit the image the survivors wanted, it was largely up to them to foster and preserve it.

Significantly, the survivors of the Escadrille failed in this endeavor, partly for lack of effort. And the lack of effort, in turn, seems to have stemmed from the lack of unit cohesion from 18 February 1918 to the Armistice, as well as in the postwar period. How it would have been had the unit continued to the Armistice and come out of the war intact, presumably to return home in a blaze of glory, is a matter of speculation. As it was, the Escadrille not only lost the continuing recognition it had received as an active combat unit, but the survivors themselves lost regular contact with each other.

As noted earlier, with the exception of Raoul Lufbery and Edwin Parsons, all Americans with the Lafayette Escadrille at the time of the transfer temporarily remained assigned to the 103d Pursuit Squadron. The American Air Service intended to use the fliers as flight and squadron commanders as soon as American units could use them. In this way some unit cohesion was maintained, but only for a short time. William Thaw, part of the heart of the squadron from its beginning, was given command of the 103d, but he left in August 1918 to take over the Third Pursuit Group. Meanwhile, David Petersen had joined the 94th Pursuit Squadron (he later took command of the 95th Squadron), Ray Bridgman had assumed command of the 22d Pursuit Squadron, and Dudley Hill took over the 128th Pursuit Squadron—he later commanded the Fifth Pursuit Group.[2] Henry Jones returned to the United States in June to serve as an instructor and test pilot. He was followed in short order by Charles H. Dolan II, the flier destined to be the last survivor of the Lafayette Escadrille. Only Robert Soubiran and Robert "Doc" Rockwell remained with the 103d to the end of the war, with each getting the chance to command the squadron before the Armistice. Christopher Ford, the last man to enter his name on the rolls of the Lafayette Escadrille, would have stayed with the 103d to the end of the war, but he was shot down and captured by the Germans in October 1918.

There is evidence that all former members of the Lafayette Escadrille active at the front after the transfer visited one another in their respective squadrons as time and circumstances permitted. Such visits were relatively rare, however. The war continued to place heavy demands on the pilots, particularly now that most of them had command positions.[3]

On 19 May 1918, a grave tragedy befell the survivors of the Lafayette Escadrille, when Raoul Lufbery jumped to his death after his plane caught fire during combat with a German aircraft. It is quite likely that had Lufbery lived, he might have made some difference in fostering a better image of the Lafayette Escadrille after the war. He had fought longer than Eddie Rickenbacker, the most famous American ace to come out of the war, and given the same criteria for confirming kills that Air Service pilots had, easily would have ended the war as the top American ace. He would certainly have received many if not most of the accolades given to Rickenbacker. Indeed, the survivors would surely have initiated a concerted effort to get him the Medal of Honor instead of Rickenbacker. As it was, an effort was made to get him the award posthumously, since, as Charles Dolan, who knew both men well, put it in a letter trying to enlist support, "Lufbery was twice the man Rickenbacker was."[4]

Surprisingly, the survivors of the Lafayette Escadrille displayed even less cohesion after the war than they had during the February–November 1918 period. Several reasons could be offered for this, but the main one seems to be disillusionment with the war itself, a feeling relatively common to veterans of the Great War, and apparently particularly acute among those who fought for idealistic motives. While one could suggest that William Dugan's return to Cuba and Didier Masson's decision to live out his life in Central America were examples of men returning to their old ways, there is evidence that few of the Lafayette fliers remained untainted by the war. A number refused to discuss the war or to have any association with their former comrades in arms. James Norman Hall, one of the elite, moved to Tahiti, and even William Thaw, a model of stability and common sense during the war, had trouble adjusting. He toyed with prospecting for a time, and got involved in lighter-than-air flying. He avoided publicity, however, and never regained his love for flying. He died at age thirty-four in relative obscurity as an insurance broker in Pittsburgh.[5]

Easily the most tragic victim of the Lafayette pilots surviving the war was Ray Claffin Bridgman, the scholarly idealist who fought well on the western front even though he hated war. He was among those who refused all association with his former comrades, and as war clouds again began gathering over Europe, he joined some fellow-traveler organizations promising peace. Disillusioned on that front, too, and dismayed by the aftereffects of World War II, the apparently stable professor of history at New York University took his own life in 1951 by jumping from the Staten Island ferry.[6]

## Battling the "Ringers"

Lacking unit cohesion between the wars, the survivors of the Lafayette Escadrille did little to actively display and promote the spirit of their squadron before the American people. Even so, all survivors looked with dismay on the growing number of individuals who, for one reason or another, falsely claimed membership in their elite unit. Efforts to stem the tide of ringers, as they were called, were many but inherently reactive. Not designed to present the true image of the squadron, they aimed at preserving the remaining portion of that image.

Some of the ringers were honest and upright men who had flown with the Lafayette Flying Corps, that unofficial brotherhood of all Americans who had flown for France in the Great War. Since the public almost invariably confused the Flying Corps with the Lafayette Escadrille, these men grew weary of making the distinction and tacitly accepted membership in the famous squadron. On the other hand, several members of the Flying Corps actively claimed membership in the Escadrille and, when in trouble, used the horrors of the war in general and their long service with the Lafayette Escadrille in particular as an excuse for bad behavior. An excellent but not exceptional example can be found in the foreword to Denison Kitchel's 1978 volume entitled *The Truth about the Panama Canal*. In writing the foreword, Representative John R. Rhodes tries to support Kitchel's credentials as a lawyer by citing a 1942 court martial case over which he had some jurisdiction. Kitchel, it seems, defended a military "officer" who faced no fewer than twenty-nine separate charges. The charges were not so much denied as excused, largely on the grounds that the defendant, in Rhodes's words, was a "flying officer of some note, a former member of the famous Lafayette Escadrille." For added measure, the defendant claimed to be the one who flew an airplane through the Arc de Triomphe during the Armistice celebrations, one of the several false claims that Rhodes, Kitchel, and the court apparently accepted at face value. Actually, the defendant had a track record of false claims, and a few minutes' research could easily have shown that one, at least—the claim about membership in the Lafayette Escadrille—was false. Instead, as Representative Rhodes puts it, "Kitchel did such a thorough job of preparation and such an outstanding job of presenting the evidence, bringing out the good side of his 'client' that the officer was acquitted on 28 of the 29 charges."[7]

As for numbers, the ringers seemed to multiply like descendants of those who came to America on the Mayflower. By the early 1930s more than four thousand had been identified, a hundredfold-plus increase over the actual membership. Claimants ranged from bums of the road to highly placed government officials, military personnel, and Hollywood personalities. Indeed, so many "survivors" of the Lafayette Escadrille appeared that some ringers sought special recognition by claiming to have been among the "original"members of the squadron or, better yet, among its founders.[8]

For obvious reasons, ringers are becoming increasingly rare. As of this writing, even the genuine survivors are down to one man. Still, it is not beyond the realm of possibility that someone, following the pattern of Walter Williams, who claimed to be the last survivor of the Civil War, will claim at a very advanced age to be the last of the Lafayette Escadrille. It is also possible that the claimant, like Williams, will be buried with full honors, even though there will be very little excuse for those providing the honors not to know that the claims are totally false. Indeed, it may well be that those promoting the truth will be castigated for their efforts, since the whole procedure, however tainted, can be passed off as representing a good thing.[9]

Overall, there was little the survivors and their friends could do to expose, let alone control, the number of ringers. The survivors were not organized, and it fell upon the more dedicated men, such as Rockwell, Parsons, Willis, and Dolan, to do what they could. For the most part, this consisted of letters to the editors of newspapers and magazines, exposing the ringers and offering the truth about the squadron. In one instance, Charles Dolan wrote *American Aviation Magazine*, saying that, "It seems no matter where we go in the world, we run into survivors who are 'Lafayette' heroes, and we are thoroughly disgusted with them and with the press for never having checked before." Dolan then went on to provide accurate details of the Escadrille and the Flying Corps, offering data as to numbers and giving the names of Escadrille members who had died and those who were still living.[10]

Dolan also made reference to the formation of a Lafayette Escadrille Corporation for the express purpose of protecting the name of the squadron. He did not state, however, that this organization was itself largely reactive, having been created to prevent a bar from exploiting the name during the 1939 New York World's Fair.[11]

In 1932 an incident occurred which promised to focus national attention on the ringer issue. In wooing and winning the consent of a woman from Charlotte, North Carolina, to be his wife, a young man claimed to be none other than Andrew Courtney Campbell, the reckless Lafayette Escadrille pilot who disappeared behind German lines in October 1917. He explained his fifteen-year disappearance by insisting that he had spent four years in a German hospital, suffering from wounds and amnesia. After a return to the States, he wandered around in a kind of daze until a fall from a freight train while taking part in the Veteran's bonus march on Washington restored his sagging memory. Pressed about his failure to contact anxious family and friends, he claimed that the war had left such a brutal imprint on his mind, he felt it best to sever old connections.[12]

The girl and her family accepted him at his word and proceeded with wedding plans on the condition that he marry under his "real" name. He agreed, which proved his undoing. The news services picked up the story. One announced that an "American Airman Reported Dead Wants to Get Married," adding that the ex-flier had written the French air ministry "to ask for a change in records."[13]

Convinced that another ringer had appeared, Rockwell, Parsons, and others joined forces. Rockwell, in Paris, got the French authorities working on the problem while Parsons, then with the F BI, mobilized resources available to him. So too did a German pilot names H. Andres, who announced through the Paris edition of the *Tribune* that he had shot Campbell down in October 1917, and had identified the body a few hours later through military papers carried by the downed flier. "I assume that some person is unrightfully misusing the name of the poor, brave flyer who died for his fatherland," Andres wrote, "and I cannot permit this."[14]

Eventually the truth won out. Using fingerprints processed by the F BI, the ringer proved to be one Clarence Stephen Wendler of Richmond, Virginia, an unstable malcontent who had deserted from the U.S. Navy in January 1920.[15]

The worldwide attention given the "new" Andrew Courtney Campbell did not do much to promote the real story of the Lafayette Escadrille. The survivors and their friends made efforts in this direction but the public quickly lost interest after the sensationalism died down. Besides, the efforts of the survivors were again largely reactive.

### The Attempts to Create a Second Lafayette Escadrille

In the distresses of 1939, when France again faced hostile German armies, two major efforts were made to create a second Lafayette Escadrille. One effort, led by Charles Sweeney, the former West Point cadet who had led the Americans in their march to the Hôtel de Ville in August 1914, was founded on the adventure and profit motives then evident in the China-based Flying Tigers. The other, led by Paul Rockwell and Harold B. Willis, both of whom had very close connections with the 1916–18 Escadrille, attempted to duplicate the devotion and self-sacrifice of the original. The latter endeavor, if successful, might have brought the spirit of the Lafayette Escadrille back into focus. As it was, both efforts failed, but for very different reasons.

Sweeney, who had picked up a reputation as a soldier of fortune between the wars, appeared in the Los Angeles area in the fall of 1939 with grandiose plans and a great deal of money.[16] His purpose, kept secret for the time being, was to enlist a number of American youths and send them to France via Canada.

Sweeney quickly enlisted the aid of Edwin C. Parsons. Then a writer and technical advisor on certain World War I aviation movies, Parsons agreed to help. As he later explained it, he had already proposed the idea to a couple of his old comrades, but, since "nothing definite had been started" and he was "really anxious to see the Escadrille tradition carried on," he willingly joined forces with Sweeney. "I had a very wide acquaintance among Southern California pilots," he wrote, "owing to my connection with several flying pictures and I passed the word. We had a quick response and, cautioning the boys about outside talk, we interviewed about thirty or forty at the hotel in Santa Monica, where Charley made his headquarters."[17]

While some of those interviewed showed "real interest" the "general attitude . . . was disappointing." "There was a definite lack of idealism or desire to get into action for the sake of a sister nation that had characterized the boys from 1914 on. Instead, the general attitude was, 'What's in it for me?' However, we finally lined up a substantial nucleus, with others to follow, and, to avoid premature publicity, took six or eight of them to Pasadena one night and put them on a Santa Fe train for the East and eventually Canada. They were provided with tickets and plenty of expense money."[18]

Since the United States government officially frowned on "recruiting for foreign governments"—a byproduct of U.S. "volunteers" in the Spanish Civil War—Sweeney and Parsons faced fines up to $1000, or a three-year prison term. To avoid detection and arrest, they used code names and warned the would-be fliers to keep quiet about the venture.[19]

In a way, the emphasis on secrecy proved their undoing. Some of the "recruits" neglected to tell their parents. One young man, for example, left the following note to explain his mysterious departure. "I have decided to take a little trip. . . . I have done nothing wrong. I am not running away from anybody or anything. I hope you will please forgive me. I am not taking any clothes because my job furnished them."[20] Anxious parents quickly sought federal help. The FBI intervened, as did the five uncles of one recruit. The latter intercepted the initial group on their way to Toronto and successfully removed "all but a couple of the boys" from the train. One "repentant" youth "told the whole story" and, as Parsons put it, "the fat was really in the fire."[21] Among other things, the Los Angeles papers had a grand time of it. Headlines announced, "ALLIES LURE L.A. BOYS INTO WAR AIR SERVICE," "PARENTS ASK G-MEN TO HALT RECRUITING BY FOREIGN AGENTS," and "NEW EVIDENCE REVEALS FOREIGN RECRUITING HERE."[22]

Sweeney and Parsons hurriedly left town, leading to more speculation about the "mystery men," their link to "big money circles" and "foreign governments." Parson, however, later expressed his belief that "the FBI could have nabbed us at any time they wanted, but someone apparently threw some water on the fire and neither of us was bothered."[23]

Meanwhile, Paul Rockwell and Harold Willis had taken steps to create a second Lafayette Escadrille. As early as the Munich crisis of 1938, they had cabled French authorities their willingness to sponsor such a unit "should war come." At the time, however, the French were uncertain about the implications of recent American declarations of neutrality and hence declined the offer.

After Germany invaded Poland in September 1939 and France again found herself at war, Rockwell and Willis renewed their offer. The French were thinking this offer over when the Sweeney scandal broke. Warned by the events in California, Rockwell and Willis fled. Rockwell arrived in Paris via Nova Scotia while Willis reached the same destination via Italy.[24]

In Paris, the two men found themselves among more than six hundred individuals and organizations applying for official permission to "conduct war charities and other forms of volunteer aid."[25] By this time, the French looked with favor on efforts aimed at social work and hospital relief. They were still fearful, however, that American combat units might clash with U.S. neutrality laws, and hence remained unwilling to approve such units.[26]

Undaunted, Rockwell and Willis set about recruiting old acquaintances and forming a committee to deal with French authorities. Col. Georges Thenault became an important member of that committee, as did Dr. Edmund Gros. There were, moreover, two important additions, men whose interest in the Lafayette Escadrille flowered after the Great War. One was Nelson Cromwell, a Paris-based lawyer of international fame. He had represented the de Lesseps Enterprise in the sale of de Lesseps' interests in a Panama canal to the United States. His personal interest in the Lafayette Escadrille had been amply manifest in his prime role in financing and building a postwar monument to the Lafayette Escadrille and the Lafayette Flying Corps in a Paris suburb.

Colonel Jacques Balsan was the other important recruit to the Rockwell-Willis committee. Balsan, who had an impressive record in World War I both as a flier and as a member of General Foch's staff, knew of the Lafayette Escadrille during the Great War, and at the time appreciated the record and motives of the squadron members. His appreciation for the squadron really flowered, however, after he met and married the recently divorced Duchess of Marlborough, a sister to the W. H. Vanderbilt who had financed the Lafayette Flying Corps.[27]

It was Balsan and Thenault who, more than any others, guided the Rockwell-Willis movement for a second Lafayette Escadrille through the vital offices in the French ministries of War and Foreign Affairs. Rockwell also assisted in this endeavor, and both Rockwell and Willis worked through the Trench and Air Association of American Volunteer Combatants in the French Army, 1914–1918, an important and powerful organization of which both were members.

These connections, together with the American Ambulance Service, an officially approved and growing organization which not only became a good recruiting base but also provided a leadership position for Harold Willis, were sufficient. By early May 1940 some forty idealistic American volunteers had been recruited for the Second Lafayette Escadrille. The new unit, it seemed, would be closely patterned after the original one. Moreover, facing increasing danger from the Germans, the French government had given its approval. The Trench and Air Association was authorized to announce the coming formation of the squadron at a special meeting with the French Aero Club on 10 May. Formal announcement by the French government was scheduled for 15 June.[28]

Given a few more weeks, the squadron would have become a reality, though perhaps a short-lived one. The Germans began their massive invasion of France on 10 May and on 15 June their victorious forces entered Paris. Rockwell and Willis were not around to witness the humiliation. They had fled Paris four days earlier.[29]

To those Americans and Frenchmen who hoped that a second Lafayette Escadrille, flying for France in World War II, would revitalize and preserve the legacy of the first one, the near miss of May–June 1940 was a great disappointment.[30] Moreover, since the fall of France precluded further attempts, the legacy of the World War I squadron in the United States more or less drifted with the ebb and flow of public opinion. And how far this public concept diverged from the true spirit of the squadron is well manifested in a remarkable movie released by Warner Brothers studios in 1958.

## The Warner Brothers' Abomination

Before its release, the Warner Brothers' movie entitled *The Lafayette Escadrille* appeared to have impressive credentials. Its director was none other than William W. Wellman, who had flown for France in the Escadrille SPA-87 from December 1917 to March 1918. Wellman knew some of the pilots then flying for the Lafayette Escadrille and could hardly have missed knowing about the spirit of the squadron. Moreover, Wellman was an excellent producer, having won an Academy Award for *Wings*, a 1926 aviation classic.

As part of the publicity for the film, Warner Brothers stated categorically that Wellman had flown with the Lafayette Escadrille, a claim Wellman apparently made no effort to correct. Indeed, the production notes issued by Warner Brothers not only stated that Wellman was a "former member of the Lafayette Escadrille," they insisted that the story was his and was "based on his own experiences." Consequently, "characters and events are for the most part authentic."[31]

Months before the movie premiered, however, a Hollywood actress told Paul Rockwell that Wellman was making a "dirty" movie about the Escadrille. Rockwell passed the information on to the survivors and then joined in directing a number of protests at Wellman. The producer, however did not take the protests kindly. In January 1957, more than a year before the premier of the movie, he told one of his old comrades: "Look Austen, no one [of the survivors] has ever seen a God damned foot of it. It's ridiculous. Whatever you've heard, they have no clips, no scenes at all. I can only tell you this. There's nothing in the picture—

whether it's a good picture or a bad picture—there's nothing in the picture that every one of those guys won't be very, very proud of."[32]

Unfortunately, the movie turned out to be even worse than the rumors indicated. It had some good clips of flying and fighting, but the story was completely out of harmony with the spirit of the Lafayette Escadrille. The hero of the film was an unstable, hot-tempered young man who fled his Boston home after stealing a car and injuring a newsboy in his getaway. A fugitive from justice, he found passage to Europe as a stowaway, although that did not prevent him from meeting three young men on the ship who were going to France to fly with the Lafayette Escadrille. In Paris, he joined them in wenching—promptly falling in love with a prostitute—and in enlisting to fly for the French.

With the Lafayette Escadrille, the hero's hot temper again got him into trouble. Detesting drill and the individual who was teaching it, he angrily struck the "officer." Arrested for this insubordination, he escaped from his forced confinement under cover of a fight staged for that purpose by his comrades in the squadron. Now a deserter, he compounded his error by killing a French soldier in an effort to acquire his uniform.

The hero then hid out with his Parisian girlfriend, paying his way by working as a pimp for one of the local brothels. During his duties as a procurer, he met and won the favor of an American general who made him a sergeant and directed him to fly with the Americans. Success in combat restored his honor and self-esteem.

The movie premiered in Washington, North Carolina, on 28 February 1958. The site was chosen to honor James H. Baugham, who had flown for France in Escadrilles N-157 and SPA-98 from December 1917 to July 1918, when he was fatally wounded in combat.[33] A. Thomas Stewart, the mayor of Washington, advertised the festivities with letterhead stationery, using both the famed Indian head insignia of the Lafayette Escadrille and a photograph of Baugham. The letterhead contained the statement "Washington's own Jim Baugham was Lafayette Escadrille's youngest member."[34] Concurrently, North Carolina Governor Luther Hodges proclaimed 28 February 1958 as "Lafayette Escadrille Day."[35]

As part of the promotions scheme, all of the surviving pilots of the Lafayette Escadrille were invited to participate in the festivities; Paul Rockwell was also invited. This proved a major miscalculation. With the exception of Henry S. Jones, they all turned it down, usually with strong words about the way the squadron was being exploited. Charles Dolan's response to Mayor Stewart was typical. "The eight survivors of the Lafayette Escadrille N-124 are opposed to the exploitation of their unit by Mr. Wellman and associates, solely for their financial benefit."[36] Rockwell wrote a number of letters, including one to the *Raleigh* (North Carolina) *News and Observer*. "I know Jim Baugham's family well, and not one of them has ever claimed that Jim belonged to the original Lafayette Escadrille. They have his official papers, his numerous medals awarded him by France, and they don't have to make any [false] claims for their hero aviator relative."[37] Other letters proved even more biting. In a letter to the *Wayneville Mountaineer*, Rockwell called the movie the "worst I have ever seen. . . . I consider Wellman's 'Lafayette Escadrille' low and subversive in that it helps destroy the morals and the morale of our youth. In producing this movie, Hollywood hit an all-time low."[38] Concurrently, the *Ashville Citizen Times* carried a letter from Edwin Parsons, in which he stated: "The trashy story of the film 'Lafayette Escadrille' in no way represents or recreates the conduct, gallant personnel or true spirit of the real Lafayette Escadrille. The living can speak for themselves, but I feel that it is an insult to the memory of our dead."[39] The same issue of the *Citizen Times* quoted Barbara Haviland Weiler, the daughter of former Lafayette Escadrille member Willis Haviland, as saying: "There was certainly more to the Lafayette Escadrille squadron than insubordination, desertion, bar lounging, and harlot seeking, as featured in the Warner Brothers' film. I feel that the movie is stupid and degrading. The name and fame of the Lafayette Escadrille is being exploited to draw people in to see a very poor movie which in no way lives up to its title."[40]

The anti-Wellman movie campaign launched by the survivors of the Lafayette Escadrille had some effect. Rockwell, Parsons, and Willis got the movie banned in France, and they no doubt hurt commercial efforts in the States.[41] They apparently jarred Wellman's conscience as well, for the producer responded to my 1960 inquiry with the claim that he never wanted the movie associated with the Lafayette Escadrille. He had intended, he said, to call it "C'est la Guerre," but was overruled by officials of Warner Brothers Studios.[42]

In retrospect, the movie has much to say about the legacy of the Lafayette Escadrille in the United States. Apparently the Warner Brothers Studios produced the movie without much fear of challenge and, as far as the public was concerned, they were quite right. The movie still makes the rounds of the late shows, and like others with strong interest in the Lafayette Escadrille, I inevitably get a few calls from well-meaning friends, sharing the news that a good movie is on about the Lafayette Escadrille and "it would be a shame to miss it."

## The Founding of the Lafayette Escadrille N-124 Society

In early June 1960, five of the eight surviving members of the Lafayette Escadrille gathered at Paul Rockwell's home in Asheville, North Carolina. It was an exclusive reunion, the only one held by the survivors and one which outsiders could hardly hope to penetrate. Only two non-squadron members were allowed full access to the meetings. I was one. The other was Capt. Louis Richard, the commander of the French Lafayette Escadron, the squadron then carrying on the tradition of the original Lafayette Escadrille.

The reunion was a festive occasion, full of laughter and stories. But it also had its serious moments. One was a meeting in which the survivors formed the Lafayette Escadrille N-124 Society. Patterned in part on the famed Society of the Cincinnati, the Society approved a constitution which stressed both the "spirit of the original squadron" and a pattern for the future. The spirit was reflected in the first paragaraph.

The Escadrille N-124, officially named the Lafayette Escadrille by the Government of France, was a unique fighting unit, and won a special place in history during the first of the great world conflicts. Its American pilots were bound to the Nation they served not by ties of birth or citizenship, but by those indefinable ones of gratitude, admiration and affection. When they gained immortal fame for the Escadrille their own country was neutral and their activities were frowned upon officially by homeland authorities. America's pioneers in aerial warfare, they stood apart from the great mass of their compatriots, and blazed the trail for others to follow in 1917.[43]

The constitution also outlined two basic purposes for the Society. One was to "perpetuate the remembrances of those days when [the pilots] acted outside the mandates of their Government and fought for a Cause in which they believed." The other was to "foster the mutual affections and bonds of friendship which have been formed under common danger and cemented by the blood of their beloved comrades." Concurrently, the constitution listed some impressive objectives for the members of the Society. They were urged to maintain "an unalterable determination to promote and cherish those ties of affection and friendship between France and the United States," and to render "permanent the deep affection and spirit of solidarity subsisting among the pilots [of the squadron]."

The issue of ringers and the other misconceptions about the Lafayette Escadrille also came up at the reunion. As a result, the Society's constitution manifests a determination to give "incessant attention to preserve inviolate the good name of the Escadrille," and to do so with "prompt and public protest when any attempt is made to exploit the name for personal or commerical gain." And there was something else:

The Society shall endeavor to see that the history of the Lafayette N-124 be accurately written according to official records and proven facts, and continue protests against misleading claims, statements, moving pictures, newspaper and newspaper articles, books, possible TV series and radio misinterpretations. Its members will provide newspaper men and other writers correct data relating to the Lafayette Escadrille N-124 whenever occasion arises, and by thus cooperating with persons interested, assure that history be truthfully presented and recorded.

The Society arranged for its perpetuation by providing succession of one relative for each original member. Initially this was to come through the eldest male line or, failing that, the next male line, and so on. Membership would pass to the female line only when the male lines had failed.

Because of its perpetuation policy, the Lafayette Escadrille N-124 Society still exists, even though at this writing all of the World War I participants save Charles H. Dolan II and Paul Rockwell have died. So far, the Society has not prospered as its founders intended. Apparently the motivation of the descendants, for the most part, is less than that which brought either the squadron or the Society into being.

## The Tradition of the Lafayette Escadrille in France

French appreciation for the Lafayette Escadrille of 1916–18 and the legacy it left in that country stands in stark contrast to the confusion and apathy of the American people towards the squadron. Viewed in retrospect, the basic reason for this contrast is obvious. Since the Lafayette pilots acted as individuals and in no way reflected the official policy of the United States government or the general will of the

American people, they could be accepted by Americans as a whole only as impetuous heroes of aviation. To have accepted them as exemplars of perceptiveness, moral courage, and devotion to a "just and noble cause" was to accept the view that those who held back were inherently less perceptive and less courageous than the volunteers. In other words, they could not accept the Lafayette Escadrille on its own terms without in some degree discrediting themselves.

The French, on the other hand, had every reason to accept the American pilots as heroes of the first order. Though few in number, they came during France's greatest struggle and in some of her darkest hours. They thus served not only as a beacon of hope, but also as a sterling certification that the cause of France, as Kiffin Rockwell once phrased it, was indeed "the cause of humanity, the most noble of all causes." As a result, the squadron inherently had an aura of grandeur about it. That aura, together with the unusually high caliber and remarkable dedication of its members gave France a group of heroes and legends the country could happily cherish and willingly adopt as a special part of its history. Thus it is not surprising that the French have kept the spirit of the Lafayette Escadrille alive, nourishing it through an elite fighter squadron that carries the name and tradition of the original Escadrille. It is also nourished through a variety of monuments, ceremonies, and a multitude of courtesies toward those who represent the squadron of 1916–18.

In 1920, the French Armée de l'Air officially designated the newly created 7th squadron of the 35th Aviation Regiment as the heir to the name and tradition of the original Lafayette Escadrille. As explained in a publication by the French Ministry of War, the step was designed to preserve the "glorious traditions" of the original unit while serving as a reminder of the "best example of Franco-American friendship since the American Revolution."[44]

A series of reorganizations just prior to the opening shots of World War II resulted in the transfer of the N-124 tradition to the 1st Escadrille of the 2/5 Groupe de Chasse. At the same time, the 2d Escadrille of this unit was given the name and tradition of the SPA-167, the *Cignones* (Storks), easily one of France's most famous fighter units of World War I.[45] It was a fitting combination. In bringing the famous Sioux Indian head insignia together with that of the Stork, the French could hardly have paid the original Lafayette Escadrille a higher tribute.

The "Lafayette Escadrille" and the "Storks" formed an integral part of French resistance to the massive German invasion of May 1940. A pilot belonging to the Lafayette was honored as the first French flier to bring down a German plane during the war, and, in the few short weeks before France fell, the combined unit received credit for no less than sixteen victories.[46]

The stunning German successes against France forced the 2/5 to move to Casablanca, where it remained until the U.S. invasion of North Africa in November 1942. Commanded by the Vichy government to oppose the American landings, it did so until its base was overrun.

Two Americans with very close connections with the original Lafayette Escadrille were among the American forces occupying French North Africa. One was Col. Harold B. Willis, the Lafayette pilot who, with Edward Hinkle, had designed the Indian head insignia in 1917. The other was Paul Rockwell, who only 2½ years earlier had worked with Willis in attempting to form a second Lafayette Escadrille in France. It could hardly have been more opportune, for both would have a significant role in revitalizing the French squadron.

Visiting the French air base at St. Denis du Sid shortly after it fell to the Americans, Colonel Willis was astonished to see his old insiginia on French aircraft. Pursuing his discovery, he asked to see the squadron commander, only to be told he was not available: "You Americans shot him down two days ago."[47]

Colonel Willis forthwith conceived the idea of equipping the "liberated" French Lafayette Escadrille with American aircraft and having it fly with the Allied forces. As chief of the French Liaison Section of the Allied Air Forces in North Africa, his voice was a powerful one, particularly after he managed to get Rockwell as his assistant.[48] Rockwell was particularly well known to the French, having won their unfailing admiration and trust over the years. In any event, the obstacles were soon overcome and on 20 December 1942 General James Doolittle, Commander of the U.S. 12th Air Force, issued the appropriate order. It stated that the "Lafayette Escadrille" was to receive twenty-five P-40 aircraft for "training and combat purposes." Moreover, "the entire French group will be under the operational control of the French and the French only, although all missions will be coordinated through proper American and British control channels."[49]

Initially, the new unit went by its official designation, the 33rd Group of the 12th Air Force. Five days after Doolittle's order, however, this oversight was corrected and the unit was officially designated the Group La Fayette, a recognition not only of its past but also of the role it was to play during the remaining months of the war. The Group La Fayette performed admirably in the months long Tunisian campaign. It then flew coastal surveillance in the western Mediterranean for almost a year. Beginning in early May 1944, however, it flew the heavier and more powerful P-47 fighters in interdiction missions against German communications and supply lines in Italy. From September 1944 to the end of the war it was back on French soil, again opposing German air forces.[50]

Returned to the French Armée de l'Air after the war, the French Lafayette Escadrille maintained its status as one of France's most elite fighter units. Among other things, it gained more combat experience in the Indochina and Algerian conflicts, and, at one point, represented the French Air Force in an international air show in Zurich, Switzerland.[51]

The French version of the Lafayette Escadrille still exists as an elite unit with a glorious tradition. Pilots are eager to enter it, even though there is a six-month probationary period before full acceptance. And that, in turn, is celebrated with appropriate ceremonies, complete with American Indian motif and dress.[52]

In addition to its ongoing emphasis on an elite fighter squadron, the French maintain and nourish the legacy of the 1916–18 Lafayette Escadrille through a variety of acknowledgments, celebrations, and monuments. Recognition ranges from simple pilgrimages to where some of the pilots fell or are buried—often with fresh flowers left as a token of appreciation—to honors that have the aura of a solemn memorial. In 1937, for example, ten members of the French Cabinet and fifty members of the Parliament gathered at Luxeuil-les-Bains, where the Lafayette Escadrille first began operations in April 1916. Their express purpose was to pay homage to the memory of the Escadrille, and for some that included a visit to the burial place of Kiffin Rockwell, one of the first Lafayette pilots to give his life for France.[53]

From a number of commemorative ceremonies, the French feeling for the Lafayette Escadrille, particularly on the part of the military, may best be found in the pomp and circumstance surrounding the unveiling of a monument to the Escadrille at Luxeuil in July 1967. An elaborate affair, it took more than a year to prepare. It was particularly significant, however, for surviving Escadrille pilots were invited as guests of the French government. Paul Rockwell was also invited, and he, along with Charles Dolan, represented the squadron. In a letter written a few days thereafter, Paul Rockwell described the event:

No people on earth could have treated us better or shown greater gratitude. The ceremony at Luxeuil . . . was magnificent. The top names in French military aviation were present, including many of my French comrades of the North Africa–Italy–South of France campaigns. General Maurin, present C-in-C of the French Air Force, for example, was a captain commanding the Escadrille Navarre in Morocco when I first met him in 1942. The USAF was well represented: General Preston who commands all our Air Forces Europe, the General commanding the 17th AF in Germany, a General and band from the 16th AF (Spain) etc., etc. General Huertaux, greatest living World War I ace was on hand, looking well despite his more than 80 years.

The Monument to the Escadrille Lafayette at the Luxeuil Base is most handsome and dignified: Carl Dolan and I unveiled it. This ceremony was followed by a banquet at the Base for over 300 guests. Carl and I went from ceremony to ceremony, and one *champagne d'honneur* after the other. I was tired at midnight, but happy.[54]

It remains to be noted that part of the visible reminders of Lafayette Escadrille in France are the result of cooperation between the French government and a community of Americans who, at one time or another, lived or fought in France and came to love that country as their own. The civilian portion of that community, represented by people like Dr. Edmund Gros, Nelson Cromwell, and the Vanderbilts is well known on both sides of the Atlantic. The historic Trench and Air Association of American Volunteer Combatants in the French Army 1914–1918, while less well known, was also an important part of that community, and in some ways was a manifestation of the forces that gave birth to the Lafayette Escadrille.

Evidence of this bridge between France and America can be found in the French-owned National Museum of Franco-American Cooperation at Blerancourt. One portion of this palace, once a royal residence, contains momentos and artifacts relating to military cooperation between the two countries. Within this wing, one room is devoted exclusively to the Lafayette Escadrille and the Lafayette Flying Corps. Among other things, this room holds the long-empty "Bottle of Death" which once contained the eighty-year-old whiskey Paul Rockwell gave in celebration of his brother's first victory.[55]

Easily the most impressive and famous monument to the Lafayette

Escadrille and the spirit of those Americans who flew for France during the Great War can be found in a Paris suburb. It, too, is the result of the cooperative effort. The French government donated the land while the Foundation du Memorial de l'Escadrille Lafayette, an organization established and led by prominent members of the Franco-American community, arranged the financing and construction.[56]

The dedication of this monument on 4 July 1928 was designed, in part, to summarize the history and the legacy of the Lafayette Escadrille, and, to a lesser degree, the follow-on Americans who flew for France. Myron T. Herrick, the former U.S. ambassador to France, presided. Dr. Edmund Gros and Commandant Georges Thenault also addressed the huge crowd. Paul Painleve, the French minister of war, was the concluding speaker.

As part of the ceremony a special testimonial by Marechal Ferdinand Foch, the supreme commander of all Allied forces on the western front at the end of the war, was presented to the audience. It read as follows:

On the 26th of April 1777, Lafayette embarked at the Point-de-Grave to place his sword and the services of his companions at the disposal of Washington. His spontaneous act was the initial cause of the participation of France in the War of American Independence.

From the very commencement of the Great War, volunteers from the United States flew to the aid of France and of the liberty of the world. On the 20th of April 1916, these pioneers grouped themselves under the French Tricolor to form an American Escadrille."

Their action, spontaneous like that of Lafayette, was the signal for the forward movement of the whole United States toward France.

All honor to these heroes of the American Escadrille, whose bravery I well know, for having so nobly reciprocated the visit which Lafayette paid to their ancestors.[57]

# Notes

## I: The Genesis of the Lafayette Escadrille

1. John R. Bolling, comp., *Chronology of Woodrow Wilson*, pp. 191–92.
2. Telegram, Minister of Foreign Affairs to the French Ambassador, Washington, D.C., 22 June 1915. Sterling Memorial Library, Yale University.
3. Edwin W. Morse, *The Vanguard of American Volunteers*, p. 132.
4. Paul L. Hervier, *The American Volunteers with the Allies*, p. 113.
5. Society of World War I Aero Historians, *Cross and Cockade Journal* (Spring 1961): 45–46, 63. This issue is devoted entirely to the Lafayette Escadrille.
6. *War Letters of Kiffin Yates Rockwell*, p. xxi. The preface to this volume was written by Paul A. Rockwell, Kiffin's brother.
7. *Atlanta Journal*, 4 August 1914; Paul A. Rockwell, interview, 7 November 1959.
8. Paul A. Rockwell, *American Fighters in the Foreign Legion*, pp. 3, 4.
9. Ibid., p. 6.
10. *New York Herald Tribune*, 13 March 1948.
11. Quoted in the preface of Rockwell, *American Fighters*.
12. Ibid., p. xiv.
13. This law, H.R. 24122 of the 59th Congress, is discussed in J. V. Best's "Status of Americans Fighting under Foreign Flag," pp. 127–31.
14. Colonel T. Bentley Mott, *Myron T. Herrick: Friend of France*, p. 144.
15. Ambassador Herrick helped organize the American Relief Clearing House, which had included the offer of pilots and airplanes to the French among its "humanitarian" activities. See the *New York Herald* (European Edition) 7 October 1915.
16. Alvey A. Adee to Joseph W. Ganson, 27 August 1915. Record Group 851/22/GA. State Department Section, Archives of the United States.
17. George C. Sharp to his son George, 15 March 1963. This letter, written in reply to some inquiries by young George in my behalf, was graciously made available to me in its entirety.
18. Paul A. Rockwell to me, 15 March 1960. The conspicuous absence of materials in the State Department Section of the National Archives dealing with the American Legionnaires and aviators indicates that the matter of their enlistments was simply not discussed, at least in normal channels. Usually, newspaper clippings dealing with Americans abroad were included in the diplomatic pouches. There are very few dispatches and no clippings in the U.S. National Archives dealing with the American volunteers.
19. *Cross and Cockade Journal* (Spring 1961), p. 46. "William C. Thaw II," *État Signaletique et des Services*, Class 1914, no. L.M.: 5.503. A typescript of this important document was graciously provided me by the French Ministry of War.
20. Irving J. Newman, "A Biography of Colonel Thaw II," p. 281; Edwin C. Parsons, *The Great Adventure*, p. 11. Parsons' book was republished in 1963 under the title, *I Flew with the Lafayette Escadrille*.

21. Col. Georges Thenault, *l'Escadrille Lafayette*, p. 10.

22. Rockwell, *American Fighters*, pp. 6–9.

23. Ibid., pp. 19–20.

24. Rockwell, interview, 7 November 1959. Rockwell was one of the Legionnaires present.

25. James Norman Hall and Charles B. Nordhoff, *The Lafayette Flying Corps*, 1: 455, 458–59.

26. *Norman Prince: A Volunteer Who Died for the Cause He Loved*, pp. 56–57; Juliette A. Hennessy, "The Lafayette Escadrille, Past and Present," p. 150; Fred T. Jane, *All the World's Aircraft*, 5:205. The *Boston Daily Globe* (29 August 1911) announced the news in large headlines: "Young Prince is an Aviator," adding, "This will be a great surprise to his personal friends."

27. Hall and Nordhoff, *Lafayette Flying Corps*, 1:4.

28. Ibid., pp. 4, 392.

29. Ibid.

30. Ibid.

31. Ibid.

32. Ibid.; Parsons, *Great Adventure*, p. 164.

33. Hall and Nordhoff, *Lafayette Flying Corps*, 1:4.

34. This rejection, as recorded by Hall and Nordhoff, must be viewed in light of the fact that Prince and Curtis were not offering their personal services except as part of a volunteer squadron. Had they applied as individuals, they would probably have been accepted without delay. Times had changed since Thaw was turned down in 1914. Indeed, several Americans had already found their way into French military aviation.

35. *New York Hearld Tribune*, 17 December 1956; Paul A. Rockwell to me, 5 July 1960.

36. James Norman Hall, *High Adventure*, pp. xii–xiii. Dr. Gros wrote the preface to this volume.

37. Parsons, *Great Adventure*, p. 13.

38. Thenault, *l'Escadrille Lafayette*, p. 10; Parsons, *Great Adventure*, p. 13.

39. Frederick C. Hild, "War Experiences of an Air Scout; the Diary of an American Volunteer with the Aviation of the French Corps," p. 38. Hild claimed that three Russians, several Englishmen, two Belgians, two Italians and a Spaniard were among his aviation classmates in the training school at Tours.

40. Ibid.

41. Le Général Directeur de l'Aéronautique Militaire to the Général Commandant en Chef, 11 November 1914. Archives des Services Historiques de l'Armée de l'Air, Versailles, France. Thenault was of the opinion that Hild deserted while still in flying school. (Paul A. Rockwell to me, 12 January 1963.)

42. *New York Times*, 28 December 1914.

43. Rockwell, interview, 1 January 1960; Rockwell, *American Fighters*, p. 187. For years the identity of the American who deserted from French aviation remained a secret. The French were apparently willing to talk about the incident, particularly to a tried and proven friend like Paul Rockwell, but they declined to disclose the name of the deserter. Rockwell learned Hild's identity quite by accident when he ran across the Hild article cited above in a North Carolina used book store. This evidence was circumstantial, of course, but when Rockwell mentioned his discovery to some of his high-placed French friends, they confirmed Hild's identity. (Rockwell, interview, 1 January 1960.)

44. Note, French Minister of Foreign Affairs, n.d., ca. July 1915. Sterling Memorial Library, Yale University.

45. Rockwell to me, 5 July 1960; Hall and Nordhoff, *Lafayette Flying Corps*, 1:458.

46. James Bach was only too happy to forget this bit of deceit, for he apparently mentioned it to no one, not even his wife. (Mrs. James J. Buck [Bach] to me, 7 August 1960.) Hall, on the other hand, expanded the tale to include combat in the 1912–13 Balkan wars.

47. Hall and Nordhoff, *Lafayette Flying Corps*, 1:458.

48. Parsons, *Great Adventure*, pp. 93–94.

49. Hall and Nordhoff, *Lafayette Flying Corps*, 1:458.

50. Ibid. An aerial gunner at this time used the pistol and carbine rather than the machine gun.

51. Quoted in Morse, *Vanguard of American Volunteers*, p. 272.

52. Hall and Nordhoff, *Lafayette Flying Corps*, 1: 455, 459.

53. Thenault, *l'Escadrille Lafayette*, p. 15.

54. Ibid.; Edward F. Hinkle, interview, 10 July 1959; Emil A. Marchal, interview, 21 January 1960. Both Hinkle and Marchal served with the Lafayette Escadrille, the former as a pilot, the latter as one of the support personnel.

55. Thenault, *l'Escadrille Lafayette*, p. 16; Hinkle, interview, 10 July 1959; Rockwell, *American Fighters*, pp. 187–88.

56. Hall and Nordhoff, *Lafayette Flying Corps*, 1: 100, 255.

57. Ibid., pp. 330–31. Lufbery was reluctant to discuss his colorful past and most of what is written in English about his early life is based on an interview Paul Rockwell had with him in the summer of 1916 (Rockwell, interview, 29 December 1959). Hall and Nordhoff got their information from this source.

58. Parsons, *Great Adventure*, p. 73.

59. Hall and Nordhoff, *Lafayette Flying Corps*, 1: 100, 225.

60. Parsons, *Great Adventure*, p. 176; *Cross and Cockade Journal* (Spring 1961), p. 53.

61. Parsons, *Great Adventure*, pp. 176–78. Edward F. Hinkle to me, 20 July 1959. Some aviation buffs have doubted Masson's story, apparently on the grounds that it sounds farfetched. Unlike Bert Hall's well-accepted tales, however, there is some evidence to support Masson, including the fact that his comrades in the Lafayette Escadrille believed him. Parsons, for example, flew for Pancho Villa at the same time Masson flew for General Huerta. The two never learned of each other's activity until they met in France but they never doubted each other, either. (Edwin C. Parsons, interview, 5 June 1960.) See also Hall and Nordhoff, *Lafayette Flying Corps*, 1:356.

62. Masson was an American citizen when he returned to France, leading one to conclude that the law precluding foreigners from serving with the French in units other than the Foreign Legion could be circumvented. Other Americans who entered regular line regiments include Pierre Boal, Emil A. Marshall (Marchal), Andrew Walbron, and William H. Waters. The date for Masson's *brevet* is found in Hall and Nordhoff, *Lafayette Flying Corps*, 1:335.

63. John R. Cuneo, *The Air Weapon, 1914–1916*, p. 153.

64. The evidence for this assertion is cumulative rather than specific, but it is based largely on the acknowledged fact that neither Prince nor Curtis offered his services in any capacity other than flying, and even then only when their entrance into aviation was seemingly assured.

65. Hall and Nordhoff, *Lafayette Flying Corps*, 1:6. By a strange coincidence, Robert Bliss, who arranged for Prince to meet M. de Sillac, was a man who impressed some of the American volunteers as disapproving of their fighting for France, at least in the trenches. According to one ex-Legionnaire, Bliss appeared "to go out of his way to be nasty" to the volunteers. (Paul A. Rockwell to me, 15 March 1960.)

66. Quoted in Hall and Nordhoff, *Lafayette Flying Corps*, 1:6.

67. Ibid.; Rockwell to Parsons, 26 October 1960.

68. Quoted in Hall and Nordhoff, *Lafayette Flying Corps*, 1:6.

69. Ibid., pp. 8, 196, 204, 391.

70. Rockwell to me, 15 December 1960. Georges Leygues eventually became premier of France.

71. Note, Minister of Foreign Affairs to the French Premier, 27 January 1916. Sterling Memorial Library, Yale University.

72. Parsons, interview, 29 October 1960; Henry J. Jones, interview, 29 October 1960. Both men flew with the Lafayette Escadrille and knew Thaw well.

73. Hall and Nordhoff, *Lafayette Flying Corps*, 1:9–10.

74. Ibid., p. 10.

75. Ibid., p. 11.

76. Directeur de l'Aéronautique Militaire to the French Minister of Foreign Affairs, 21 August 1915. Sterling Memorial Library, Yale University.

77. Note, French Minister of Foreign Affairs, 15 September 1915. Sterling Memorial Library, Yale University; Hall and Nordhoff, *Lafayette Flying Corps*, 1: 196, 391.

78. Ibid., pp. 100–101.

79. Ibid., pp. 455–56. Herbert Malloy Mason, Jr., *The Lafayette Escadrille*, p. 42.

80. Note, French Minister of Foreign Affairs to the Premier, 27 January 1916. Sterling Memorial Library, Yale University.

81. Hall and Nordhoff, *Lafayette Flying Corps*, 1:11.

82. Directeur de l'Aéronautique Militaire to the Minister of Foreign Affairs, 21 August 1915. Sterling Memorial Library, Yale University.

83. Hall and Nordhoff, *Lafayette Flying Corps*, 1:48.

84. Directeur de l'Aéronautique Militaire to the Minister of Foreign Affairs, 21 August 1915.

85. Dudley Hill of Peekskill, New York, occasioned the first point. Hill passed his medical examination in September 1915 but later, in training, he was found to have defective vision in one eye. Rather than release him from active duty, the French wanted to make him a mechanic. Not one to let a thing like this stand in his way, Hill worked his way up to pilot status with the Lafayette Escadrille. See Hall and Nordhoff, *Lafayette Flying Corps*, 1: 11, 12.

86. Note, French Minister of Foreign Affairs to the Premier, 27 January 1916.

87. Quoted in Hall and Nordhoff, *Lafayette Flying Corps*, 1:12.

88. Parsons, *Great Adventure*, pp. 14–15; Rockwell, interview, 29 December 1959.

89. Mason, *Lafayette Escadrille*, p. 53.

90. *New York Times*, 25 December 1915. In the last sentence of the above quote, Mr. Viereck was referring to that portion of the Hague Convention which stated that "a neutral power, which receives in its territory troops belonging to a belligerent nation shall intern them, so far as possible, at a distance from the theatre of war."

91. Hervier, *American Volunteers*, p. 113.

92. James R. McConnel, *Flying for France*, pp. 16–17; Hall and Nordhoff, *Lafayette Flying Corps*, 1:16.

93. Thenault, *l'Escadrille Lafayette*, p. 28.

94. Paul Rockwell, who worked for the French Public Information after illness forced his release from active duty with the Foreign Legion, and who is the man best qualified to speak on this particular subject, wrote me as follows: "The French authorities, and especially the military, never recognized the publicity and propaganda value of the Foreign Legion ranks. I worked closely with the *Section d'Information* of French Army GHQ and other official propaganda agencies, from 1915 to the Armis-

tice, and was constantly urged, almost pressured to write about political affairs and the exploits of the French Army as a whole. Even in 1918, after we had gotten this country into the war, I was often asked to write almost scholarly dissertations about the Alsace-Lorraine question, the ancient historical importance of Verdun ('France since the days of Charlemagne'), etc., etc." (Rockwell to me, 15 December 1960.)

95. Thenault, *l'Escadrille Lafayette*, p. 26.

96. The number *nine* is worth remembering. With eventually more than four thousand men claiming membership in the Lafayette Escadrille, a significant number of them sought extra distinction by also claiming that they were among the "originals."

97. *Cross and Cockade Journal* (Spring 1961), p. 43; Rockwell, interview, 31 December 1959.

98. Hall and Nordhoff, *Lafayette Flying Corps*, 1:79.

99. Ibid., pp. 81–83.

100. Edwin C. Parsons, interview, 29 October 1960; Hall and Nordhoff, *Lafayette Flying Corps*, 1:83.

101. Parsons, *Great Adventure*, p. 89.

102. Ibid., pp. 86–87.

103. Rockwell, interview, 7 November 1959.

104. Marcelle Guerin, interview, 19 January 1960; McConnell, *Flying for France*, p. 96.

105. Like his son Victor, John Jay Chapman was one of those rare individuals filled with compassion for his fellow men. A friend of the family told me that Mr. Chapman once playfully struck a friend, causing an eye to pop out of its socket. So grieved was Chapman at being the cause of this misfortune that he thrust his offending fist into a burning fire. (Madame Guerin, interview, 19 January 1960.) See the *Cross and Cockade Journal*, (Spring 1961), p. 44.

106. *Victor Chapman's Letters from France*, p. 117. The quotation is from a letter to Alice Weeks, who had a son in the Foreign Legion. While in the Legion, Chapman had a friend with an ulcerated stomach. Moved by his friend's desire to stay at the front and his need for fresh milk, Chapman scoured the countryside until he found a milch cow, which he promptly purchased and gave to his friend. (*Victor Chapman's Letters*, p. 34; Rockwell, interview, 1 January 1960.) In the preface to *Victor Chapman's Letters*, John Jay Chapman wrote that his son "never really felt he was alive except when he was in danger."

107. Parsons, *Great Adventure*, pp. 104–5.

108. *Victor Chapman's Letters*, p. 102.

109. *Cross and Cockade Journal* (Spring 1961), p. 144. Thenault tells the story of the unveiling of a certain statue of Thomas Jefferson on the University of Virginia campus. The ceremony, attended by President Woodrow Wilson, revealed a chamber pot on Jefferson's head. Having played a prominent part in this prank, McConnell was among those expelled from school. (Thenault, *l'Escadrille Lafayette*, p. 23.)

110. Hall and Nordhoff, *Lafayette Flying Corps*, 1:341. The quotation is from McConnell, *Flying for France*, p. 15.

111. Hall and Nordhoff, *Lafayette Flying Corps*, 1:343; Rockwell, interview, 1 January 1960.

112. Hall and Nordhoff, *Lafayette Flying Corps*, 1:391; Parsons, *Great Adventure*, p. 163.

113. Rockwell to Parsons, 26 October 1960; Parsons, *Great Adventure*, p. 168; Rockwell, interview, 1 January 1960; Parsons, interview, 29 October 1960.

114. Emil A. Marchal, interview, 20 January 1960; Rockwell, interview, 1 January 1960. According to Marchal, who witnessed the event and discussed it with me with his diary in hand, Hall shook his fist at the American pilots when he left the squadron, shouting, "You'll hear from me yet."

115. Hall and Nordhoff, *Lafayette Flying Corps*, 1: 196–97; Rockwell, interview, 1 January 1960; Rockwell to Parsons, 26 October 1960.

116. Rockwell, interview, 7 December 1978.

### II: The Air War

1. Hall and Nordoff, *Lafayette Flying Corps*, 1:17.

2. See Cuneo's *Air Weapon*, for an excellent discussion of early efforts to make the airplane an instrument of war. Reichsarchiv, *Der Weltkrieg, 1914 bis 1918*, vol. 1, *Die Grenzschlachten in Westen*, pp. 126, 664–86; Walter Raleigh and H. A. Jones, *The War in the Air*, 1:411; État Major de l'Armée, Service Historique, *Les Armées Françaises dans la Grande Guerre*, 1:31. These figures are "nominal" strengths of the various air services and do not include training planes, experimental craft, etc., owned by the military. The basic, official sources have been used, since writers usually include all available aircraft in the totals and hence make the numbers look impressive. The British, for example, had 116 airplanes attached to the military besides the 63 they sent to France, but, in the words of the official historian, these "were impressive only by their numbers. About twenty of them, more or less old fashioned, were in use at the Central Flying School for training; the rest were worn out or broken, and were fit only for the scrap heap." (Raleigh and Jones, *War in the Air*, 1:411.)

3. Raleigh and Jones, *War in the Air*, 1;213; Cuneo, *Air Weapon*, p. 157.

4. Cuneo, *Air Weapon*, p. 142.

5. Gustave Crouvezier, *l'Aviation Pendant la Guerre*, p. 18; Raleigh and Jones, *War in the Air*, 1:304; Cuneo, *Air Weapon*, pp. 92–93.

6. Cuneo, *Air Weapon*, p. 92.

7. Raleigh and Jones, *War in the Air*, 1:260.

8. Cuneo, *Air Weapon*, p. 94.

9. Hall, *High Adventure*, pp. 179–80.

10. Winston S. Churchill, *The World Crisis*, p. 296.

11. Cuneo, *Air Weapon*, p. 154.

12. Raleigh and Jones, *War in the Air*, 2:87–88.

13. They did not. See Cuneo, *Air Weapon*, p. 156.

14. Charles Dollfus and Henri Bouché, *Histoire de l'Aéronautique*, p. 287.

15. Andrew Boyle, *Trenchard*, p. 128.

16. Cuneo, *Air Weapon*, p. 185.

17. Ibid., p. 156.

18. Quoted in ibid., pp. 160–61.

19. Raleigh and Jones, *War in the Air*, 1:328.

20. In 1915 the SPAD Aviation Company attempted to combine the advantages of both the pusher and the tractor types as far as the machine gun was concerned. It was basically a single-engine tractor, but by means of some rather unorthodox bracing, a nacelle, capable of carrying a man and a machine gun, stuck out in front of the engine like an oversized propeller hub. It was not much of a success and it was certainly no comfort to the observer or gunner up front, who found himself in great danger on landing; the tractor type with a "conventional" landing gear system—two main

wheels up front with a single tail wheel in back—was notorious for ending nose down, particularly when landing on soft or unprepared landing fields.

21. Raleigh and Jones, *War in the Air*, 1:262.

22. These weapons were not completely ineffective. On 25 July 1915, for example, Capt. Lanoe G. Hawker of the Royal Flying Corps won the Victoria Cross for attacking three German Albatroses with his rifle-firing Bristol Scout, destroying one, damaging one, and sending the remaining one racing for safety.

23. Aaron Norman, *The Great Air War*, p. 98. Since the Gun Bus was used for some scouting and light bombing, Norman does not classify it as strictly a fighter.

24. Jean Ajalbert, *La Passion de Roland Garros*, 1:253–63. Most World War I aviation experts treat Garros as an ace, but that is not supported by the careful work of Ajalbert.

25. Cuneo, *Air Weapon*, p. 160. The Germans later blamed their own unfavorable showing in the first half of 1915 on French use of the deflector plates, but as Cuneo makes clear, the German problem was much more basic, touching on such weighty matters as organization and doctrine. The French, for their part, did not even begin to use the deflector plates to any appreciable degree until after Garros was captured by the Germans.

26. Anthony Fokker and Bruce Gould, *Flying Dutchman: The Life of Anthony Fokker*, pp. 124–26.

27. Ibid., pp. 126–28, 138.

28. Cuneo, *Air Weapon*, p. 173.

29. For the politicians' reactions, see Raleigh and Jones, *War in the Air*, 2:150. Cuneo, *Air Weapon*, p. 232.

30. The pusher never lost its vulnerability from the rear. As for the top-mounted Lewis machine gun, it was notoriously prone to jamming, primarily because of the force of the windstream on the circular drum of ammunition. As will be shown later, jamming was a constant complaint of the Lafayette Escadrille pilots.

See William E. Barrett, *The First War Planes*, p. 42, on the merits of the French and British craft. One must not overestimate the performance of the Fokker Eindecker, an error that often plagued British and French airmen. In April 1916, one of the Eindeckers fell into British hands and was matched against the French Morane monoplane. According to an eyewitness, "Both machines took off together, and it was immediately clear that the Morane was all over the Fokker. It climbed quicker, it was faster on the level, and when the two machines began a mock fight over the aerodrome, the Morane had everything its own way. A cheer went up from the ground. The bogey was laid. A description of the machine, its size, power, capabilities, was circulated at once to everyone in the Corps. It did a great deal to raise the morale and prepare the way for the Allied air supremacy later that year." (Cecil Lewis, quoted in Cuneo, *Air Weapon*, pp. 232–33.)

31. According to William E. Barrett, Nungesser's injuries included the following: "A fractured skull, concussion of the brain, five fractures of the upper jaw, two fractures of the lower, shell splinter in the right arm, both knees dislocated, bullet wound in the mouth, atrophy of the calf, injury to the lower tendons of the left leg, collar bone dislocation, left wrist dislocated, right ankle dislocated, contusion of the chest" (*First War Planes*, p. 58). Like so many fighter pilots, Nungessser was proud of his exploits and wore his many medals even in the air. He also limped heavily, causing his medals to jangle. As one author put it, he sounded "rather like a walking ironmongers shop." (Vigilant [pseud.], *French War Birds*, p. 99).

32. Laurence L. Driggs, *Heroes of Aviation*, pp. 179, 183–84.

33. Quoted in ibid., p. 185.

34. Cuneo suggests that one of the main factors in the decline of French aviation during and after the Battle of the Somme was the failure of the French pilots to overcome the individualism that had made them famous (*Air Weapon*, p. 269). There is considerable logic to this conclusion. As long as the opponents used teamwork, individualism was bound to be detrimental—and dangerous.

35. Henry S. Jones, interview, 29 October 1960.

36. In June 1960, while enjoying an intimate luncheon with five of the eight surviving members of the Lafayette Escadrille, I happened to mention that in seven years of flying with the United States Air Force I had never had an accident or even a forced landing. The oldtimers were stunned by what seemed an incredible announcement.

37. McConnell, *Flying for France*, p. 87.

38. Parsons, interview, 29 October 1960; Jones, interview, 29 October 1960.

39. Edward F. Hinkle was once missing for twenty-four hours. When he returned to the N-124, he found his possessions already divided up among his comrades. The man inheriting his best uniform had already lengthened the sleeves. (Hinkle, interview, 10 July 1959.)

40. Quoted in Parsons, *Great Adventure*, p. 249.

### III: Off to the Front: In the Vosges and Verdun Sectors

1. McConnell, *Flying for France*, p. 27.

2. Col. Charles Salesse, "La Groupe d'Aviation de Chasse 11/5, en 1939–1940," unpublished MS, p. 2. Archives des Services Historiques de l'Armée de l'Air, Versailles, France.

3. Jacques Mortane, "Le Commandant Happe," pp. 458–59; Thenault, *l'Escadrille Lafayette*, p. 24; Mortane, "Le Commandant Happe," p. 458.

4. Mortane, "Le Commandant Happe," p. 458; Rockwell, interview, 1 January 1960. Colonel Rockwell was appointed historian of the Escadrille Americaine by the original members at the gathering the evening before Chapman, Rockwell, Prince, and McConnell left for Luxeuil-les-Bains. This is a strong indication that the group sensed a destiny with history.

5. Thenault, *l'Escadrille Lafayette*, p. 25.

6. *Cross and Cockade Journal* (Spring 1961), p. 12.

7. McConnell, *Flying for France*, pp. 25, 26.

8. *Victor Chapman's Letters*, p. 171.

9. Ibid.

10. Ibid.; McConnell, *Flying for France*, p. 26.

11. *Cross and Cockade Journal* (Spring 1961), p. 12; Thenault, *l'Escadrille Lafayette*, p. 34.

12. Thenault, *l'Escadrille Lafayette*, p. 34.

13. McConnell, *Flying for France*, p. 85; Thenault, *l'Escadrille Lafayette*, p. 35.

14. Thenault, *l'Escadrille Lafayette*, p. 36.

15. Parsons, *The Great Adventure*, p. 6.

16. *War Letters of Kiffin Yates Rockwell*, pp. 126–27.

17. Under the French system, fellow airmen could not confirm victories. Only ground personnel, including balloonists, could qualify as witnesses. For this reason, any victory taking place an appreciable distance behind German lines was certain to go unconfirmed. (Edwin C. Parsons to me, 15 October 1960.)

18. McConnell, *Flying for France*, p. 43.

19. Parsons, *Great Adventure*, p. 6.

20. Ibid., p. 7.

21. Quoted in Churchill, *World Crisis*, p. 262.

22. Quoted in ibid.

23. Jere King, *Generals and Politicians*, pp. 89–95.

24. Boyle, *Trenchard*, p. 166.

25. Hans Ritter, a German critic and the author of *Der Luftkrieg*, estimated that it would take 720 machines of the 1916 model to effectively patrol a block of airspace 12 miles long by 15,000 feet in height. If a patrol of two machines could handle a block six-tenths of a mile by 1,500 feet, 120 patrols (240 machines) would be in the air at a given time. Assuming each plane would fly twice a day for two-hour intervals, 720 planes, not counting reserves, would be necessary. (See Cuneo, *Air Weapon*, p. 214.)

26. General von Hoeppner, *Deutschlands Krieg in der Luft*, p. 52.

27. Thenault, *l'Escadrille Lafayette*, pp. 39, 40, 41; McConnell, *Flying for France*, pp. 34, 35–36.

28. Driggs, *Heroes of Aviation*, p. 10.

29. McConnell, *Flying for France*, p. 36.

30. Boyle, *Trenchard*, p. 166.

31. Thenault, *l'Escadrille Lafayette*, pp. 41–42. The term "nervous and troubly" comes from a diary entry by Clyde Balsley, dated 9 June 1916. It is included as an apt description of the turbulance caused by heavy artillery. See "The Diary of Clyde Balsley," *Cross and Cockade Journal* (Summer 1977), p. 117.

32. Rockwell, *American Fighters*, p. 189; *Victor Chapman's Letters*, p. 180.

33. The evidence for this assertion is cumulative rather than specific. Kiffin Rockwell, not the type to pick on anyone, wrote his brother that "a friend" had succeeded in bringing down a German machine but declined to name him, even though Paul Rockwell knew Hall well (Rockwell, *American Fighters*, p. 190). Chapman likewise mentions "one of my fellows who . . . fell upon a Boche and brought him down" (*Victor Chapman's Letters*, p. 180). Thenault, writing with the squadron diary at hand, does not even mention the victory, nor does McConnell. Finally, for reasons not clear, Hall himself, who later put forth the most exaggerated claims about his combat record, passes this genuine victory by with only one sentence (Bert Hall, *En l'Air*, p. 68).

34. Thenault, *l'Escadrille Lafayette*, pp. 42, 43.

35. Ibid., p. 44.

36. Rockwell, *American Fighters*, p. 190; Parsons, *Great Adventure*, p. 157.

37. Thenault, *l'Escadrille Lafayette*, pp. 44–45.

38. The quotation is from *Victor Chapman's Letters*, p. 35; Rockwell, *American Fighters*, p. 190.

39. *Cross and Cockade Journal* (Spring 1961), p. 19.

40. Parsons, *Great Adventure*, p. 100.

41. Hall and Nordhoff, *Lafayette Flying Corps*, 1:332.

42. Parsons, *Great Adventure*, p. 73.

43. Hall and Nordhoff, *Lafayette Flying Corps*, 1: 107–9, 286–87.

44. Ibid., p. 287.

45. Ibid., p. 422.

46. N-124 *Journal de Marche*, 25 August to 25 November 1916; Rockwell, interview, 1 January 1960. The *Journal de Marche* is the official log or diary of the squadron.

47. Hall and Nordhoff, *Lafayette Flying Corps*, 1: 265, 266; Parsons, *Great Adventure*, pp. 38–39.

48. Colonel Charles H. Dolan II told me that Hill "was paid to stay away from home" (interview, 5 June 1960).

49. Hall and Nordhoff, *Lafayette Flying Corps*, 1:255; Parsons, *Great Adventure*, pp. 174–75.

50. Parsons, *Great Adventure*, pp. 109–10. Victor Chapman, it seems, exhibited in fullest measure some of the virtues and defects of many World War I airmen. Though blessed with remarkable idealism and truly impressive devotion to duty, he nonetheless was far from being an ideal soldier. He was individualistic, reckless, and his enthusiasm could hardly be tamed.

51. Ibid.

52. Balsley kept a diary which surfaced only in recent years. Unfortunately, the entries are erratic and ended before the flight in which he was wounded. The diary was reproduced in its entirety in the Summer 1977 issue of *Cross and Cockade Journal*. The quotation is from Parsons, *Great Adventure*, p. 119.

53. Hall and Nordhoff, *Lafayette Flying Corps*, 2:60.

54. Quoted in Parsons, *Great Adventure*, pp. 120–21.

55. Hall and Nordhoff, *Lafayette Flying Corps*, 2:66. Balsley's experiences at Vadelaincourt, which he describes in some detail, are outstanding examples of the sufferings that attended the huge casualty lists of World War I.

56. Ibid., pp. 60–72.

57. Ibid. Hall and Nordhoff give Balsley considerable credit, suggesting that he "rendered a great service to his country" for he "helped to make clear and unmistakable to the French people, America's friendship and her desire to help" (*Lafayette Flying Corps*, 2:109). He also served his own country well after he left the French. He returned to the United States, took a captain's commission, and ended the war as an administrator in the Pursuit Division, U.S. Air Service.

58. *Victor Chapman's Letters*, pp. 40, 41; Paul A. Rockwell, interview, 1 January 1960.

59. McConnell, *Flying for France*, p. 43; *Victor Chapman's Letters*, pp. 37–42. This description of Chapman's death is taken from a letter written by Kiffin Rockwell to Chapman's parents, dated 10 August 1916, and from a letter by Chouteau Johnson to his mother, dated 23 July 1916. The original of Johnson's letter is in the Paul Rockwell Collection, Asheville, North Carolina. It remains to be noted that mystery still surrounds Chapman's death. It began when the Germans did not release Chapman's name among the fallen fliers, a custom practiced by both sides. After the war, Frederick Zinn, one of Chapman's friends from Foreign Legion days, was sent into the battle areas to locate the graves of American aviators. He found a grave near where Chapman fell, bearing the name of Clyde Balsley and the date, 23 June 1916. Since Chapman was carrying a letter to Balsley, intending to deliver it along with the oranges, it was assumed that Chapman's body had been found. But when the body was exhumed, it was wearing a pair of German military boots such as Chapman never possessed. A committee, which included Paul A. Rockwell, was appointed by John Jay Chapman, Victor's father, to look into the matter. Rockwell explained what happened in a letter to me. "I was one of the committee that examined the body and evidence (we sent a chart of the teeth to Victor's American dentist, whose report was negative), and we decided it was not Victor. However, the remains were buried in the American Cemetery at Suresness under Victor's name. We could not be absolutely sure, and anyway it was the body of a brave man fallen in battle" (Rockwell to me, 12 January 1963). Because of this doubt, the casket marked with Victor Chapman's name in the crypt of the beautiful Lafayette Memorial near Paris is vacant.

60. The question is examined at some lengh in the Spring 1961 issue of *Cross and Cockade Journal*.

61. Rockwell, interview, 7 November 1959.

62. Chouteau Johnson to his mother, 23 July 1916 (original in the Paul A. Rockwell Collection); Rockwell, *American Fighters*, p. 192; McConnell, *Flying for France*, pp. 44–45.

63. Parsons, *Great Adventure*, p. 112.

64. Quoted in *Victor Chapman's Letters*, p. 27.

65. Both quotations are in ibid., p. 28.

66. Hall and Nordhoff, *Lafayette Flying Corps*, 1: 255, 456. Unfortunately only one of Hall's four citations is presently available. For some reason, Hall and Nordhoff did not feel obligated to include them all in their short biographical sketch of Bert Hall in the first volume of their book, even though they customarily did this. Moreover while the French Ministry of War graciously provided me with copies of the personal military records of almost all of the Lafayette Escadrille pilots, Bert Hall's was not among them. Paul A. Rockwell was told by a French intelligence officer in the 1920s that Hall's *État Signaletique et des Services* had been removed from the files for study, perhaps by American authorities, and was never returned. (Rockwell to me, 12 January 1963.)

67. Rockwell, *American Fighters*, pp. 190–91. There is a natural tendency for nations to be too liberal with awards and decorations in wartime. Indeed, these trinkets usually retain only a fraction of their intended value. Also, one must make allowance for those unit commanders who embellish their own record by awarding decorations for the slightest achievement. Of this latter weakness, however, there is no evidence in the history of the Lafayette Escadrille. Captain Thenault, it seems, leaned the other way and often refused recognition to men who could easily have had it elsewhere (Edward F. Hinkle, interview, 10 July 1959). "When he awarded a decoration, it was well earned" (Rockwell to me, 12 January 1963).

68. Hall and Nordhoff, *Lafayette Flying Corps*, 1:191.

69. Dolan, interview, 5 June 1960.

70. Driggs, *Heroes of Aviation*, p. 196. Nungesser's exact status with the Lafayette Escadrille and his reasons for flying with the squadron are still uncertain. His name was duly recorded in the *Journal de Marche* and in the monthly report of men and equipment submitted to higher headquarters. On the other hand, the men of the N-124 never regarded him as other than a passing and unofficial member of the unit.

71. Thenault, *l'Escadrille Lafayette*, p. 49. It is significant that Thenault does not mention Hall's victory.

72. Ibid.

73. Jacques Mortane, *Deux Grands Chevaliers de l'Aventure: Marc Pourpe, Raoul Lufbery*, p. 261.

74. Ibid., pp. 261–62.

75. McConnell, *Flying for France*, p. 65.

76. Mortane, *Deux Grands Chevaliers*, pp. 261–62.

77. Ibid., pp. 262–63.

78. Hall and Nordhoff, *Lafayette Flying Corps*, 1:33.

79. Thenault, *l'Escadrille Lafayette*, p. 49.

80. Ibid., pp. 49–50.

81. McConnell, *Flying For France*, pp. 134–35.

82. Ibid., p. 135.

83. Hall and Nordhoff, *Lafayette Flying Corps*, 1:343.

84. Rockwell, interview, 1 January 1960; Rockwell to Parsons, 26 October 1960.

85. Parsons, *Great Adventure*, p. 140.

86. Rockwell, *American Fighters*, p. 67. Adolph Bressett Beaufort and his South American "Republic" of Counani declared war on Germany in 1914. Beaufort personally brought a small army of less than a hundred men to England, where he picked up a few more recruits and fed his men by taking collections in British movie houses. Made up mostly of adventurers with little or no discipline, the Counani army was considered an outcast by the British and Belgians, although the French finally took it in on the condition that it lose its identity and become part of the Foreign Legion. A special correspondent for the *Chicago Daily News* and a Legionnaire himself called the truculant Counani army "one of the strangest human interest narratives of the war," subheadlining his article, "POLYGLOT RECRUITS VENT VALOR ON ONE ANOTHER UNTIL THEY AT LAST REACH FRONT" (*Chicago Daily News*, 3 January 1915).

87. Hall and Nordhoff, *Lafayette Flying Corps*, 1:379; Rockwell, interview, 7 December 1978.

88. It is difficult to convey the terror that an in-flight fire could cause a pilot who carried no parachute, although as a former pilot, I do not find it beyond imagination. McConnell wrote that "falling in flames . . . is the worst death an aviator can meet" (McConnell, *Flying for France*, pp. 86–87).

89. Parsons, *Great Adventure*, p. 142; Parsons, interview, 29 October 1960.

90. Ibid.

91. *Journal de Marche*, 24 August 1916, 25 August to 28 August 1916.

92. Ibid., 9 September 1916.

93. *War Letters of Kiffin Yeates Rockwell*, pp. 152–53.

94. Thenault, *l'Escadrille Lafayette*, pp. 51–52.

95. *Journal de Marche*, 22 May to 12 September 1916.

96. Thenault, *l'Escadrille Lafayette*, pp. 51–52.

97. Ibid, p. 51.

98. Cuneo, *Air Weapon*, pp. 429–30.

### IV: Vosges and Somme Sectors

1. Thenault, *l'Escadrille Lafayette*, p. 53.

2. A large number of the American volunteers wrote regularly to Alice Weeks, treating her like a mother. Mrs. Weeks, in turn, treated them as her sons, seeing to their needs and worrying about their safety. For the volunteer's view, see *Victor Chapman's Letters*. For the other side, see Alice Weeks, *Greater Love Hath No Man*.

3. Hall and Nordhoff, *Lafayette Flying Corps*, 1:69; Rockwell to me, 13 February 1960.

4. Parsons, *Great Adventure*, pp. 147–48.

5. Thenault, *l'Escadrille Lafayette*, p. 56; Marchal, interview, 20 January 1960.

6. Thenault, *l'Escadrille Lafayette*, p. 56. "Bert Hall 'suscribed' 100 francs, but as usual never paid up" (Rockwell to me, 12 January 1963).

7. Thenault, *l'Escadrille Lafayette*, p. 56; Parsons, *Great Adventure*, p. 147.

8. Marchal, interview, 20 January 1960.

9. Parsons, *Great Adventure*, p. 147; Marchal, interview, 20 January 1960.

10. Guerin, interview, 20 January 1960. Madame Geurin knew many pilots of the N-124.

11. Hinkle, interview, 10 July 1959.

12. Parsons, *Great Adventure*, pp. 150–51.

13. Ibid., p. 149. One individual who turned his back on Soda to prove she wasn't really as bad as everyone claimed, offered to show me teeth marks he still carried as a token of his mistaken trust.

14. Hall and Nordhoff, *Lafayette Flying Corps*, 1:411.

15. Parsons, *Great Adventure*, p. 153.

16. McConnell, *Flying for France*, p. 83.

17. Ibid. p. 84.

18. Thenault, *l'Escadrille Lafayette*, p. 57.

19. Ibid., p. 59.

20. Parsons, *Great Adventure*, p. 146; McConnell, *Flying for France*, p. 84.

21. Thenault, *l'Escadrille Lafayette*, p. 58.

22. McConnell, *Flying for France*, pp. 92–93.

23. Thenault, *l'Escadrille Lafayette*, p. 59.

24. McConnell, *Flying for France*, pp. 93–94.

25. Ibid.; Hall and Nordhoff, *Lafayette Flying Corps*, 1:409.

26. McConnell, *Flying for France*, p. 96.

27. Ibid., pp. 96–97.

28. Ibid., p. 98.

29. Ibid., p. 99; Rockwell, *American Fighters*, p. 199.

30. McConnell, *Flying for France*, p. 99; Hall and Nordhoff, *Lafayette Flying Corps*, 1:410. The appreciation felt by the French for the total sacrifice of such men as Chapman and Rockwell was unquestionably heartfelt and sincere. In 1937 several members of the French senate made a sort of pilgrimage to Kiffin Rockwell's grave. Also, when Rockwell returned to Luxeuil and his brother's tomb in June 1959, he found the grave covered with fresh flowers even though no one was aware of his coming (Rockwell to me, 30 June 1959).

31. Chouteau Johnson to his mother, 24 September 1916. Original in the Paul A. Rockwell Collection, Asheville, North Carolina. For Lufbery's reaction, see McConnell, *Flying for France*, p. 96. The rain is documented in the *Journal de Marche*, 26 September to 3 October 1916; Mortane, *Deux Grands Chevaliers*, pp. 274–75. Prince's citation is quoted in Hall and Nordhoff, *The Lafayette Flying Corps*, 1:391.

32. *Journal de Marche*, 26 September to 6 October 1916; Mortane, *Deux Grands Chevaliers*, pp. 274–75.

33. Mortane, *Deux Grands Chevaliers*, p. 276; McConnell insists that Lufbery "and the Boche, who was an excellent pilot, had tried to kill each other one or two occasions before" (*Flying for France*, p. 101).

34. Mortane, *Deux Grands Chevaliers*, p. 277.

35. Ibid.

36. Ibid., p. 278.

37. Ibid.

38. Raleigh and Jones, *War in the Air*, 2:452.

39. Ibid.

40. Thenault, *l'Escadrille Lafayette*, p. 60.

41. Ibid.; *Journal de Marche*, 11 October 1916.

42. Raleigh and Jones, *War in the Air*, 2:452; Thenault, *l'Escadrille Lafayette*, p. 60.

43. Thenault, *l'Escadrille Lafayette*, p. 61.

44. Ibid., pp. 61–62; Mortane, *Deux Grands Chevaliers*, p. 281; Raleigh and Jones, *War in the Air*, 2:453.

45. Hall and Nordhoff, *Lafayette Flying Corps*, 1:391. Because of Prince's fatal accident following the Oberndorf mission, the type of machine he shot down and where it fell was not logged in the *Journal de Marche*. Mortane, *Deux Grands Chevaliers*, p. 281.

46. Parsons, *Great Adventure*, pp. 183–85.

47. Ibid.

48. Ibid.

49. Ibid.

50. Hall and Nordhoff, *Lafayette Flying Corps*, 1:355; Mortane, *Deux Grands Chevaliers*, p. 282. There are various accounts of Prince's accident and subsequent death, but easily the most valuable is that contained in Mortane, which is really what Lufbery passed on to his friend.

51. Mortane, *Deux Grands Chevaliers*, pp. 282–83.

52. Thenault, *l'Escadrille Lafayette*, p. 62; Parsons, *Great Adventure*, p. 172.

53. Rockwell to me, 13 April 1959, 12 January 1963.

54. Thenault, *l'Escadrille Lafayette*, p. 63; McConnell, *Flying for France*, pp. 112–13.

55. Raleigh and Jones, *War in the Air*, 2:453.

56. *Journal de Marche*, 15 October 1916.

57. Thenault, *l'Escadrille Lafayette*, p. 64.

58. James E. Edmonds, *History of the Great War: Military Operations, France and Belgium*, 1: 12, 33, 36.

59. Cyril Falls, *The Great War*, p. 207.

60. Quoted in Raleigh and Jones, *War in the Air*, 2:472.

61. Cuneo, *Air Weapon*, p. 245.

62. Quoted in ibid., pp. 244, 253–54.

63. Ibid., pp. 258, 260.

64. Raleigh and Jones, *War in the Air*, 2:282.

65. Cuneo, *Air Weapon*, p. 260.

66. Ibid., p. 264.

67. Ibid.; Dolan to me, 17 November 1962.

68. Cuneo, *Air Weapon*, p. 269.

69. McConnell, *Flying for France*, p. 115.

70. Thenault, *l'Escadrille Lafayette*, p. 68.

71. Ibid.

72. McConnell, *Flying for France*, p. 117.

73. Ibid.

74. Marchal, interview, 20 January 1960. It is worth noting that when Marchal spoke with me he used his wartime diary as a reference.

75. *Cross and Cockade Journal* (Spring 1961), p. 60.

76. Ibid.

77. In July 1918, still serving with the French, Marchal (he then spelled his name Marshall) was asked to carry an urgent message to a newly arrived American division that was firing upon a French brigade. Although few expected him to survive the trip, Marchal made his way through heavy machine-gun fire and reached his destination. On the way back, however, his thigh was shattered by machine-gun bullets. Marchal lived out the war and then some in a French military hospital, honored by the French government with expressions of gratitude, citations, the Medaille Militaire, Croix de Guerre, Crois de Blesses and other medals. See the *Cross and Cockade Journal* (Spring 1961), p. 60. It is worth noting that this biographical sketch of Emil Marchal was written by Paul Rockwell.

78. Hall and Nordhoff, *Lafayette Flying Corps*, 1:390; Frederick H. Prince, Jr., interview, 5 June 1960.

79. Ibid. Prince, who died in 1962, was a man of remarkable vitality. Although he had suffered a recent heart attack, he arose from his sickbed to attend the reunion of Lafayette Escadrille survivors held at Asheville, North Carolina, in June 1960. At this

reunion, he engaged Edwin C. Parsons, who had recently fractured his ankle, in a playful sword fight, using walking canes. Prince also seriously approached me about the possibility of getting a ride in an Air Force jet trainer.

80. Rockwell, interview, 1 January 1960.

81. Ibid.; "Willis Haviland," *État Signaletique et des Services*, Class 1917, no. L.M.:11.731.

82. Rockwell, interview, 1 January 1960.

83. Ibid.; Mrs. Robert Soubrian, interview, 7 November 1959; *Cross and Cockade Journal* (Spring 1961), p. 54.

84. Rockwell, interview, 1 January 1960; Hall and Nordhoff, *Lafayette Flying Corps*, 1:435.

85. Hall and Nordhoff, *Lafayette Flying Corps*, 1:36–37.

86. Telegram, Ambassador Jules Jusserand to the French Minister of Foreign Affairs, no. 782, n.d., ca. 3 November 1916. Sterling Memorial Library, Yale University.

87. Ibid.

88. Telegram, Ambassador Jusserand to the French Minister of Foreign Affairs, no. 849, n.d., ca. 22 November 1916. Sterling Memorial Library, Yale University.

89. Memo, French Minister of War to the Premier and the Minister of Foreign Affairs, no. 8017, 16 November 1916. Sterling Memorial Library, Yale University.

90. Hall and Nordhoff, *Lafayette Flying Corps*, 1:38, gives credit to Dr. Gros, as does the doctor himself in his introduction to James Norman Hall's *High Adventure*. According to Parsons and others, however, the doctor was "willing and able to take the spotlight and bows" (Parsons to me, 19 October 1959). Paul Rockwell wrote me that the honor may belong to a one-time member of the French embassy in Washington who "told me he suggested the name. . . . He was not boasting, just made a casual remark" (Rockwell to me, 12 January 1963). At any rate, the name was a natural. Perhaps some credit should go to Theodore Roosevelt, who, in an article appearing in *Colliers Magazine* in July 1916, called the men of the N-124 "LaFayettes of the Air."

91. Parsons to me, 19 October 1959.

92. Quoted in the *Journal de Marche*, 9 December 1916.

93. Thenault, *l'Escadrille Lafayette*, p. 75.

94. Ibid., p. 67.

95. Parsons, interview, 29 October 1960; Jones, interview, 29 October 1960. In his interview, Parsons spoke of diving a SPAD in excess of 300 miles per hour in order to escape some German fighters. The plane was never the same after that, but, in his words, "at least it held together." SPAD stood for the Societé Pour Aviation et des Derives.

96. Reginald Sinclaire, interview, 19 December 1960. Sinclaire, who flew with the French for more than a year, had considerable experience with the SPAD. See Barrett, *First War Planes*, p. 63.

97. Parsons, *Great Adventure*, p. 290.

98. *Journal de Marche*, 23 October to 30 November 1916.

99. Mortane, *Deux Grands Chevaliers*, pp. 287–88.

100. Thenault, *l'Escadrille Lafayette*, p. 74.

101. Parsons, *Great Adventure*, p. 195.

102. Ibid., pp. 197–99. Unless otherwise noted, information used to describe this particular experience was taken from this source.

103. *Ronald Wood Hoskier: Literary Fragments and Remains in Prose and Verse*, p. ix. The foreword to this memorial volume was written by Ronald's father.

104. Quoted in Hall and Nordhoff, *Lafayette Flying Corps*, 1:277.

105. Mortane, *Deux Grands Chevaliers*, p. 289. Aviation writers have generally given credit for killing Leffers to a French ace named de la Tour, and I was once heavily criticized for suggesting that Lufbery deserved the credit. Nevertheless, since Mortane, writing with official sources at hand, knew both Lufbery and de la Tour, his conclusion has considerable weight. It is worth noting that the *Fraternité d'Armes Franco-Américaine*, an official publication of the French Ministry of War, also credits Lufbery with the kill (p. 106).

106. *Journal de Marche*, 1 to 31 January 1917.

107. Mortane, *Deux Grands Chevaliers*, p. 291.

108. Philip C. Brown, "Pavelka of the Lafayette," *Cross and Cockade Journal* (Summer 1978), p. 108.

### V: From St. Just to Chaudun

1. Parsons, interview, 29 October 1960.

2. Ibid.; Edwin C. Parsons, "Flying As It Was," pp. 16, 30, 32.

3. Parsons, interview, 29 October 1960; Hall and Nordhoff, *Lafayette Flying Corps*, 1:376.

4. Grace Ellery Channing, ed., *War Letters of Edmond Genêt*, p. viii. It is worth noting that Edmond Charles ("Citizen") Genêt was awarded the first patent for an "aeronautical device" issued in the United States. Apparently the device had something to do with airship design and caused considerable furor in scientific circles. See Charles B. van Pelt, "The Army's Introduction to the Air Arm," pp. 243, 246n.

5. *War Letters of Edmond Genêt*, p. xviii.

6. Ibid., p. xix.

7. Parsons, *Great Adventure*, p. 208.

8. Hall and Nordhoff, *Lafayette Flying Corps*, 1:243.

9. *War Letters of Edmond Genêt*, p. 181. Of Genêt's desertion, Parsons wrote: "It was desertion with a noble purpose, from a safe and easy berth at home to the post of danger in the trenches of the Western Front" (*Great Adventure*, p. 208).

10. Ibid., pp. 209–10.

11. Basil H. Liddell Hart, *The Real War*, p. 321.

12. C.R.M.F. Cruttwell, *A History of the Great War*, p. 898.

13. King, *Generals and Politicians*, p. 159. Note that Nivelle, like Falkenhayn in the Battle of Verdun, fell victim to the attractive but desperately dangerous idea that one can simply call off an offensive at will.

14. E. L. Spears, *Prelude to Victory*, pp. 41-42; Thenault, *l'Escadrille Lafayette*, p. 77.

15. Thenault, *l'Escadrille Lafayette*, p. 77.

16. Parsons, *Great Adventure*, pp. 238, 245.

17. Ibid.

18. *War Letters of Edmond Genêt*, pp. 234, 278.

19. Ibid., p. 280.

20. Thenault, *l'Escadrille Lafayette*, p. 79; *Journal de Marche*, 1 to 31 March 1917.

21. Hall and Nordhoff, *Lafayette Flying Corps*, 1: 456, 40.

22. Rockwell, interview, 1 January 1960; Rockwell, *American Fighters*, p. 151; Rockwell to me, 12 January 1963; Parsons, *Great Adventure*, p. 246.

23. *Journal de Marche*, 19 March 1917.

24. Quoted in Rockwell, *American Fighters*, p. 252.

25. Parsons, interview, 29 October 1960; Jones, interview, 29 October 1960; *Journal de Marche*, 19 March 1917. A portion of the telephone message was dutifully logged in the *Journal*.

26. Parsons, *Great Adventure*, p. 247.

27. Quoted in Rockwell, *American Fighters*, p. 253.

28. Ibid.; Thenault, *l'Escadrille Lafayette*, p. 65.

29. Hall and Nordhoff, *Lafayette Flying Corps*, 1:390. Frederick H. Prince, Sr., had considerable influence with the French because he had floated some French war loans in the United States. (Dolan to me, 25 January 1963).

30. Rockwell, interview, 1 January 1960.

31. Hall and Nordhoff, *Lafayette Flying Corps*, 1:131.

32. Ibid.; Rockwell, interview, 1 January 1960.

33. Hall and Nordhoff, *Lafayette Flying Corps*, 1:324–25; Caroline Ticknor, ed., *New England Aviators*, 1:34.

34. Hall and Nordhoff, *Lafayette Flying Corps*, 1:324.

35. Ibid., p. 493; Harold B. Willis, interview, 5 June 1960; Hall and Nordhoff, *Lafayette Flying Corps*, 1:493.

36. Thenault, *l'Escadrille Lafayette*, p. 106.

37. Hinkle to me, 29 May 1959.

38. Hinkle to me, 22 May 1959.

39. Parsons, interview, 29 October 1960.

40. Parsons, *Great Adventure*, p. 254; Rockwell, interview, 1 January 1960.

41. Hall and Nordhoff, *Lafayette Flying Corps*, 1:223–24; Rockwell, interview, 31 December 1959.

42. Kenneth Marr, interview, 16 September 1960.

43. Parsons, *Great Adventure*, p. 254; Hall and Nordhoff, *Lafayette Flying Corps*, 1:354; Parsons, interview, 29 October 1960; Jones, interview, 29 October 1960.

44. Rockwell, interview, 1 January 1960; "Thomas S. Hewitt," *État Signaletique et des Services*, Class 1917, no. L.M.:11.826; Parsons, interview, 29 October 1960; Jones, interview, 29 October 1960; Rockwell, interview, 1 January 1960.

45. Thenault, *l'Escadrille Lafayette*, pp. 78, 75; Parsons to me, 13 January 1963; Hinkle to me, 29 May 1959.

46. Hinkle, interview, 10 July 1959.

47. Spears, *Prelude to Victory*, pp. 453, 542.

48. Thenault, *l'Escadrille Lafayette*, p. 86.

49. Parsons, *Great Adventure*, pp. 257, 258.

50. Raoul Lufbery to Mrs. Harper, n.d., quoted in *War Letters of Edmond Genêt*, p. 321.

51. Ibid.

52. Parsons, *Great Adventure*, p. 258.

53. Apparently Genêt's age was something of a mystery. At Genêt's funeral, Thenault gave 1890 as his year of birth, an obvious error since Thenault himself later declared that Genêt was twenty-four years old when he died. Genêt's official army record gives his birth date as 2 November 1893, but it must be remembered that he had to lie about his age to get into the Foreign Legion. The correct date is no doubt that given by his family in the short biography contained in *War Letters of Edmond Genêt*—9 November 1896. Walter Lovell to Paul Rockwell, 16 April 1917, quoted in *War Letters of Edmond Genêt*, p. 323. Thenault, *l'Escadrille Lafayette*, p. 87.

54. *War Letters of Edmond Genêt*, pp. xxii, 329–30.

55. Quoted in Parsons, *Great Adventure*, p. 259.

56. *Journal de Marche*, 17 to 23 April 1917.

57. Parsons, *Great Adventure*, p. 260; *Ronald Wood Hoskier*, p. 7.

58. Parsons, *Great Adventure*, p. 261. This event took place while de Laage and Dressy were in the Dragoons. To appreciate the deed, one must realize that Dressy's family, in the words of Paul Rockwell, "had been peasants and retainers on the de Laage lands for many generations and the relationship was very close, almost a family one" (Rockwell to me, 12 January 1963).

59. Quoted in the *Journal de Marche*, 23 April 1917; Parsons, *Great Adventure*, p. 260.

60. Mortane, *Deux Grands Chevaliers*, pp. 294–95; *Journal de Marche*, 24 April 1917.

61. As often happened in aerial combat, Johnson did not see his victim hit the ground, primarily because he had other things to worry about. Thus in his report of the mission he told of firing fifty rounds which sent the German ship into a "vertical dive" (*Journal de Marche*, 26 April 1917). Such incidents make it very difficult to determine just how many combats ended in a downed airplane, even with the squadron log at hand. On at least one occasion, Lufbery didn't even bother to claim several victories, since they fell behind German lines and would not be confirmed anyway. "I know I got them," he told a friend who had seen three of them hit the ground, "and that is what counts." (Dolan, interview, 25 September 1962.)

62. *Journal de Marche*, 1 to 30 May 1917; Dolan to me, 25 January 1963.

63. *Journal de Marche*, 2 May 1917.

64. Mortane, *Deux Grands Chevaliers*, pp. 296–97.

65. Ibid., p. 296.

66. Entry in the diary of Emil A. Marchal under date of 23 May 1917. (Marchal, interview, 20 January 1960).

67. Quoted in Thenault, *l'Escadrille Lafayette*, p. 99. A striking characteristic of the interviews I had with survivors of the Lafayette Escadrille was the reverential respect they had for de Laage.

68. By the time the United States entered the war in April 1917, some eighty-four Americans had found their way into French aviation. Naturally, not all of them could fit into one squadron. This oversupply grew rapidly after America entered the war, primarily because for many months thereafter it was the quickest way to get flying training and into combat. With some degree of overlap, one can fit these men into three basic groups. The first and most unique was made up of those who entered the French service before the United States entered the war and before it was apparent that the country might do so. The second group comprises those who entered the French service after it was apparent that the United States would fight and that they would be a part of the conflict one way or another. The third group consisted of those who hurried to France after 6 April 1917 in order to fly and fight as quickly as possible. Because the Lafayette Escadrille came into being as an elite unit and because new men were carefully looked over before they were allowed to join, it remained an elite squadron throughout its existence. In a way, it was like a good social club. Nevertheless, as Edwin C. Parsons put it, "For such a small barrel, we had our share of bad apples" (Parsons to me, 13 December 1960).

69. "Andrew Courtney Campbell," *État Signaletique et des Services*, Class 1917, no. L.M.:11.835.

70. Parsons, *Great Adventure*, p. 299. Corrective measures included a fist fight in the barracks (Parsons, interview, 29 October 1960).

71. Hall and Nordhoff, *Lafayette Flying Corps*, 1:156.

72. Ibid., p. 145; Rockwell, interview, 1 January 1960.

73. The citation is quoted in Hall and Nordhoff, *Lafayette Flying Corps*, 1:144; 29 October 1960; Dolan, interview, 5 June 1960.

74. Jones, interview, 29 October 1960.

75. Hall and Nordhoff, *Lafayette Flying Corps*, 1:221; "John A. Drexel," *État Signaletique et des Services*, Class 1917, no. L.M.:11.962. There is evidence of some resentment on the part of the men of the Lafayette Escadrille at Drexel's transfer and commission as a major. Since he had no service experience other than that gained with the Service Aéronautique, they tended to regard the episode as a rather sad example of the manner in which the American Air Service handed out rank by preference instead of merit.

76. Dolan, interview, 5 June 1960.

77. Dolan to me, 25 January 1963; Dolan, interviews, 5 January 1960, 15 September 1962.

78. Hall and Nordhoff, *Lafayette Flying Corps*, 1:210–11; Rockwell, interview, 1 January 1960; Dolan, interview, 5 June 1960; Dolan to me, 25 January 1963. After the war, Dolan went on to win an enviable reputation in military and civil aviation, one of the few World War I pilots to do so.

79. Dolan to me, 25 January 1963; "Henry S. Jones," *État Signaletique et des Services*, Class 1917, no. L.M.:11.969; Jones, interview, 29 October 1960.

80. Hall and Nordhoff, *Lafayette Flying Corps*, 1:294; Jones, interview, 29 October 1960. After the war, Jones joined the F. W. Woolworth Company, eventually becoming manager of one of the firm's largest stores.

81. Hall and Nordhoff, *Lafayette Flying Corps*, 1:85; *Cross and Cockade Journal* (April 1961), p. 59.

82. Parsons, interview, 29 October 1960: Jones, interview, 29 October 1960.

83. *Journal de Marche*, 3 June 1917.

84. *Les Armées Françaises*, vol. 2, p. 192; Cruttwell, *History of the Great War*, p. 415.

85. See vol. 2, chapter 4 of *Les Armées Françaises* for an excellent description of the extent of the mutinies and the efforts to shore up the French army.

## VI: From Chaudun to the End at La Noblette

1. Mortane, *Deux Grands Chevaliers*, p. 298.

2. Jones, interview, 29 October 1960; Thenault, *l'Escadrille Lafayette*, p. 112.

3. Parsons, *Great Adventure*, p. 268; Parsons, interview, 29 October 1960.

4. Dolan to me, 7 March 1961. French antiaircraft shells exploded with a white burst, while those of the Germans were black. The quotation is from Parsons, *Great Adventure*, p. 273.

5. Dolan, interview, 15 September 1962; Dolan to me, 25 January 1963.

6. *Journal de Marche*, 4 June to 15 July 1917. It will be recalled that it was virtually impossible for French fliers to get confirmations if the enemy aircraft fell behind enemy lines beyond the observing range of French front-line trenches.

7. James Norman Hall, *My Island Home*, pp. 170–71.

8. Rockwell, interview, 1 January 1960; Parsons, *Great Adventure*, p. 275.

9. *Journal de Marche*, 24 June 1917. Within the Lafayette Escadrille, it was customary for a new pilot flying his first sortie over the lines to be escorted by two veteran pilots, one flying above and one below the novice. This was not always possible, however. (Dolan to me, 7 March 1973).

10. Unless otherwise noted, the information on this particular event was taken from the *Journal de Marche*, 26 June 1917; and Hall, *My Island Home*, pp. 181–85.

11. Parsons, *Great Adventure*, p. 282.

12. Thenault, *l'Escadrille Lafayette*, p. 94; Hall and Nordhoff, *Lafayette Flying Corps*, 1:256.

13. Hall, *My Island Home*, p. 183.

14. Mortane, *Deux Grands Chevaliers*, p. 298.

15. Ibid. One Captain Dourner, flying a SPAD, had observed the fight from a distance, and upon landing, put into operation the machinery which resulted in the confirmation. Thus, the formalities were taken care of by the time Lufbery landed.

16. Ibid., p. 301. The page in the *Journal de Marche* covering 3 to 6 June 1916 has a telegram attached in which Lufbery informs Captain Thenault that he is in the "local disciplinaire place de Chartres."

17. *Journal de Marche*, 16, 25 June 1917.

18. Hall and Nordhoff, *Lafayette Flying Corps*, 1:329; Mortane, *Deux Grands Chevaliers*, p. 301.

19. Thenault, *l'Escadrille Lafayette*, p. 95.

20. Parsons, *Great Adventure*, pp. 268–69; *Journal de Marche*, 7 July 1917.

21. Thenault, *l'Escadrille Lafayette*, p. 91.

22. "Lawrence Rumsey," *État Signaletique et des Services*, Class 1915, no. L.M.:1167.

23. Parsons, *Great Adventure*, p. 285; Rockwell, interview, 1 January 1960.

24. Hall and Nordhoff, *Lafayette Flying Corps*, 1:383.

25. Ibid., pp. 349, 351.

26. Ibid., p. 315.

27. Rockwell, interview, 1 January 1960.

28. Ministry of War, *Les Armées Françaises*, vol. 2, pp. 642, 646.

29. Raleigh and Jones, *War in the Air*, 4:138.

30. *Journal de Marche*, 17 July 1917.

31. Ibid.; Hall and Nordhoff, *Lafayette Flying Corps*, 1:215. Doolittle was eventually invalided out of the French army, and to his dismay, his wounds prevented him from successfully offering his services to the American Air Service. (Parsons, *Great Adventure*, p. 286.)

32. Thenault, *l'Escadrille Lafayette*, p. 100.

33. Raleigh and Jones, *War in the Air*, 4:163.

34. Parsons, *Great Adventure*, pp. 288–89. Since fighter pilots of that era were generally not enthusiastic about the idea of low-level or "fighter-bomber" flying anyway, they often yielded to the temptation to jettison their bombs and grenades "at the earliest convenience" (Jones, interview, 29 October 1960).

35. Falls, *Great War*, p. 301.

36. Falls, *Great War*, p. 301; *Journal de Marche*, 31 July to 4 August 1917.

37. *Journal de Marche*, 6 to 9 August 1917.

38. This is a qualified conclusion on my part. The French First Army remained in place, but it is clear from the withdrawal of select aviation units that French thoughts were elsewhere.

39. Ministry of War, *Les Armées Françaises*, vol. 2, pp. 732–33.

40. Parsons, *Great Adventure*, p. 297.

41. Ibid., p. 296. The citation can be found in a number of sources, including Hall and Nordhoff.

42. *Journal de Marche*, 16 to 17 August 1917.

43. Quoted in Hall and Nordhoff, *Lafayette Flying Corps*, 1:494.

44. Parsons, *Great Adventure*, p. 306.

45. Ibid., pp. 306–7. Willis remained a prisoner until October 1918, when on his fourth attempt he made good his escape in the best tradition of Yankee ingenuity. Doctoring his prison garb to look as much as possible like a guard's uniform, he used the confusion of a larger break on a dark night to join with the search for escaping prisoners. He quickly deserted the search crew and, joining with a U.S. naval lieutenant by the name of Isaacs, whose ship had been torpedoed in the Atlantic, he finally succeeded in making his way across the Rhine River into Switzerland. He arrived back in Paris just in time to join his Lafayette comrades in the Armistice celebrations. See Hall and Nordhoff, *Lafayette Flying Corps*, 2:294–313, for Willis's first-person account. See also Edouard Victor Isaacs, *Prisoner of the U-90*.

46. Thenault, *l'Escadrille Lafayette*, p. 105.

47. *Journal de Marche*, 20 August 1917; "Stephen Bigelow," *État Signaletique et des Services*, Class 1917, no. L.M:11.787. Even so, Bigelow received a citation for his part in the day's struggle.

48. Parsons, *Great Adventure*, pp. 302–3.

49. Ibid., p. 303; Dolan, interview, 15 September 1962.

50. *Journal de Marche*, 24 September 1917; Dolan to me, 7 March 1963.

51. Parsons, *Great Adventure*, p. 304; Dolan, interview, 15 September 1962.

52. Hall and Nordhoff, *Lafayette Flying Corps*, 1:350–51.

53. *Journal de Marche*, 4 September 1917; Mortane, *Deux Grands Chevaliers*, p. 303.

54. *Journal de Marche*, 19 September 1917.

55. Ibid., 22 September 1917; Mortane, *Deux Grands Chevaliers*, p. 302.

56. Thenault, *l'Escadrille Lafayette*, p. 114; Parsons, interview, 29 October 1960; Jones, interview, 29 October 1960.

57. Parsons, *Great Adventure*, p. 305.

58. Ministry of War, *Les Armées Françaises*, vol. 2, p. 912.

59. *Journal de Marche*, 30 September to 8 December 1917.

60. Ibid., 1 October 1917; Parsons, *Great Adventure*, pp. 325–26. See chapter 8 for a sequel to the Campbell disappearance.

61. Parsons, *Great Adventure*, pp. 311, 325–26.

62. "Andrew C. Campbell," *État Signaletique et des Services*, Class 1917, no. L.M.:11.835.

63. Hall and Nordhoff, *Lafayette Flying Corps*, 1:85–86; Parsons interview, 29 October 1960; Jones, interview, 29 October 1960.

64. Quoted in Hall and Nordhoff, *Lafayette Flying Corps*, 1:90.

65. Parsons, *Great Adventure*, p. 300.

66. Hall and Nordhoff, *Lafayette Flying Corps*, 1:237; "Christopher Ford," *État Signaletique et des Services*, Class 1918, no. L.M.:11.175.

67. Hall and Nordhoff, *Lafayette Flying Corps*, 1:237.

68. *Journal de Marche*, 15 to 16 October 1917; Mortane, *Deux Grands Chevaliers*, p. 303.

69. *Journal de Marche*, 24 October 1917. We cannot assume that Lufbery was alone on these patrols, but he did prefer to fight alone. When he mixed it up with a German pilot, his comrades knew they were supposed to stay out of the fight, unless, of course, Lufbery himself was shot down. "I am quite capable of taking care of my own fights," he said. (Dolan to me, 7 March 1963.)

70. Ibid.

71. Thenault, *l'Escadrille Lafayette*, p. 116.

72. Mortane, *Deux Grands Chevaliers*, p. 303. It is worth noting that Mortane, who knew Lufbery well and apparently had access to considerable information about Lufbery and his flying, makes no mention of the remarkable feat described above.

73. *Journal de Marche*, 2 December 1917.

74. Mortane, *Deux Grands Chevaliers*, p. 304.

75. Hinkle, interview, 10 July 1959.

76. Guerin, interview, 20 January 1960.

77. Parsons, *Great Adventure*, p. 151. Whiskey and Soda died of the mange shortly after the war.

78. Thenault, *l'Escadrille Lafayette*, p. 117.

79. *Journal de Marche*, 9 December 1917 to 7 January 1918. Except for the entries in the *Journal de Marche*, there is no specific evidence in any of the sources examined in this study that suggests that these French fliers were officially assigned to the Lafayette Escadrille. Apparently they were on temporary assignment, or they may have been members of sister squadrons, more or less on loan to the SPA-124.

### VII: The Transfer

1. Channing, ed., *War Letters of Edmond Genêt*, pp. 225–26.

2. Ibid., p. 318.

3. Thenault, *l'Escadrille Lafayette*, p. 82.

4. Telegram, Ambassador Jules Jusserand to the French Minister of Foreign Affairs, no. 373, 6 April 1917. Archives des Services Historiques de l'Armée de l'Air.

5. Ibid.

6. Telegram, Minister of War to État-Major Beauvais, no. 465, c.k., 10 April 1917. Archives des Services Historiques de l'Armée de l'Air.

7. Thenault to M. le Général Commandant en Chef, 17 April 1917. Archives des Services Historiques de l'Armée de l'Air.

8. Ibid.

9. Ibid.

10. *New York Times*, 12 April 1917. The headlines introducing this article read as a flat announcement that the squadron was being formed.

11. Rockwell, *American Fighters*, p. 296; Salesse, "La Groupe d'Aviation de Chasse 11/5 en 1939–40," p. 20.

12. Parsons, *Great Adventure*, p. 255.

13. Alfred Goldberg, ed., *A History of the United States Air Force, 1907–1957*, p. 15.

14. Arthur Sweester, *The American Air Service*, p. 16; John J. Pershing, *My Experiences in the World War*, 1:27.

15. These missions, and particularly the French ones, naturally used the reputation of the Lafayette Escadrille to further stimulate public interest in combat aviation. See Sweester, *American Air Service*, p. 59, and Goldberg, *History*, p. 14.

16. Edgar S. Gorrell, *The Measure of America's World War Aeronautical Effort*, p. 1.

17. Sweester, *American Air Service*, p. 68.

18. Gorrell, *Measure*, p. 4; Dr. C. D. Walcott of the National Advisory Committee for Aeronautics, quoted in Sweester, *American Air Service*, p. 45.

19. Quoted in Hall and Nordhoff, *Lafayette Flying Corps*, 1:40–41.

20. Commandant Féquant to l'Aide Général Chef du Service Aéronautique at Grand Quartier Général, 5 September 1917. Archives des Services Historiques de l'Armée de l'Air.

21. Commandant Féquant to l'Aide Général Chef du Service Aéronautique, 5 September 1917. Féquant's admiration for his American friends can be measured by the fact that this officer, a national hero who rose to the rank of full general, wished to be buried in the crypt of the Lafayette Escadrille memorial near Paris. His wish was granted, and he rests in the crypt with the more than sixty young Americans who gave their lives flying for France.

22. Memo, l'Aide-Major Général Chef du Service Aéronautique to the Groupe de Chasse 13, 15 September 1917. Archives des Services Historiques de l'Armée de l'Air.

23. See Henry G. Pearson, *A Businessman in Uniform: Raynal Cawthorne Bolling.*

24. Ibid., p. 143.

25. The "Commission" was made up of Maj. R. H. Goldthwaite, Lt. R. S. Beam, and Dr. (Major) Edmund Gros, who acted as head of the delegation. (Hall and Nordhoff, *Lafayette Flying Corps*, 1:53).

26. Hqs, Air Service Line of Communications, A.E.F., special order no. 34, 11 September 1917. Quoted in Hall and Nordhoff, *Lafayette Flying Corps*, 1:53.

27. In all, 38,770 men sought military pilot training with the American Air Service between 14 July 1914 and 2 June 1918. Of this number, 18,004 were accepted. (Sweester, *American Air Service*, pp. 98, 102.)

28. Ibid., p. 99.

29. Quoted in ibid., p. 101.

30. This assertion is bound to be challenged by many of those who lack experience with combat aviation. The supporting evidence, however, can be had in abundance and is unmistakably clear. As every fighter pilot knows, there are no firm criteria for determining in advance which pilots will be "tigers." As Dr. William R. Emerson of the Franklin D. Roosevelt Library, a top-level military historian and a former fighter pilot, once put it, "Only one man in a hundred can *fly* fighters. Most just burn gas" (interview, 10 January 1963). Moreover, experience has shown that the elite can include a thoroughly undisciplined youth like Frank Luke, a poor physical specimen like the incomparable Georges Guynemer, or even a person lacking certain flying skills. Example: "Buzz" Buerling, the well-known British ace of World War II, of whom it was said that he had to shoot down two Germans every time he went aloft to show a net gain since he invariably washed out his own fighter trying to land it. Indeed, one could make an interesting if not too credible case for the view that the so-called heroes of air fighting tend to fall into what one might call an unstable category.

31. Dolan, interview, 15 September 1962.

32. Hqs, A.E.F., special order no. 113, 1 October 1917. Quoted in Hall and Nordhoff, *Lafayette Flying Corps*, 1:54. Of the men making up the commission, Major Gros (the doctor) could be expected to look after the interests of the American fliers, Major Goldthwaite had been on the earlier commission, and Major Hoffman was a man who clearly appreciated the position of the Lafayette pilots.

33. Hall and Nordhoff, *Lafayette Flying Corps*, 1:55.

34. For some reason, the actual recommendations of rank do not appear as part of the commission report, although at one time they must have been an integral part of it. It is possible, however, to partially reconstruct the recommendations by adding one rank to those actually given. See p. 18. This is not completely accurate, for it appears that the commission gave no recommendations higher than major, that Foulois initially reduced all ranks by one grade, but that some ranks were later awarded as originally recommended.

35. Edmund Gros ed., "A Brief History of the Lafayette Flying Corps," unpub-

lished MS, p. 12. Record Group 120, Army and Air Corps Branch, National Archives of the United States.

36. Parsons, *Great Adventure*, p. 313.

37. Hall and Nordhoff, *Lafayette Flying Corps*, 1:55.

38. Quoted in ibid., p. 55.

39. Colonel Bolling to the Undersecretary of State for Military Aeronautics, 10 October 1917. Record Group 120, Army and Air Corps Branch, National Archives of the United States.

40. Hall and Nordhoff, *Lafayette Flying Corps*, 1:56.

41. Rockwell, *American Fighters*, p. 296; Hall, *My Island Home*, p. 200.

42. Harold B. Willis to Paul A. Rockwell, n.d., ca. November 1917. Original in the Paul A. Rockwell Collection. Rockwell, *American Fighters*, p. 296.

43. Quoted in Hall and Nordhoff, *Lafayette Flying Corps*, 1:56.

44. Ibid.; Memo, Général Directeur de l'Infanterie for the French Premier and the Minister of War, 11 December 1917. Archives des Services Historiques de l'Armée de l'Air.

45. Quoted in Hall and Nordhoff, *Lafayette Flying Corps*, 1:58.

46. Telephone message, Général Commandant en Chef (Aéronautique) to Général Chef Mission Française attached to Headquarters, A.E.F., 24 December 1917. A written copy of the message is in the Archives des Services Historiques de l'Armée de l'Air.

47. Pearson, *Businessman in Uniform*, p. 195; William W. Hoffman, interview, 3 October 1962.

48. William W. Hoffman to me, 20 October 1959.

49. Pearson, *Businessman in Uniform*, p. 169.

50. Hall and Nordhoff, *Lafayette Flying Corps*, 1:56.

51. Ibid., pp. 56–57; Hoffman, interview, 3 October 1962.

52. Hall and Nordhoff, *Lafayette Flying Corps*, 1:57.

53. In the course of this study, I met several Americans who made this category.

54. Telegram, Commander 6th A.I.C., to Major Gros, n.d., ca. January 1918. Record Group 120, Army and Air Corps Branch, National Archives of the United States.

55. Hoffman to me, 20 October 1959; Rockwell, interview, 1 January 1960.

56. Rockwell, interview, 1 January 1960.

57. Harold B. Willis to Paul Rockwell, n.d., ca. November 1917.

58. Rockwell to me, 10 October 1959.

59. Hoffman, interview, 3 October 1962. To the best of my knowledge, General Foulois nowhere specified in writing his program as I have outlined it above. Since he apparently left much of the initiative for the agreement to the French, his program must be reconstructed from his reactions to various proposals and counterproposals.

60. Général Commandant en Chef, G.Q.G. des Armées du Nord et du Nord Est to S/Secretaire de l'Aéronautique Militaire et Maritime, 12 February 1918. Archives des Services Historiques de l'Armée de l'Air.

### VIII: The Legacy

1. Quoted in Mason, *Lafayette Escadrille*, p. 105.

2. All biographical information showing unit designations of the Lafayette pilots during their service with the French can be found in vol. 1 of Hall and Nordhoff, *Lafayette Flying Corps*.

3. The evidence for this assertion is cumulative rather than specific. Letters of the period and subsequent interviews with a number of the survivors support the assertion.

4. Charles H. Dolan to Commandant Georges Thenault, 5 September 1931. Crehore Collection, USAF Academy, Colorado.

5. *Cross and Cockade Journal* (Spring 1961), p. 47.

6. Falnes to me, March 1960; Rockwell, interview, 1 January 1960.

7. Denison Kitchel, *The Truth about the Panama Canal*, pp. 11, 12.

8. Rockwell, interviews, 8 December 1978, 12 April 1979. Paul Rockwell has extensive newspaper clippings concerning ringers. The Crehore Collection at the Air Force Academy also has a number of clippings dealing with this unique group. A surprising number of articles in each collection use the words *original member* and *founder.*

9. See *Time Magazine*, 4 January 1960, for a revealing article on the accolades given Walter Williams.

10. *American Aviation Magazine*, 15 December 1939. Clipping in the Crehore Collection.

11. Ibid.; Rockwell, interview, 7 December 1979.

12. Ibid.; Rockwell has a number of newspaper clippings concerning this event.

13. *San Antonio* (Texas) *Light*, 25 September 1932. Clipping in the Rockwell Collection.

14. Quoted in Mason, *Lafayette Escadrille*, p. 288.

15. *Asheville* (North Carolina) *Citizen Times*, 4 October 1932. Clipping in the Rockwell Collection.

16. Rockwell, interviews, 1 January 1960, 7 December 1978; Edwin C. Parsons to Major Robert Hays, 16 August 1964. Copy in my collection. Rockwell and Parsons both felt that the money came from Frederick H. Prince, Sr., the father of Lafayette Escadrille pilots Norman Prince and Frederick H. Prince, Jr., who intended the new squadron be named after his fallen son.

17. Parsons to Major Hays, 16 August 1964.

18. Ibid.

19. Ibid.

20. *Los Angeles Examiner*, 27 February 1940.

21. Parsons to Major Hays, 16 August 1964.

22. *Los Angeles Examiner*, 27 February 1940, 28 February 1940.

23. Ibid.; Parsons to Major Hays, 16 August 1964.

24. Rockwell, interviews, 7 December 1978, 12 April 1979.

25. Ibid.; *New Canaan* (Connecticut) *Advertiser*, 7 December 1939. Clipping in the Paul A. Rockwell Collection.

26. Rockwell, interviews, 7 December 1978, 12 April 1979.

27. Ibid.; Rockwell to me, 21 September 1966, 14 January 1980.

28. Rockwell, interview, 7 December 1978.

29. Ibid.

30. In virtually all interviews with the survivors and with Col. Paul Rockwell, the subject of the 1939 Rockwell/Willis effort to found a second Lafayette Escadrille was discussed. The interviewees invariably expressed regret at the failure of the enterprise.

31. Warner Brothers Studios, "Production Notes on 'Lafayette Escadrille,' " n.d., ca. 1958. When I wrote Warner Brothers in 1960 asking about the research done to provide authenticity for the film, a copy of the production notes was provided without further comment.

32. Stenographic notes, telephone conversation between William Wellman and Austen Crehore, 29 January 1957. Copy in the Charles Dolan Collection.

33. Hall and Nordhoff, *Lafayette Flying Corps*, 1:114–15.

34. A copy of the letterhead stationery can be found in the Austen Crehore Collection, USAF Academy, Colorado.

35. Rockwell, interview, 7 December 1978.

36. Charles H. Dolan to Mayor Stewart, 24 February 1958. Copy in the Crehore Collection.

37. *Raleigh* (North Carolina) *News and Observer*, 5 March 1958. Clipping in the Paul A. Rockwell Collection.

38. *Waynesville* (North Carolina) *Mountaineer*, 5 March 1958. Clipping in the Paul A. Rockwell Collection.

39. *Asheville* (North Carolina) *Citizen Times*, 23 March 1958. Clipping in the Paul A. Rockwell Collection.

40. Ibid.

41. Rockwell, interviews, 1 January 1960, 7 December 1978.

42. William Wellman to me, 5 December 1960. Wellman gave the following explanation. "A few years ago I wrote a story called 'C'est la Guerre,' a story of one pilot in the *Lafayette Flying Corps*—It was a tragedy and was made as such and unfortunately when Warner-Bros got through changing the title and the story, the whole thing became a Little Boy Blue affair and one that I am terribly ashamed of."

43. MS, "Constitution of the Lafayette Escadrille N-124 Society," distributed at the Lafayette Escadrille Reunion, Asheville, North Carolina, 3 to 6 June 1960. (All attendees at the reunion were provided copies of this document.) Unless otherwise noted, the remainder of this section dealing with the N-124 Society is based on this document.

44. Minister of War, *Revue Historique de l'Armée, Numero Special, Fraternité d'Armes Franco-Américaine*, p. 107.

45. Ibid., p. 108.

46. Ibid.

47. Captain Louis Richard, interview, 3 June 1960. At the time of this interview, Richard was commander of the French fighter unit carrying the name and tradition of the 1916–18 Lafayette Escadrille.

48. Rockwell to me, 20 July 1967.

49. Memo, Maj. Gen. J. H. Doolittle, Commander, 12th Air Force, to Deputy Commander in Chief for Air, 20 December 1942. Copy in the Paul A. Rockwell Collection.

50. *Fraternité d'Armes Franco-Américaine*, pp. 108–12.

51. Rockwell to me, 20 July 1967; Rockwell, interview, 7 December 1978.

52. Richard, interview, 3 June 1960; Capt. Michael H. Ghesquiere, interview, 18 January 1960. At the time of the interview, Ghesquiere was second-in-command of the unit carrying the tradition of the original Lafayette Escadrille.

53. *New York Herald Tribune*, 24 May 1967.

54. Rockwell to me, 20 July 1967.

55. Rockwell, interview, 7 December 1978. The bottle, under careful security, was brought to the July 1967 celebration at Luxeuil-les-Bains.

56. Ibid.; Rockwell, interview, 12 April 1979.

57. I own copies of the program for the dedication and the memorial brochure. The former lists the speakers; both contain the Foch testimonial.

# Bibliography

Sources on the Lafayette Escadrille tend to fall into two distinct categories. On the one hand, individuals who were either in the squadron or closely associated with it have left a surprisingly large number of letters, memorandums, articles, books, and photographs. With few exceptions, these primary sources are basically reliable. On the other hand, a sizeable group of secondary sources, made up mostly of newspaper and magazine articles and books, purport to tell the story of the Lafayette Escadrille or some of its individual members. As a rule, authors within this group, usually writing for profit, have tended toward sensationalism.

There have always been serious discrepancies between the two groups of sources both in emphasis and content, particularly since the spirit of the Lafayette Escadrille has been seriously misinterpreted in the United States. As a result, it is safe to say that at this time a credible history of the Lafayette Escadrille cannot be written without careful emphasis on primary sources. In this regard, I found my research greatly enhanced by three invaluable controls. The first consisted of the eight surviving members of the squadron who were alive when the basic research for this book was underway. With one exception, all were willing to be interviewed at length and to answer letters. Nor did they mind having their memories tested against each other and against source documents. Col. Paul A. Rockwell, of Asheville, North Carolina, was another primary control. Having known all of the squadron members well, and having served as the unofficial historian of the Lafayette Escadrille, his remarkable memory and equally impressive collection of documents proved uniquely invaluable. In an almost endless process of checking and crosschecking, I never found him to have made a serious error in fact or judgment. The third control came in the form of the squadron's *Journal de Marche*, its official log or diary, found in a private home in Paris. Many incidents otherwise seemingly acceptable had to be omitted when the *Journal* made no mention of them.

It remains to be noted that I have not cited all sources examined in the preparation of this history, nor are all listed in the bibliography. This is particularly true of the many books on World War I aviation I have studied over the years. The latter were included only if they helped understand the air war or had relevance to the Lafayette Escadrille.

## Archives and Personal Collections

*Archives des Services Historiques de l'Armée de l'Air*, Versailles, France. This archive contains a large quantity of miscellaneous material on the Lafayette Escadrille, including letters, leave requests, combat reports, etc. Most of the material is of marginal value since groups of records such as the combat reports are not complete. The archives do contain some very important documents relating to the transfer of the Lafayette Escadrille pilots to the American Air Service, primarily from the French position.

*Archives, Bureau Central d'Incorporation et d'Archives de l'Armée de l'Air*, Compiègne, France. This archive contains official documents related to the Lafayette Escadrille, including the personal history cards filled out by the American volunteers and a monthly log and report book, listing the men and aircraft assigned to the squadron at given times. This latter source, made up of several small books, was the only document available to me that gave the roster of nonflying as well as flying personnel.

*Archives, Ministère de la Guerre*, Paris, France. From this source I obtained invaluable typescript copies of the *État Signaletique et des Services* (official service records) of all but five of the American pilots who flew with the Lafayette Escadrille.

*National Archives of the United States*, Washington, D.C. Since the Lafayette Escadrille was an official French unit, this archive contains comparatively few documents relating to the squadron. Of those it does contain, the most important ones are those concerned with the transfer of the squadron members to the American Air Service. The State Department section of this archive contains almost no reference to the American pilots flying for France, a significant omission.

*Microtext Reading Room, Sterling Memorial Library, Yale University*, New Haven, Connecticut. While in France in 1960 I was allowed entry into a "closed" archive on the condition that I not disclose its identity. The French government, however, graciously microfilmed pertinent documents for my use, and, since the French placed no restriction on the film itself, it has been placed in the Yale University Library. It is filed under France: Lafayette Escadrille.

*Personal collection of Austen Crehore*, Air Force Academy, Colorado. Crehore flew for France in squadrons other than the Lafayette and was active in preserving the tradition of the Lafayette Flying Corps. His collection has a few significant documents relating to the Lafayette Escadrille. A prime asset, however, is a fine collection of news clippings, many of them detailing events in the lives of Lafayette Escadrille survivors after the war.

*Personal collection of Madame Jean Paul Deudon*, Paris, France. Madame Deudon, the daughter of the French commander of the Lafayette Escadrille, Georges Thenault, kept many of her father's papers, including those used in the preparation of his book *l'Escadrille Lafayette*. Among this collection was the invaluable N-124 *Journal de Marche*, the official log or diary of the squadron. This priceless document is now on display in the

National Air and Space Museum, Washington, D.C., the generous gift of Madame Georges Thenault, Madame Deudon, and the French government.

*Personal collection of Colonel Charles H. Dolan II, Hawaii.* Besides keeping documents and photographs relating to his own tour of duty with the Lafayette Escadrille and the American Air Service, Colonel Dolan, who looked after many of his fellow Lafayette pilots after the war, fell heir to some of their material as well. His collection is extensive.

*Personal collection of Madame Marcelle Guerin, Monte Carlo, Monaco.* As a young American girl living in France, Marcelle Guerin knew several of the Lafayette Escadrille pilots and regularly corresponded with them. Their letters to her form the foundation of her collection, which also includes newspaper clippings, photographs, etc.

*Personal collection of Rear Adm. (Ret.) Edwin C. Parsons, Osprey, Florida.* Admiral Parsons, who wrote extensively about the Lafayette Escadrille in the period between the wars, kept an impressive collection of articles, documents, medals, citations, etc., most of which relate to his duty with the French Service Aéronautique.

*Personal collection of Col. Paul A. Rockwell, Asheville, North Carolina.* Colonel Rockwell, whose brother was one of the original Lafayette Escadrille pilots, was the unofficial historian of the squadron both during and after the war. Over the years he collected an incredible amount of published and unpublished material relating to the squadron, including letters, orders, newspaper clippings, citations, books, pamphlets, etc. For anyone researching the Lafayette Escadrille, the value of this collection can hardly be overestimated.

*Personal collection of Mrs. Robert Soubiran, Washington, D.C.* Through various means, Robert Soubiran, who flew with the Lafayette Escadrille, acquired and copyrighted an impressive collection of photographs relating to the Lafayette Escadrille. The Soubiran collection is now located in the library of the National Air and Space Museum, Washington, D.C.

### Personal Interviews

Crehore, Austen B., New York City, 27 December 1960. Mr. Crehore flew with the French in Escadrille SPA-94 from December 1917 to the Armistice. Although he manifested some animosity toward the Lafayette Escadrille during the interview—he felt the squadron had had more than its share of glory—he did much to keep alive the tradition of those who flew for France.

Deudon, Madame Jean Paul, Paris, France, 14 January 1960. Madame Deudon, the daughter of the French commander of the Lafayette Escadrille, related to me her father's feelings about the squadron.

Dolan, Charles H., II, Asheville, North Carolina, 4 June 1960, 5 June 1960; New Haven, Connecticut, 15 September 1962; Air Force Academy, Colorado, 12 April 1966. Colonel Dolan flew with the Lafayette Escadrille from May

1917 to February 1918. His aviation experience, both military and civil, has been extensive. He is the last surviving member of the Lafayette Escadrille.

Emerson, William R., New Haven, Connecticut, 10 January 1963. Dr. Emerson, a ranking military historian, flew fighter aircraft in World War II.

Ghesquiere, Captain Michael H., Freibourg, Germany, 18 January 1960. At the time of the interview, Captain Ghesquiere was a flight commander in the Lafayette Escadron, a crack French fighter unit that inherited the name and the tradition of the original Lafayette Escadrille.

Guerin, Madame Marcelle, Monte Carlo, Monaco, 20 January 1960. In France during World War I, Madame Guerin knew several of the Lafayette pilots and maintained a close association with them.

Hinkle, Edward F., Mount Clemens, Michigan, 10 July 1959. Hinkle, who was over forty years of age when he joined the Service Aéronautique, flew with the Lafayette Escadrille from March 1917 to June 1917.

Hoffman, Maj. William W., New York City, 3 October 1962. Major Hoffman was a member of the American army commission that helped arrange the transfer of Lafayette Escadrille pilots from the Service Aéronautique to the American Air Service.

Jones, Henry S., Asheville, North Carolina, 4 June 1960; Osprey, Florida, 29 October 1960. Jones flew with the Lafayette Escadrille from May 1917 to February 1918.

Lufbery, Charles, Wallingford, Connecticut, 10 July 1962. Charles Lufbery is a brother of Raoul Lufbery, the triple ace of the Lafayette Escadrille.

Marchal, Emil A., Pegomas, France, 20 January 1960. Due to an error, Marchal, an American and a nonflier, was assigned to the Lafayette Escadrille. He learned to appreciate the squadron before returning to the trenches.

Marr, Kenneth, Luke Air Force Base, Arizona, 16 August 1960. Marr flew with the Lafayette Escadrille from March 1917 to February 1918.

Martin, Oliver R. W., Paris, France, 11 January 1960. Martin, a French pilot during the Great War, became well acquainted with the Lafayette Escadrille pilots. Later one of France's leading scientists in astronautics, he contributed much to the understanding and appreciation of the American pilots by his countrymen.

Parsons, Rear Adm. Edwin C., Asheville, North Carolina, 4 June 1960; 5 June 1960; Osprey, Florida, 29 October 1960; New Haven, Connecticut, 12 September 1961. Parsons, one of the aces of the Lafayette Escadrille, flew with the squadron from January 1917 to February 1918. Unlike his fellow Americans in the SPA-124, he did not transfer to the American Air Service.

Prince, Frederick H., Jr., Asheville, North Carolina, 4 June 1960. The brother of Norman Prince, one of the original members of the Lafayette Escadrille, Frederick Prince flew with the squadron from October 1916 to February 1917.

Richard, Captain Louis, Asheville, North Carolina, 4 June 1960. Captain Richard was the commander of the Lafayette Escadron when he came to the United States in June 1960 to participate in a reunion of Lafayette Escadrille pilots.

Rockwell, Col. Paul A., Washington, D.C., 7 November 1959; Asheville, North Carolina, 30 December 1959; 1 January 1960; 4 June 1960; 5 June 1960; 7 December 1978; 12 April 1979. Colonel Rockwell, appointed the unofficial historian of the N-124 by the original members of the unit, personally knew every pilot who flew with the Lafayette Escadrille.

Soubiran, Mrs. Robert, Washington, D.C., 7 November 1959. Mrs. Soubiran is the widow of Robert Soubiran, a former Lafayette Escadrille pilot.

Willis, Col. Harold B., Asheville, North Carolina, 4 June 1960. Colonel Willis flew with the Lafayette Escadrille from February 1917 until the following August, when he was shot down and captured by the Germans.

### Personal Correspondence

Bertin, Col. Jean, Assistant Air Attaché to the French Embassy, Washington, D.C., one letter, May 1960, to me.

Buck, Mrs. James J., one letter, August 1960, to me. Mrs. Buck's husband, the late James J. Bach (later changed to Buck) served in the French Foreign Legion and the Service Aéronautique. He would have become a member of the Lafayette Escadrille except for his capture by the Germans on 23 September 1915.

Connett, William B., First Secretary to the American Embassy, Paris, France, one letter, February 1960, to me.

Cousins, William S., Secretary, Fondation du Memorial de l'Escadrille Lafayette, one letter, January 1960, to me.

Crehore, Austen B., four letters, November 1960–April 1961, to me. Prior to his death in 1962, Crehore collected newspaper clippings on the so-called ringers, people falsely claiming membership in the Lafayette Escadrille and the Lafayette Flying Corps.

Deudon, Madame Jean Paul, one letter, September 1960, to me. Madame Deudon's father commanded the Lafayette Escadrille throughout its existence.

Dolan, Col. Charles H., thirty-five letters, September 1939–December 1978, to me. Dolan flew with the Lafayette Escadrille from May 1917 to February 1918. He is the lone survivor.

Falnes, Oscar J., Assistant Chairman, Department of History, New York University, one letter, March 1960, to me.

Guerin, Madame Marcelle, six letters, January 1960–January 1963, to me. As a young American girl in France, Marcelle Guerin knew several of the Lafayette Escadrille pilots.

Hinkle, Edward F., fourteen letters, May 1959–March 1963, to me. Hinkle flew with the Lafayette Escadrille from March 1917 to June 1917.

Hoffman, Maj. William W., eight letters, October 1960–February 1963, to me. Hoffman was a member of an American army commission that helped arrange the transfer of the Lafayette Escadrille pilots to the American Air Service.

Hoover, J. Edgar, Director, Federal Bureau of Investigation, one letter, April 1961, to me.

Jones, Henry S., five letters, December 1959–February 1963, to me. Jones flew with the Lafayette Escadrille from May 1917 to February 1918.

Lufbery, Charles, one letter, February 1963, to me. Charles Lufbery was a brother of the Lafayette Escadrille ace Raoul Lufbery.

Marchal, Emil A., five letters, March 1959–January 1963, to me. Marchal served with the Lafayette Escadrille as *personnel non-navigant*.

Marr, Kenneth, three letters, August 1959–January 1961, to me. Marr flew with the Lafayette Escadrille from March 1917 to February 1918.

Parsons, Rear Adm. Edwin C., 42 letters, May 1959–March 1963, to me. Parsons flew with the Lafayette Escadrille from January 1917 to February 1918.

Prince, Frederick H., Jr., two letters, November 1959–March 1960, to me. Prince flew with the Lafayette Escadrille from October 1916 to February 1917.

Rockwell, Col. Paul A., 119 letters, May 1959–January 1980, to me. Rockwell, who knew personally every pilot who flew with the Lafayette Escadrille, was regarded by the pilots as the historian of the unit.

Sharp, George C., one letter, to his son George, 10 January 1963. Sharp, U.S. ambassador to France, 1914–19, wrote this letter in response to some inquiries made by his son on my behalf.

Soubiran, Mrs. Robert, seven letters, November 1959–May 1960, to me. Mrs. Soubiran's husband flew with the Lafayette Escadrille from October 1916 to February 1917.

Thenault, Sarah Spencer, four letters, December 1959–September 1962, to me. Mrs. Thenault is the widow of the late Colonel Georges Thenault, the commander of the Lafayette Escadrille.

Wellman, William, one letter, 5 December 1960, to me. Wellman was the director and producer of *The Lafayette Escadrille*, a Warner Brothers' movie which had its premiere in 1958.

Willis, Col. Harold B., three letters, May 1959–July 1960, to me. Colonel Willis flew with the Lafayette Escadrille from March 1917 to August 1917.

## Articles

Balsley, Clyde, and P. Adams. "Story of the Lafayette Escadrille." *Bellman* 25 (20 July 1918): 68–72. Brief and rather shallow account of the Lafayette Escadrille. Balsley flew with the Escadrille from May to June 1916.

Best, J. V. "Status of Americans Fighting under Foreign Flag." *Law Notes* 22 (October 1918): 127–31. Best attempts to analyze the status of American volunteers under the terms of laws disenfranchising Americans taking an oath of allegiance to foreign states. Unfortunately, Best draws no firm conclusions.

"The Diary of H. Clyde Balsley." *Cross and Cockade Journal* 18, no. 2 (Summer

1977):97–123. Balsley flew with the Lafayette Escadrille for less than a month before he was severely wounded and eventually invalided out of the Service Aéronautique.

Genêt, Edmond C. C. "La Mort de McConnell." *La Guerre Aérienne* (26 April 1917), p. 379. Genêt was McConnell's companion on the ill-fated flight that ended with McConnell's death.

Hall, Bert. "Fast Fighting and Narrow Escapes in the Air." *The American Magazine* 86 (September 1918):43–45. Grossly exaggerated account by a member of the Lafayette Escadrille who not only was known for taking literary license but who also, by his own confession, was "not a literary cuss."

Hennessy, Juliette A. "The Lafayette Escadrille: Past and Present." *The Airpower Historian* 4, no. 3 (July 1959):150–61. Generally accurate description of the Lafayette Escadrille with valuable emphasis on the tradition of the squadron in the American Army Air Corps and the U.S. Air Force.

Lovell, Walter. "Mon Premier Combat." *La Guerre Aérienne* (22 November 1917), p. 629. Lovell, a Lafayette Escadrille pilot, did not meet any German fliers on this sortie, but his willingness to continue the flight alone, mechanical trouble, and a fuel shortage almost proved his undoing.

Lufbery, Raoul G. "Mon Premier Combat." *La Guerre Aérienne* (27 November 1917), pp. 35–36. Lufbery's personal account of his first combat, which took place while he was flying bombers.

———. "Un Boche Abattu." *La Guerre Aérienne* (10 January 1918), p. 139. Lufbery's description of his first confirmed victory.

"Lufbery Vanquished in a Battle with Huge German Plane." *Literary Digest* 57 (8 June 1918):42–44. Popular but reasonably accurate account of Lufbery's spectacular death.

McConnell, James R. "Flying for France." *The World's Work* 33 (November 1916):41–53; (March 1917):479–509. Well-written but brief history of the Lafayette Escadrille and the fliers in it. Much of this material appeared in McConnell's book of the same title.

———. "Soldats due Ceil pour la France." *La Guerre Aérienne* (3 May 1917), pp. 389–91; (10 May 1917), pp. 415–16; (17 May 1917), pp. 430–31. Valuable first-hand account of the early exploits of the Lafayette Escadrille.

———. "Verdun." *La Guerre Aérienne* (27 September 1917), pp. 722–24; (11 October 1917), pp. 762–63; (15 November 1917), pp. 797–98. Excellent description of the air battle over Verdun in 1916 and the role played by the men of the N-124.

Masson, Didier. "Le Premier Essai d'Aviation a la Guerre," *La Guerre Aérienne* (22 November 1917), pp. 19–21. Delightful narrative by a pioneer airman who flew for General Obregon in 1913.

Mortane, Jacques. "l'As Lufbery, Mecanicien de Marc Pourpe." *La Guerre Aérienne* (12 July 1917), p. 546. Mortane knew Lufbery well and here describes the flier's unusual life before he became a pilot.

————. "Le Commandant Happe." *La Guerre Aérienne* (31 May 1917), pp. 458–459. Excellent article by an outstanding aviation writer about one of the most incredible airmen who ever lived.

————. "Les Heroes Disparus: Marc Pourpe." *La Guerre Aérienne* (4 December 1916), p. 55. Brief description of the tragedy that triggered Lufbery's thirst for vengence.

————. "l'Escadrille La Fayette." *La Guerre Aérienne* (22 February 1917), pp. 227–31. One of the better descriptions of the Lafayette Escadrille. Mortane knew and respected the American pilots.

————. "Quelques Citations des 'As' Americains." *La Guerre Aérienne* (19 July 1917), p. 577. Some of the citations won by pilots of the Lafayette Escadrille. This special issue of *La Guerre Aérienne* is devoted entirely to the Lafayette Escadrille.

Newman, Irving J. "A Biography of Colonel Thaw II." *Popular Aviation* 16 (November 1934):281–83. Few Lafayette pilots performed as well as did William Thaw, yet few were more unwilling to stand in the limelight. For this reason, this short biography makes a valuable contribution.

Parsons, Edwin C. "Flying As It Was." *The Sportsman Pilot* 12 (October 1940):16, 31–32. Delightful article describing Parson's hectic experiences trying to train unwilling fliers for Pancho Villa.

————. "Glory Grabbers." *For Men* (June 1939), pp. 21–27. A well-written article designed to scotch the increasing numbers of individuals falsely claiming membership in the Lafayette Escadrille. Worthy of a better magazine.

Pourpe, Marc. "Comment Je Connus Lufbery." *La Guerre Aérienne* (20 December 1917), p. 100. Portion of a letter or other early document written by Pourpe and describing his fateful meeting with Raoul Lufbery in Saigon in 1912.

Rockwell, Paul A. "Deux Morts: Pavelka et Trinkard." *La Guerre Aérienne* (31 January 1918), pp. 190–91. Pavelka is of particular interest since he flew with the Lafayette Escadrille. Rockwell knew both men well.

————. "l'Escadrille La Fayette." *La Guerre Aérienne* (19 July 1917), pp. 562–76. Extremely valuable article. He describes the unit, its early successes and some of its losses. This weekly issue of *La Guerre Aérienne* is devoted entirely to the Lafayette Escadrille.

————. "Le Sergent Douglas MacMonagle." *La Guerre Aérienne* (13 December 1917), p. 76. Rockwell knew MacMonagle well.

————. "Le Sergent Pilote Paul Pavelka." *La Guerre Aérienne* (13 September 1917), pp. 703–4. Rockwell details some of the airman's most remarkable adventures.

————, and Felix B. Grundy. "Deux Nouvelles Victimes." *La Guerre Aérienne* (10 May 1917), pp. 431–32. An account of the deaths of Edmond Genêt and Ronald Hoskier.

Roosevelt, Theodore. "Lafayettes of the Air." *Colliers* 57 (29 July 1916):16. Roosevelt was no neutral, and he proves it with his declarations of sympathy and admiration for these fliers.

## Books

Ajalbert, Jean. *La Passion de Roland Garros.* 2 vols. Paris: les Éditions de France, 1926. Better-than-average biography of the airman who played an unusual but significant role in the development of the fighter airplane.

Barrett, William E. *The First War Planes.* Greenwich, Connecticut: Fawcett Publications, 1960. Shallow narrative, but interesting photographs and valuable performance data of many World War I aircraft.

Bolling, John R., comp. *Chronology of Woodrow Wilson.* New York: Frederick A. Stokes Co., 1927. Chronological outline of the main events in the life of Woodrow Wilson. Also contains some of Wilson's most important speeches.

Bornecque, Henri, and René de Valforie. *Les Ailes dan la Bataille.* Paris: Librairie Hachette, 1920. An elementary approach to military aviation but a valuable and indeed successful attempt to explain the role of aircraft in battle.

Boyle, Andrew. *Trenchard.* New York: W. W. Norton and Co., 1962. Best available biography of Britain's premier World War I airman.

de Brunoff, ed. *l'Aéronautique Pendant la Guerre Mondiale, 1914–1918.* Paris: M. de Brunoff, 1919. Well-written, beautifully illustrated volume covering French aerial activities, including both military and naval operations, during the Great War.

Channing, Grace E., ed. *War Letters of Edmond Genêt.* New York: Charles Scribner's Sons, 1918. Valuable and touching collection of letters by a young member of the Lafayette Escadrille whose whole life was a tragic adventure. The preface contains valuable biographical data on Genêt.

Churchill, Winston S. *The World Crisis, 1914–1918.* Oxford: The Clarendon Press, 1934. A great book by a great writer, but it must be viewed in light of the fact that Churchill had some powerful prejudices as well as some mistakes to explain away. This volume is a condensation of a six-volume work published between 1923 and 1929.

Crouvezier, Gustave. *l'Aviation pendant la Guerre.* Paris: Librairie Militaire Berger-Levrault, 1916. Contains much excellent information on the early development of World War I aviation.

Cruttwell, C.R.M.F. *A History of the Great War.* Oxford: The Clarendon Press, 1934. An excellent interpretative account of World War I, although in certain areas, such as the offensive plans of the belligerents, it contains errors hardly pardonable sixteen years after the armistice.

Cuneo, John R. *Winged Mars.* Vol. 1, *The German Air Weapon, 1870–1914.* Harrisburg, Pa.: The Military Service Publishing Co., 1942. Valuable work on the actual and theoretical role of "military" aircraft prior to World War I with most of the emphasis, as the title suggests, on the German side. A competent military history.

———. *Winged Mars.* Vol. 2, *The Air Weapon, 1914–1916.* Harrisburg, Pa.: The Military Service Publishing Co., 1947. Superb work. A rare and unusually successful attempt to fit the air weapon into the war which started its spectacular rise to prominence.

Dollfus, Charles, and Henri Bouché. *Histoire de l'Aéronautique.* Paris: l'Illustration, 1932. Monumental work. Beautifully written and illustrated volume depicting the history of aeronautics from the period of the early legends to 1932.

Driggs, Laurence L. *Heroes of Aviation.* Boston: Little, Brown and Co., 1918. Well-written book explaining the value of air supremacy and describing some of the more remarkable exploits of leading pilots in the war. Contains a chapter on the formation of the Lafayette Escadrille and its subsequent achievements.

Eberhardt, Walter von, ed. *Unsere Luftstreitkräfte, 1914–1918.* Berlin: C. A. Weller, 1930. Monumental work. Massive, well-written and beautifully illustrated. Contains a fairly reliable list of German airmen who fell in battle.

Edmonds, Sir James E. *History of the Great War: Military Operations, France and Belgium.* 23 vols. London: MacMillan and Co.; H M S Office, 1922–48. Official British history of the war. Although some portions are still controversial, it is easily the best and most reliable of the official histories.

État Major de l'Armée, Service Historique. *Les Armées Françaises dans la Grande Guerre.* 11 vols. Paris: Imprimerie Nationale, 1922–37. Official French history of the war. The number of "volumes" is deceiving. Actually, there are eleven *tomes* subdivided into *volumes*, of which there are more than ninety.

Falls, Cyril B. *The Great War.* New York: G. P. Putnam's Sons, 1961. Perhaps the best single-volume history of the war.

Fokker, Anthony, and Bruce Gould. *Flying Dutchman: The Life of Anthony Fokker.* New York: Henry Holt and Co., 1931. Readable and very informative biography by the young Dutchman who designed and built some excellent fighter planes in the Great War.

*For France.* Garden City, New York: Doubleday, Page and Co., 1917. A compilation of articles, speeches, etc., which indicate that many Americans, including some in very high positions, were far from neutral in the early years of the war.

Gisclon, Jean de. *l'Escadrille La Fayette au La Fayette Squadron, 1916–1945.* Paris: Editions France Empire, 1975. The best existing work dealing with the tradition and legacy of the Lafayette Escadrille in France.

Goldberg, Alfred, ed. *A History of the United States Air Force, 1907–1957.* Princeton, New Jersey: D. Van Nostrand Co., 1957. Valuable one-volume history of the U.S. Air Force, but too brief, and suffers the deficiencies of virtually all "official" histories.

Gorrell, Edgar S. *The Measure of America's World War Aeronautical Effort.* Northfield, Vermont: Norwich University, 1940. Technical but readable description of America's fumbling efforts to build a huge air armada.

Hall, Bert. *En l'Air.* New York: The New Library, 1918. A gross exaggeration of Hall's exploits. Probably ghost-written.

———, and John J. Niles. *One Man's War: The Story of the Lafayette Escadrille.* New York: Henry Holt and Co., 1928. Must be used with extreme caution, particularly as a primary source. Although once a member of the Lafayette Escadrille, Hall is basically unreliable.

Hall, James Norman. *High Adventure*. Boston: Houghton Mifflin Co., 1918. Interesting and beautiful account of Hall's experiences in France, but of marginal historical value since Hall disguised both persons and events.

———. *My Island Home*. Boston: Little, Brown and Co., 1952. Hall's autobiography, written shortly before his death.

———, and Charles B. Nordhoff, *The Lafayette Flying Corps*. 2 vols. Boston: Houghton Mifflin Co., 1920. Designed to be the official history of the Lafayette Flying Corps, this masterful work contains mostly biographical data on American pilots who flew for France in the Great War. The authors are understandably gentle toward those who did not perform well, but having based their work on official records and having known most of the pilots, the volumes are basically reliable.

Hervier, Paul Louis. *The American Volunteers with the Allies*. Paris: Éditions de la Nouvelle Revue, 1918. This volume, originally published in French, is backed by better-than-average research, although the author is sometimes guilty of sensationalism.

Hoeppner, General von. *Deutschlands Krieg in der Luft*. Leipzig: K. F. Koehler, 1921. Excellent and remarkably detailed work by the officer who reorganized the German air service after it was badly mauled by the Allies at the Battle of the Somme.

Hoskier, Ronald Wood. *Ronald Wood Hoskier: Literary Fragments and Remains in Prose and Verse*. Boston: The McKenzie Engraving Co., n.d., ca. 1927. Small memorial volume containing some of Hoskier's more promising writings together with biographical data supplied by his father.

Hudson, James J. *Hostile Skies: A Combat History of the American Air Service in World War I*. Syracuse, New York: Syracuse University Press, 1968. Academically sound and very readable account of the U.S. Air Service in France. Contains a number of references to the Lafayette Escadrille.

Isaacs, Edouard Victor. *Prisoner of the U-90*. Boston: Houghton Mifflin Co., 1919. Contains the story of Harold B. Willis's escape from a German prison camp.

Jane, Frederick T. *All the World's Aircraft*. Vol. 5, 1913, vol. 8, 1917. London: S. Low, Marstand Co., 1913, 1917. The standard reference works on the aircraft of the years indicated.

Jordanoff, Assen. *Men and Wings*. Buffalo, New York: Curtiss-Wright Corp., 1942. Brief but well-written history of aviation, spotlighting the milestones of progress from the eighteenth century to the opening years of World War II.

King, Jere. *Generals and Politicians*. Berkeley: University of California Press, 1951. Brilliant study of the civil-military relationship in France during World War I.

Kitchel, Denison. *The Truth about the Panama Canal*. New Rochelle, New York: Arlington House Press, 1978. This volume contains an interesting foreword by Representative John J. Rhodes.

Liddell Hart, Basil H. *The Real War*. London: Faber and Faber, 1930. A standard work by one of the best-known military writers of the twentieth century.

McConnell, James R. *Flying for France*. Garden City, New York: Doubleday, Page and Co., 1917. Delightful personalized account of flying with the Lafayette Escadrille by an idealistic airman who later died in combat.

*Man the Destroyer*. Vol. 2, *The Book of Progress Series*. New York: Cricks Publishing Corp., 1915. Chapter 5 of this volume contains the answer to the once-perplexing problem of the identity of the American who deserted from French aviation in 1914, thereby creating a spirit of distrust on the part of the French that later proved most difficult to overcome.

Mason, Herbert Molloy. *The Lafayette Escadrille*. New York: Random House, 1964. Generally reliable account of the Escadrille, although, as a commercial venture, it suffers from the customary tendency toward sensationalism.

Mauer, Mauer, ed. *The U.S. Air Service in World War I*. 2 vols. Washington, D.C.: Office of Air Force History, 1978. Mostly excerpts from documents etc. A valuable addition to the history of the U.S. Air Service, it contains very little about the Lafayette Escadrille.

Ministère de la Guerre. *Revue Historique de l'Armée, Numero Special, Fraternité d'Armes Franco-Américaine*. Paris: Ministère de la Guerre, 1957. This impressive volume, an official publication of the French War Department, deals with Franco-American military cooperation from the War of American Independence through World War II.

Morse, Edwin W. *The Vanguard of American Volunteers*. Vol. 2, *America in the War*. New York: Charles Scribner's Sons, 1919. An attempt to tell the story of Americans fighting for France, 1914–17, by focusing attention on select individuals.

Mortane, Jacques. *Les As, Peints par Eux-Memes*. Paris: Alphonse Lemerre, 1917. The lives of some of the aces of the war as told in some of their own writings.

————. *Duex Grands Chevaliers de l'Aventure: Marc Pourpe, Raoul Lufbery*. Paris; Éditions Baudiniere, 1938. Rare volume containing invaluable information on the early life of Lufbery.

Mott, Colonel T. Bentley. *Myron T. Herrick: Friend of France*. Garden City, New York: Doubleday, Doran and Co., 1929. A sympathetic and informative biography of the United States ambassador to France, 1912–14.

Neumann, Georg P. *Die deutschen Lufstreitkraefte in Weltkriege*. Berlin: E. S. Mittler und Sohn, 1920. Authoritative history of the evolution of German military aviation during the war.

Norman, Aaron. *The Great Air War*. New York: The Macmillan Co., 1968. One of the better books on World War I aerial combat, although like almost all commercial ventures on the subject, the patterns and trends of the air fighting are more or less lost in the storytelling.

*Norman Prince: A Volunteer Who Died for the Cause He Loved*. Boston: Houghton Mifflin Co., 1917. Brief memorial volume issued by the Prince family to demonstrate Norman's "tenderly affectionate nature and his constant thoughtfulness and solicitude for those he left at home." Of marginal historical value.

Oughton, Frederick. *The Aces*. New York: G. P. Putnam's Sons, 1960. Shallow work, with imagination often taking the place of research.

Parsons, Edwin C. *The Great Adventure*. Garden City, New York: Doubleday, Doran and Co., 1937. Very valuable first-person account of flying with the Lafayette Escadrille. Parsons cannot always be accepted at face value, however.

Pearson, Henry G. *A Businessman in Uniform: Raynal Cawthorne Bolling*. New York: Duffield and Co., 1923. Useful biography of a solicitor for United States Steel who played a prominent role in the early American Air Service in France.

Pershing, John J. *My Experiences in the World War*. 2 vols. New York: Frederick A. Stokes Co., 1931. Standard postwar memoir.

Raleigh, Walter, and H. A. Jones. *The War in the Air*. 6 vols. Oxford: The Clarendon Press, 1922–37. Official British history of the air war. Easily the best and most complete work of its kind.

Reichsarchiv. *Der Weltkrieg, 1914 bis 1918*. Berlin: E. S. Mittler und Sohn, 1925–42. Official German history of the war. Very valuable, although in some matters, such as the cause of the German collapse in 1918, it leaves much to be desired.

Ritter, Hans. *Der Luftkrieg*. Leipzig: K. F. Koehler, 1926. Balanced view of the air war by a critic who seems to have had an unusual grasp on the theoretical uses of airpower.

Rockwell, Paul A. *American Fighters in the Foreign Legion*. Boston: Houghton Mifflin Co., 1930. Unusually fine work by an American who fought with the Legion in World War I and who had a keen sense of perception and honesty about the men and events he describes. Contains valuable information on the origins of the Lafayette Escadrille.

Schaeffer, Ernst. *Pour le Mérite*. Berlin: Union deutsche Verlagsgesellschaft, 1931. Valuable history of those German airmen who won their nation's highest decoration.

Spaight, James M. *The Beginnings of Organized Air Power*. London: Longmans, Green and Co., 1927. Fine review of the organization of the British Air Ministry, enhanced by brief descriptions of the air organizations of France, Germany, and the United States.

Spears, E.L. *Prelude to Victory*. London: Jonathan Cape, 1939. Dealing primarily with the ill-fated Nivelle offensive of 1917, this is one of the best books about World War I.

Sweester, Arthur. *The American Air Service*. New York: D. Appleton and Co., 1919. Well-written and generally reliable study of the American Air Service. Considering when the book was published, it is remarkably candid about both successes and failures.

Thenault, Colonel Georges. *l'Escadrille Lafayette*. Paris: Librairie Hachette, 1939. Though somewhat ill organized, this volume by the officer who commanded the Lafayette Escadrille throughout its existence is essential to any researcher of the Lafayette Escadrille.

*Victor Chapman's Letters from France.* New York: The MacMillan Co., 1917. Selected letters written by Chapman prior to his death in 1916. The memoir, written by his father, contains valuable biographical data.

Voisin, Général Andre Paul. *La Doctrine de l'Aviation Française au cours de la Guerre, 1915–1918.* Paris: Berger-Levrault, 1932. A rare and able attempt to determine and analyze French air doctrine during the war.

*War Letters of Kiffin Yates Rockwell.* Garden City, New York: The Country Life Press, 1925. Valuable collection of letters by one of the original members of the Lafayette Escadrille prior to his death in September 1916.

Weeks, Alice S. *Greater Love Hath No Man.* Boston: Bruce Humphries, 1939. Valuable collection of reminiscences, letters, etc., written and collected by a woman who lost her only son in the Foreign Legion and who knew and liked many of the young Americans who fought for France.

Whitehouse, Arch. *Legion of the Lafayette.* Garden City, New York: Doubleday and Co., 1962. Popular, over-dramatized account of the Lafayette Escadrille.

### Miscellaneous: Pamphlets, Journals etc.

Franco-American Committee. *European War: The Franco-American Flying Corps.* Paris: Bishop and Garrett. n.d., ca. October 1916. Small brochure issued by the Franco-American Committee in an attempt to recruit Americans for the Service Aéronautique. Tries to make the Lafayette Flying Corps look as attractive as possible.

*Lafayette Escadrille Memorial.* Paris: Herbert Clarke, 1928. Official pamphlet issued by the Memorial de l'Escadrille Lafayette Association to celebrate the dedication of the impressive Lafayette Escadrille memorial near Paris.

Society of World War I Aero Historians. *Cross and Cockade Journal.* Truly excellent journal dealing with World War I aviation. Vol. 18, no. 2 (Summer 1977) and 19, no. 2 (Summer 1978) have articles dealing with the Lafayette Escadrille. (The former contains the entries of Clyde Balsley's diary, a document lost to fire shortly thereafter.) Vol. 2, no. 1 (Spring 1961) is devoted entirely to the Lafayette Escadrille.

Warner Brothers Studios, Burbank, California. "Production Notes on the Lafayette Escadrille." Mimeographed statement describing the Warner Brothers movie entitled "The Lafayette Escadrille." Excellent example of the prevailing ignorance about the squadron and a Hollywood effort that only compounded the problem.

### Newspapers

*Atlanta Journal,* 1914.
*Boston Daily Globe,* 1911.
*Chicago Daily News,* 1914–18.

*Denver Post*, 1914–18.
*Volontaire Étranger*, 1932.
*New Haven Register*, 1960.
*New York Herald* (European Edition), 1914–18.
*New York Herald Tribune*, 1950–56, 1967.
*New York Times*, 1914–18.

# Index